MEMORIALS

AND

CORRESPONDENCE

OF

CHARLES JAMES FOX.

☞ *The Author of this work gives notice that he reserves to himself the right of translating it.*

MEMORIALS

AND

CORRESPONDENCE

OF

CHARLES JAMES FOX.

EDITED

BY LORD JOHN RUSSELL.

VOLUME III.

AMS PRESS
NEW YORK

Reprinted from the edition 1854, London
First AMS EDITION published 1970
Manufactured in the United States of America

International Standard Book Number:
    complete set: 0-404-05470-6
    volume 3: 0-404-05473-0

Library of Congress Catalog Card Number: 75-115362

AMS PRESS, INC.
New York, N.Y. 10003

PREFACE

THIS Volume contains the Correspondence of Mr. Fox from the end of 1792, when the French Revolution began to produce the most serious effects on the domestic and foreign policy of this country, to the spring of 1804, when Mr. Fox, in junction with the Grenvilles, entered into systematic opposition to Mr. Addington's administration.

The letters are almost entirely those of Mr. Fox, and are little interrupted by other matter.

Lord Holland's work, as an editor, does not reach to this period. Mr. Allen had selected the letters of Mr. Fox to Lord Holland, which he thought worthy of publication, but had done nothing further. In order to elucidate the quotations and allusions I have had recourse to the assistance of a learned friend, who has furnished the greater portion of the notes. The reader will feel with me the high value of the aid I have thus received.

Mr. Fox, it will be seen, during this period, devoted himself with ardour to his classical studies. Mrs. Fox, in a postscript to one of her husband's letters, tells Lord Holland that his uncle is as much absorbed in Greek as Dr. Parr, and reads two or three books of Homer in a morning.

His political opinions are expressed with great warmth of feeling against the policy of the war, and an excess of apprehension for the constitution of his country. I have made some remarks on this subject in the course of the Volume.

I have received a remonstrance from General Ewart on the mention made of his father, Mr. Ewart, in a passage of one of Mr. Fox's letters in a former Volume. Mr. Fox asserts that Mr. Ewart died mad. This, it appears, was not the case; the mistake arose from the circumstance that in the last illness of Mr. Ewart, he suffered severely from gout, and was at times delirious.

London,

November, 1854.

CORRESPONDENCE OF

CHARLES JAMES FOX.

BOOK THE SIXTH.

—◆—

WE have now arrived at a period of the history of
this country and of Europe, of the highest interest.
The French Revolution, in its origin, in its career, in
the wars which attended its course, and in the consequences which it produced, forms the most important
epoch in modern history. It is far from my intention
to attempt in this place even a slight outline of that
great change in the state of Europe; but with
respect to its effects on the policy of England, on the
Whig party, and on the personal position of Mr. Fox,
the nature of the present work renders it incumbent
upon me to make some remarks.

At the beginning of December, 1790, Louis XVI.,
alarmed at the progress of the democratic factions in
France, wrote a letter addressed to the Emperor of
Germany, the Empress of Russia, the Kings of
Prussia, Spain, and Sweden, suggesting a congress
of the principal sovereigns of Europe, supported by

an armed force, as the best means of establishing a better order in France, and preventing the contagion of dangerous principles.*

There can be no doubt that this appeal to foreign states, against his own subjects, was a step at variance with the duty of a constitutional sovereign to the laws and to the people. It placed him in the light of a conspirator against his own country.

In May, 1791, the Emperor of Germany concerted measures to meet the alleged danger. He proposed that 35,000 Germans should march into Flanders, 15,000 into Alsace, that 15,000 Swiss should move towards Lyons, 15,000 Piedmontese towards Dauphiny, that 20,000 Spaniards should be placed on the frontier ; he promised the co-operation of Prussia, and that England would remain neutral. The French Parliaments were to be recalled into life in order to give legality to the future Constitution.

It is obvious that nothing could be more futile than such a plan. To imagine that 100,000 men, dotted over five points of frontier, could overcome the strong will of a nation like France, was a mistake so preposterous that it was evident the Emperor of Germany neither knew the force with which he had to deal nor his own strength.

In August, 1791, the Emperor and King of Prussia met at Pilnitz, for the purpose, it was supposed, of making arrangements with respect to Poland. The Count d'Artois, however, presented himself at Dresden, and urged the two sovereigns to

---

* "Memoires tirés des Papiers d'un Homme d'État," vol. i., p. 96.

interfere actively in the affairs of France. The Emperor was averse to such interference, but the King of Prussia was eager for war. The result of their concert was a declaration that the two sovereigns were desirous to co-operate in efficacious measures to enable the King of France to consolidate in perfect liberty a monarchical government suited to the rights of sovereigns and the welfare of the French people. The monarchs of Europe were invited to act with mutual concord and the necessary forces in order to attain this end. Accordingly, Russia, Spain, and the petty princes of Italy, expressed their entire accordance ; England alone, while not averse to the objects of this levy of sovereigns, declared for a policy of neutrality.

Nothing could be worse in principle than the declaration of Pilnitz. It laid down as a practical doctrine that the despotic sovereigns of Europe were to fix the bounds and prescribe the measure of the liberties of the people of France. While such was the unjustifiable nature of the principle, the means adopted were mischievous and dangerous in the extreme. Encouragement was given to the French princes and emigrant nobles who assembled at the head of more than 20,000 men on the frontiers of France with a view of promoting insurrection and beckoning on the great powers to the invasion, perhaps the partition of France.

Very little reflection might have sufficed to convince the statesmen of England that such a declaration ought not to be viewed with indifference. One of

two consequences must follow : either the armies of
Germany, of Russia, of Italy and of Spain would
succeed in their invasion, or France, roused to resistance by so insolent an attempt, would drive back
the aggressors, with shame, to their own frontiers.
In the former case, the independence of France would
have been destroyed, and there could be little doubt
that the monarchs who had just risen from their
shameless feast upon the spoils of Poland, would have
sought, with similar rapacity and with equal disregard
of right and justice, a gratification of their selfish
cupidity in the rich provinces of France. Indeed
cotemporary testimony leaves no room to doubt that
the hatred of liberty which the sovereigns of the
North avowed, was not stronger than the love of
plunder, which they concealed. Such a termina-
tion of the projects of the allies, looked upon as an
example, was odious and pernicious. As a disturb-
ance of the balance of power in Europe it must
have been the prelude to new convulsions and pro-
tracted wars. But in the event of the discomfiture
of the allies by the French, other consequences not
less important were sure to follow. The French, in
the very heat and fervour of a democratic revolution,
which was to establish new maxims of government,
new rules of foreign policy, to abolish old privileges,
old restrictions, and old conventions, were not likely
to be satisfied with the mere repulse of an invasion.
The attempt to confine the action of the French
people within the circle drawn by rulers of foreign
states, was sure to cause a terrible rebound. The

weapons by which their assailants might be punished
were ready to the hands of the impassioned and
reckless men who swayed the destinies of France.
The subversive theories and democratic aspirations,
which had shaken the monarchy and uprooted the
nobility of France, were fermenting in the bosoms of
many of the subjects of the assembled and affrighted
sovereigns of Europe. It could not but happen that
if the military nation who were called to arms in the
name of French independence should obtain the
victory over their enemies, they would extend the
limits of the ancient monarchy and scatter to the winds
the treaties by which Europe was bound together.

Yet this was the struggle the approach of which
was looked upon by the ministers of England with
some complacency towards the invaders, but not the
slightest apprehension of the invaded. It was in vain
that Machiavel had told them that the attempt to
oppress a nation amid the throes and heavings of
internal disorders was sure to end in failure. It was
in vain that the spectacle was exhibited before them
of a mighty people frenzied to the utmost pitch of
enthusiasm, and of embattled armies prepared to
quench that enthusiasm in blood. In their little
wisdom they presumed that it was possible and even
easy to allow the conflict to take place, and yet to
preserve undisturbed all the parchment treaties and
formal precedents by which the state of Europe was
regulated.

Events followed each other rapidly. On the 25th of
July, 1792, the Duke of Brunswick, then at the head

of an army of invasion, promulgated his celebrated proclamation. It was therein declared that the French national guards, if they should fight against the allied troops and were taken with arms in their hands, should be punished with death as rebels—that the members of municipalities should be responsible on pain of losing their heads, for all crimes which they should not in a public manner have attempted to prevent : that the inhabitants of towns and villages, who should dare to defend themselves against the allied forces, should be punished with all the rigours of war, and that their houses should be demolished : that their Imperial and Royal Majesties made personally responsible for all events, on pain of losing their heads pursuant to the sentences of court martial, without hope of pardon, " all the members of the National Assembly, of the departments, of the districts, of the municipalities, the national guards of Paris, justices of the peace, and others whom it may concern :" further that if any the least outrage were done to the royal family, if they were not immediately placed in safety and set at liberty, their Imperial and Royal Majesties will inflict on those who shall have deserved it, "the most exemplary and ever memorable vengeance and punishment, by giving up the city of Paris to military execution and exposing it to total destruction, and the rebels who shall be guilty of illegal resistance shall suffer the punishments which they shall have deserved."*

The atrocious spirit of this proclamation, while it

* Adolphus, Hist. of George III.

roused the French nation to resistance, does not appear to have excited any other feeling in the English Ministry, than a gentle and benevolent wish that the Duke of Brunswick might be successful, and that England might be able to say, she did not do it. The first witness whom I shall quote to this purpose, is Lord Grenville, the ablest and one of the most upright of Mr. Pitt's colleagues. The following extracts are taken from his letters to his brother, the Marquis of Buckingham.

" Jan. 6th, 1792.

" The solution of the French enigma which you state, is that it is a war of bullying on both sides, the two parties being equally afraid of each other. In the meantime there certainly are some in France who wish the war, but very many more who fear it, and the ruin of their finances is approaching with very rapid strides indeed."

" Sept. 20th, 1792.

" The Duke of Brunswick's progress does not keep pace *with the impatience of our wishes,* but I doubt whether it was reasonable to expect more."

" Oct. 11th, 1792.

" *We are all much disappointed with the result of the great expectations that had been formed from the Duke of Brunswick's campaign.* According to the best accounts I can get, of a business involved in almost inextricable mystery, the flux which had got into his camp was the true cause of his retreat.

Whatever be the cause, *the effect is equally to be regretted.*"

"I bless God, that we had the wit to keep ourselves out of the glorious enterprise of the combined armies, and that we were not tempted by the hope of sharing the spoils in the division of France, nor by the prospect of crushing all democratical principles all over the world with one blow. But having so sturdily resisted all solicitations to join in these plans, we have been punished for our obstinacy by having been kept in profound ignorance of the details by which they were to be executed, and even of the course of events as far as that could be done, which occurred during the progress of the enterprise. Now that it has failed, we must expect these deep politicians to return to the charge, and to beg us to help them out of the pit into which they wanted to help us. But they have as yet been in no hurry to begin this pleasant communication, and most assuredly we are in no disposition to urge them on faster."

Yet it was now obvious that the struggle was becoming one of the most fearful nature. The procession of the 10th of August, and the massacres of September, showed how dreadful a contest was begun. Still at the beginning of November, Lord Grenville wrote as a spectator :—

"*Nov. 7th*, 1792.

"The Emperor must feel that he has now got an enemy whom he must devour, or be devoured by it.

And the governing party at Paris have very many very obvious reasons for continuing the war. The rest of the empire will give their contingent, unless they have been lucky enough to be forced to sign a capitulation of neutrality. The king of Sardinia and Italy will defend themselves as they can, which will probably be very ill. What Spain will do, she does not know and therefore certainly we do not. Portugal and Holland will do what we please. *We shall do nothing.* . . . . All my ambition is that I may at some time hereafter, when I am freed from all active concern in such a scene as this is, have the inexpressible satisfaction of being able to look back upon it, and to tell myself that I have contributed to keep my own country at least a little longer from sharing in all the evils of every sort that surround us. *I am more and more convinced that this can only be done by keeping wholly and entirely aloof, and by watching much at home, but doing very little indeed;* endeavouring to nurse up in the country a real determination to stand by the Constitution when it is attacked, as it most infallibly will be if these things go on ; and, above all, trying to make the situation of the lowest orders among us as good as it can be made."

The next witness is Mr. Dundas, who writes thus, in 1791 :—

THE RT. HON. HENRY DUNDAS TO RICHARD BURKE, Jun. Esq.

"LONDON, *September* 20*th*, 1791.

. . . . . "You will naturally feel that my situation prevents me entering into any of the

discussions you are so good as to lay before me. The
line of the British Government, to adhere to an
honest and fair neutrality, being taken, and every-
where announced, it is impossible for any member of
Government to give way to any indulgence of any
speculations on the subject of French affairs. I had
a visit from your father this morning, and I took
occasion to express to him my surprise at the contents
of your last letter; never having heard, and at this
moment not believing, that this country ever interfered, directly or indirectly, to prevent the Emperor
moving any of his troops in any manner he pleased.
I need not repeat to you again, that I cannot enter
into the discussion of that subject; but I could not
refrain saying this much in answer to your letter. I
could say a great deal more, but I must not. When
I see a single step that looks like any of those great
powers taking a part, I shall believe it, but not till
then."

Lastly, Mr. Pitt, in the financial debate of February,
1792, said, " We must not count with certainty on
the continuance of our present prosperity; but un-
questionably there never was a time in the history of
this country when, from the situation of Europe, we
might more reasonably expect fifteen years of peace
than we may at the present moment."*
While such was the conduct and the view of the
Ministry, the members of the Whig Opposition were
becoming widely separated from each other. Mr.

---

* Parliamentary Debates, Feb. 1792.

Burke's " Reflexions on the French Revolution " had
produced an open rupture between him and Mr. Fox.
In the celebrated and painful scene which occurred in
the House of Commons on the 6th of May, 1791,
these statesmen unfolded views the most opposite to
each other. While Mr. Fox lauded the attempt of
the French to establish a free government, Mr. Burke
adjured his countrymen to beware the baleful example.
When Mr. Burke pronounced the words, " Fly from
the French Constitution!" Mr. Fox, who sate near
him, whispered that there was no loss of friendship.
Mr. Burke at once replied, " Yes there was; he knew
the price of his conduct; he had done his duty at the
price of his friend : their friendship was at an end."
When Mr. Burke had finished Mr. Fox rose to reply,
but was so much agitated that tears trickled down
his cheeks, and for some minutes he could not proceed. In broken accents he endeavoured to express
the pain he felt at what had occurred; referring with
deep feeling to the days of his boyhood, when he had
received instructions from Mr. Burke, and formed a
friendship which had lasted twenty-five years, for the
last twenty of which they had acted together, and
lived on terms of the most familiar intimacy. On a
subsequent day Mr. Burke, in his turn, complained
" of being obliged to stand upon his defence by that
right honourable gentleman who, when at the age of
fourteen years, had been brought to him, and evinced
the most promising talents, which he had used his
best endeavours to cultivate; and this man, who had
arrived at the maturity of being the most brilliant

and powerful debater that ever existed, had described
him as having deserted and abandoned every one of
his principles!"

While Mr. Burke complained of being accused of
deserting his principles, Mr. Fox resented the imputation that, because he rejoiced in the overthrow of
the despotism of France, and did not admire the
Quebec Bill, he must be tainted with Republican
principles. It was in one of these debates that he
compared his opponents, who fulsomely and constantly praised the Constitution, to Regan and Go-
neril, who abounded in panegyrics on their father;
while he, like Cordelia, " should say he loved the
Constitution just as much as a subject of Great
Britain ought to love a government under which he
enjoyed such blessings."

In these discussions Mr. Fox showed himself frank,
open, and generous : anxious to preserve the friendship, while he dissented from the views, of Mr. Burke.
Their divergence of sentiments regarding the French
revolution was indeed such, that as soon as any
practical question should arise, in which the French
revolution was an element, their political separation
was sure to ensue. Indeed, it was easy to foresee,
that in the event of a struggle between the Governments of England and France, Mr. Burke would be
the fiery advocate of war, while Mr. Fox would be no
less sincerely the strenuous friend of peace.

It must, however, be related in this place, that in
June, 1792, an effort was made to form a coalition
between Mr. Pitt and Mr. Fox. The matter is

noticed in Lord Malmesbury's diary, in various passages, of which extracts shall here be given. On June the 10th, 1792, Lord Malmesbury writes: " Long *téte-à-téte* conversation with the Duke of Portland. He agreed that the circumstances of the times made a coalition with Pitt a very necessary measure; that the security of the country required it, as well relative to its foreign as to its internal situation. . . . . In short, the result of two hours' discussion was, that a coalition was so desirable a measure, that not only every overture tending towards one should be listened to, but even overtures made to promote it, were it practicable." Soon after this Mr. Dundas expressed a wish for a permanent union. He held out the prospect of four vacant cabinet places,—the Chancellor, the Secretary of State for Home Affairs, the President of the Council and Privy Seal, besides two or three Privy Councillors' places in the House of Commons, and the Lord Lieutenancy of Ireland. On June 13th we find again in Lord Malmesbury's diary: " Duke of Portland said he had seen Fox for two hours. Fox, he said, was a friend to coalition ; that he only wished it to be brought about in such a way as it should appear they had not acceded to Pitt's ministry, but went to it on fair and even conditions, to share equally with him all the power, patronage, &c." Such being the disposition, various conferences took place, both as to the principles on which the two parties were to join, and on the distribution of offices. The principles chiefly in question related to the measures of

Parliamentary Reform, the Abolition of the Slave
Trade, the Repeal of the Test Act, and the system to
be observed relative to French politics. With respect
to several of these questions, Mr. Fox and Mr. Pitt
were agreed in opinion; while the Duke of Portland,
Lord Loughborough, and Lord Malmesbury differed
from both of them. The next entry in the diary is so
curious that I shall give it entire:

"Saturday, June 16th. Dinner at Lord Loughborough's with Fox. While Lord Loughborough was
engaged with his company (which were foreigners) I
talked with Fox, and afterwards carried him to Burlington House. He had not heard of the last meeting
with Pitt; he was full of doubts and misgivings, and
did not make himself (as he generally does) practicable. He seemed *a little hurt* at the first advance
not having been made to him; but this I collected
from his manner, not from any direct impression.
He doubted Pitt's sincerity, and suspected he had no
other view than to weaken their party and strengthen
his own; that to divide the Opposition was his great
object. He doubted also the King's having consented
willingly to dismiss the Chancellor, and seemed to
think it *possible* a new Administration might be made
through him, from which Pitt was to be excluded.
He contended, that it was impossible ever to suppose
Pitt would admit him to an equal share of power;
and that, whatever might be his own feelings or
readiness to give way, he could not, for the sake of
the honour and *pride* of the Party, come in on any
other terms. Pitt *must* have the Treasury, he said,

and he, on his part, had friends in the House of
Commons he *must* attend to. These friends I conceived to be Sheridan, Grey, Erskine, and Lord
Robert Spencer. After stating these doubts and
difficulties, and dwelling on them with a degree of
peevishness and obstinacy very unlike him, he however ended by saying that he loved *coalitions ;* that,
as a party man, he thought it a good thing for his
Party to come into office, were it only for a month ;
and, under the particular circumstances of the
country, he thought it of very great importance that
a strong administration should exist. He reasoned
on foreign politics with his usual ability, and on the
same system as formerly. When we got to Burlington
House he was not inclined to speak, and it was with
great difficulty I could lead him and the Duke of
Portland into discourse. Fox repeated merely what
he had said to me on the way, spoke *with acrimony* of
Pitt, and repeatedly said 'the pride of the Party must
be saved.' I observed, *purposely*, that I conceived, if
the Duke of Portland and he were agreed, they necessarily must lead the Party, and that *all* their friends
would follow them. The Duke seemed to acquiesce ;
but Fox was silent and embarrassed, and said, with a
degree of harshness very unlike his usual manner, that
he did not believe that Pitt was sincere, and that, even
if he was sincere, he did not believe any coalition
could take place. I endeavoured to bring him to—
at least, give the proposal fair play—by urging its
importance as to public concerns, which he admitted ;
and I contended that he had no option as a party

man, but either of coming in now, or of waiting till
public calamity or national distress drove Pitt from
office, and that then he necessarily must come in to
support the very measures which Pitt had not been
equal to carry through for the public safety; that,
therefore, it was not unreasonable to argue, that his
coming into an equal share of power now with Pitt,
was not only likely to prevent these public evils
which threatened the community at large, but to
insure to him and his friends a much more permanent
and secure possession of office than if they waited till
the King, against his will, and driven to it by distress,
was forced to take them in; that, coming in now, *his
power* necessarily must increase, from the palpable
good effects it would produce; that on his coming in
then it would diminish, from perhaps an unpopular
and difficult task being put upon him, and from his
not possessing the confidence of the Crown. This
had some effect upon him. I left him and the Duke
alone; and I was glad to learn that the next morning,
when he called again at Burlington House, he was
more accommodating and less taciturn than the
preceding evening."

On the following day, the 17th, we find that Mr.
Pitt stated some doubts about Fox, and these he said
might be got over. He was a little apprehensive of
Fox's opinions relative to the French revolution; and
hinted that he was afraid he had gone too far: that
this was an objection to his coming at once into the
Foreign Department, because it would look like a
change of system. On the next day, the 18th, Lord

Fitzwilliam being invited to give an opinion, insisted on the indispensable necessity of Pitt's resigning the Treasury for another Cabinet office. He expressed his dislike to Sheridan, said he might have a lucrative place, but never could be admitted to one of trust and confidence. On the 21st, the Duke of Portland told Lord Malmesbury that Fox was much more practicable, and said "it was *so damned right a thing* that it must be done." He however still held out on the impossibility of his acting under Pitt. When things had reached this point Mr. Burke interfered and put an effectual stop to the whole proceeding. He professed himself a warm advocate for a coalition, but observed " Mr. Fox's coach stops the way," and declared that the principles broached by Grey, &c., and not disavowed by Fox, had necessarily drawn a line of division in the party ; that it was necessary to declare this distinctly and decidedly, and that for better security and in order to give a convincing mark of it to the public, Lord Loughborough should be made Chancellor and represent the party in the cabinet. On the other hand, Mr. Pitt's friends objected to the measure of coalescing with Fox, and on the 27th of June, the whole of the projected arrangement was at an end. Upon the 5th of July, Lord Loughborough related to Lord Malmesbury a conversation he had had a few days before with Fox, in which he said Fox appeared more harsh, impracticable, and opinionative, than he could have supposed him to be. That he saw no chance of anything being done while Fox remained in his present temper of mind. Fox had said to him, that although it should be the united opinion of all his friends that he ought to come into office, leaving Pitt in the post he now fills, he still should maintain his own, and although in that case he should so far defer to theirs as not to refuse coming into office rather than prevent an arrangement, yet that if that was to happen he would go into the House of Lords and not remain in the House of Commons. In the course of the summer a proclamation against sedition was issued. Before the terms were finally settled, the Duke of Portland was consulted, and held a meeting of his friends at Burlington House. The Duke of Bedford, who had been invited, asked if Mr. Fox was expected. On being told that he was not, the Duke took up his hat, and saying, "Then I am sure I have no business here," left the room.*

On July 30th, we find that Lord Malmesbury dined with Fox at St.Anne's Hill with no one present but Mr. Thomas Grenville. Fox argued much on what appeared to him to be the insincerity of Pitt, who he said only wished to separate and break up the party. "All this was said," adds Lord Malmesbury, "in great good humour. Much talk on foreign politics. We agreed on the general principle, but differed on particular points. His leanings about French politics are not quite correct. His opinion of the King of Prussia much too low. His partiality for a Russian connexion very great. . . . . Fox made Pitt's quitting the Treasury a *sine quá non*, and was so

* See Lord Holland's "Memoirs of the Whig Party," vol. i. Burke's Works, vol. vi.

opinionative and fixed about it that it was impossible
even to reason with him on the subject."

No more seems to have passed on this subject for
four months. On the 11th of December, Charles
Fox, the Duke of Devonshire, Lord Malmesbury,
Mr. Grenville and Lord Fitzwilliam dined at Burlington House. Fox treated the prevailing alarm as
totally groundless, said that there was not only no
insurrection or imminent danger of invasion but no
unusual symptoms of discontent or proneness to complain in the people. He did not doubt the necessity
of assisting the Dutch if attacked, but he seemed
inclined to think the opening the Scheldt was not a
sufficient motive for war, and would not even be considered as such by the Dutch themselves. The rest
entirely disagreed with these opinions, and Lord
Fitzwilliam even blamed the Ministry for their
supineness. On a subsequent day, Sir Gilbert Elliot,
Lord Malmesbury, and Mr. Elliot of Wells dined with
the Duke of Portland. They all urged upon the
Duke their entire disapprobation of Fox's conduct and
principles, and urged the Duke to come to a fair and
short explanation with Fox, and separate from him
amicably but decidedly. When, however, they urged
the Duke of Portland to answer their appeal, he said
nothing. " I," says Lord Malmesbury, " although
I have often seen him benumbed and paralysed, never
saw him or any one else so completely so before. All
was one dead silence on his part : he seemed in a
trance, and nothing could be so painful as these two
hours, for our conversation lasted as long as that,

reckoning intervals of ten and fifteen minutes silence."
Yet one thing he did say, and that was that he was
against anything that could widen the breach, and
put it out of Fox's power to return, and drive him
into desperate opposition.

On the 18th, Lord Fitzwilliam left London " from
difficulty how to act, and distress of mind relative to
Fox." But Mr. Burke, implacable and furious, pursued
his purpose of separation.   On the 22nd he harangued
for an hour to Lords Loughborough, Malmesbury, and
Porchester, Sir Gilbert Elliot, Wyndham, Dr. Lawrence and Elliot of Wells.   He represented Fox as
seduced by his abilities to believe that a government like ours was not a proper one for great abilities
to display themselves in, that by working on his
ambition they had made him approve and praise the
French Revolution, &c.   Wyndham tried in vain to
stem this torrent of falsehood and misrepresentation.
On the same day we find this passage in Lord
Malmesbury's diary: " Fox carried me home; he
expressed great horror of the ' décret,' of the 15th
Dec. 1792, issued by the National Convention.   He
thought war likely.   The Dutch he considered as
adverse to it.   He was in very good humour, and
talked with great liberality on the difference of opinion
between him and some of his friends."

On the 24th the Duke of Portland agreed to separate from his friend, manifesting at the same time
" the great violence that this determination did to his
private affection, and attachment to Mr. Fox." *

* Lord Malmesbury, vol. ii. p. 419—454.

It is clear, from this account, that the separation
between Mr. Fox and a portion of his political friends
was no new project, and that Mr. Burke had long
endeavoured to remove Fox by representing him as
the obstacle to a coalition.   In the arrangements for
that purpose, Mr. Fox's honour and that of his
friends appear to have received very little consideration.   It would seem to have been in Mr. Pitt's
contemplation, that Fox should serve under him
in the House of Commons; and that he should
undergo some probation before he should be judged
qualified to hold the seals of the Foreign Office.
Mr. Fox in the course of these negotiations was
occasionally, as Lord Loughborough terms it, "harsh
and opinionative;" that is to say, he was not ready
at once to sacrifice his own position and that of his
friends to enable Lord Loughborough to hold the
great seal.   Had Mr. Pitt offered directly to Mr. Fox
the Foreign Office, with the leadership of the House
of Lords, there can be little doubt that Mr. Fox,
however reluctant, would have accepted the offer.
What might then have happened, whether Mr. Fox
would have brought Mr. Pitt round to his pacific
opinions, and whether any attempts of that kind could
have averted war, it is now impossible to say.

The Duke of Portland, Lord Fitzwilliam and
Mr. Wyndham, separated from Mr. Fox with the
greatest reluctance; these ties could not be torn
asunder without leaving a wound which bled, and a
scar which defaced.   The kind unaffected nature of
Mr. Fox had bound his friends to him with no

common affection, and his letters show how deep was the sorrow which followed a political breach.

While Mr. Fox was thus deserted by the panic-struck followers of Mr. Burke, Mr. Grey and others eager for parliamentary reform united themselves into a society called the "Association of the Friends of the People." The movement was unfortunate, the consequences disastrous. At such a time prudence counselled delay; Mr. Fox himself was never among the most forward in the cause of Parliamentary Reform and did not join the Association.* The following letter from Lord Carlisle refers to it:—

"GROSVENOR PLACE, *July* 23rd, 1792.

"DEAR FOX,

"The actual state of the Party appears to different people in such a different point of view that I flatter myself you will excuse this application to you, and that I endeavour, by your help, to ascertain its real condition; and, according to the lights you bestow, regulate my ideas, which I confess have been perplexed by events which have lately taken place.

"I submit, therefore, to your consideration the evident necessity of clearing away all doubt upon the following important point:—Whether those persons who originally favoured and adhere to the Association are to be deemed separated from the Party, or still belonging to it, though with a more relaxed connection; to gather, if occasion offers, the fruits of

* See Lord Holland's "Memoirs of the Whig Party," vol. i.

our common labours; or, on the contrary, to be
looked upon no longer sharers of our political
fortunes?

"Persuaded you will deal with me with your usual
frankness and sincerity, I think it right, on my part,
to advertise you that I do not make this requisition to
you under the seal of private friendship, but in order
that I may be at liberty to make free use of the
authority of your judgment and opinion.

"If I am authorised to consider all party connection dissolved between the Opposition and the
Associators, by the conduct they have thought fit to
adopt, I might entertain the hope, that at least one
great obstacle was removed (however others might
subsist) to the construction, by some means, of a
stronger Government than the country is at present
possessed of, the want of which all moderate men,
friends and supporters of the Administration, are ready
to admit; and I think I shall not be suspected of
hypocrisy when I assert, that, under the present circumstances, the adding that strength to Government
(if possible) is required of us all as a conscientious
discharge of public duty.

"Believe me to be, dear Fox,
"Ever yours most sincerely and affectionately,
"CARLISLE."

Thus while Mr. Fox, deeply attached to the Constitution, attached to peace, but no less to the honour
of the country, gave to his friends the most patriotic
counsels, the great Whig Party which he led broke

off into two divisions—the one imbibed even more than the Minister those alarms of democracy which there wanted nothing but firmness and calm temper to dissipate; the other embracing speculations of reform, for which the country was little prepared, frightened the lovers of peace, and weakened the influence of their honest and wise leader. Mr. Fox was left almost alone; his party broken, his popularity gone, his friends deserting him, his eloquence useless, his name held up to detestation.

In this situation, which might have overcome the fortitude of a man much less distinguished for sensibility than Mr. Fox, he held on his course with unvarying firmness, keen sagacity, and an eloquence as fraught with feeling as with argument. He bore aloft the standard of Whiggism, amid the attacks of his enemies and the desertion of his followers. He was purely and simply a Whig: devoted to the popular principles of that party, and embracing them all the more closely amid the fears of the timid, and the wild plans of the enthusiast.

When war was proposed, he thus analysed, in a speech in Parliament, the reasons on which it had been defended :—

" The grounds were three : the danger of Holland; the decree of the French Convention of November 19th; and the general danger to Europe from the progress of French arms. With respect to Holland, the conduct of ministers afforded a fresh proof of their disingenuousness; they could not state that the Dutch had called upon us to fulfil the terms of our alliance; they were obliged to confess that no such requisition had been made, but added that they knew the Dutch were very much disposed to make it. Whatever might be the words of the treaty, we were bound in honour by virtue of that treaty to protect the Dutch if they called upon us to do so, but neither by honour nor the treaty till then. . . . . . . The plain state of the matter was that we were bound to save Holland from war, or by war, if called upon, and that to force the Dutch into a war, at so much peril to them, was not to fulfil, but to abuse the treaty. . . . . . . The decree of the 19th November he considered as an insult, and the explanation of the Executive Council as no adequate satisfaction; but the explanation showed that the French were not disposed to insist upon that decree, and that they were inclined to peace, and then our Ministers, with haughtiness unexampled, told them they had insulted us, but refused to tell them the nature of the satisfaction that we required. It was said we must have security, and he was ready to admit that neither a disavowal by the Executive Council of France, nor a tacit repeal by the Convention, on the intimation of an unacknowledged agent, of a decree which they might renew the day after they repealed it, would be a sufficient security. But, at least, we ought to tell them what we meant by security; for it was the extreme of arrogance to complain of insult without deigning to explain what reparation we required, and he feared an indefinite term was here employed not for the purpose of obtaining, but of precluding satisfaction. Next, it was said they must withdraw their troops from the Austrian Netherlands before we could be satisfied. Were we then come to that pitch of insolence as to say to France, ' You have conquered part of an enemy's territory who made war upon you; we will not interfere to make peace; but we require you to abandon the advantage you have gained, while he is preparing to attack you anew? ' Was this the neutrality we meant to hold out to France? 'If you are invaded and beaten we will be quiet spectators; but if you hurt your enemy, if you enter his territory, we declare against you.' If the invasion of the Netherlands was what now alarmed us—and that it ought to alarm us if the result was to make the country an appendage to France, there could be no doubt—we ought to have interposed to prevent it in the very first instance, for it was the natural consequence of a war between France and Austria. With respect to the general danger of Europe, the same arguments applied, and to the same extent. To the general situation and security of Europe we had been so scandalously inattentive; we had seen the entire conquest of Poland and the invasion of France with such entire indifference, that it would be difficult now to take it up with the grace of sincerity; but even this would be better provided for by proposing terms before going to war."

Mr. Fox went on to argue on that which appears to have been with many the real, though unavowed object of the war; namely, a change in the internal government of France. His arguments on this subject, supported by references to Vattel, as a great authority on the law of nations, are familiar to the world.

Mr. Fox, with no less force, pointed out the imprudence of a war against opinion. For notwithstanding ministerial disclaimers, the fear of French principles, horror at French crimes, and disgust at French excesses, were constantly put forth as incentives to war. But how could war extirpate those principles, or arrest those crimes? Unless by complete conquest it was obvious that war could effect no such cure. On the contrary, the love of country, the enthusiasm of independence, the thirst of glory, which were excited by war, confirmed and cemented that Jacobin ascendancy, which without such stimulants and such aids would probably have sunk before the moral indignation of the French people. Austria, Prussia, and England put every Frenchman attached to his country in the alternative of either abetting the reign of terror, or of being denounced as the agent and tool of a foreign invader.

I come now to consider the last, but perhaps the most prevailing reason for rushing into war with France; namely, the existence of sedition and discontent at home, fomented by foreign emissaries.

Taking the evidence known to us on this subject, there seems never to have been a more unfounded fear than that which induced the great majority of the nation to fear the overthrow of their Constitution by a small minority enamoured of French Jacobin principles. The crimes and excesses committed in France produced horror and disgust, rather than approbation and enthusiasm; and the most ordinary vigilance of the most ordinary magistrates would have been sufficient to maintain order in Great Britain.

At a later period, indeed, when the war had inflamed the passions of its opponents, some violent men appear to have meditated a revolution; but their designs were so shallow, their party so insignificant, and their plans so immature, that even the prejudiced juries of those days refused to convict of High Treason the leaders in these abortive conspiracies.

But let us again consult Lord Grenville's letters. On the 14th of November, 1792, he writes to his brother :—

"*November 14th*, 1792.

"Our laws suppose magistrates and grand juries to do this duty; and if they do it not, I have little faith in its being done by a government such as the Constitution has made ours. If you look back to the last time in our history that these sort of things bore the same serious aspect that they do now—I mean the beginning of the Hanover reigns—you will find that the Protestant succession was established, not by the interference of a Secretary of State or Attorney-General, in every individual instance, but by the exertions of every magistrate and officer, civil or military, throughout the country. I wish this was more felt and understood; because it is a little hard to be forced to run the hazards of doing much more than one's duty, and then to be charged with doing less. As to what you mention of overt acts, these

things are all much exaggerated, where they are not
wholly groundless. The report of what is called
' Cooper's Ass Feast ' (Walker's I never heard of),
and of the Scotch Greys being concerned in it,
reached me *by accident;* for of all the King's good
subjects who are exclaiming against its not being
noticed, not one thought it worth his while to apprise
the Secretary of State of it. I took immediate steps
for inquiring into it; and am satisfied that the whole
story has no other foundation than Mr. Cooper having
invited two officers to dine with him in a small company, and having given them, by way of curiosity, as
a new dish, a piece of a young ass roasted. I
inquired, in the same manner, about the riot stated to
have happened at Sheffield; and learn from Lord
Loughborough, who lives in the county, and is enough
on the *qui vive* on the subject, that there was nothing
which, even in the most peaceable times, could
deserve the name of a riot. That supposed at Perth
I never heard of yet, though Dundas has been within
a short distance of that place.

" It is not unnatural, nor is it an unfavourable
symptom, that people who are thoroughly frightened,
as the body of landed gentlemen in this country are,
should exaggerate these stories as they pass from one
mouth to the other; but you, who know the course
of this sort of reports, ought not too hastily to give
credit to them."

Notwithstanding this plain and true testimony to
the peaceable state of the country, on the 13th of

December following the King was advised, on opening
the session, to address his Parliament in the following
terms :—

" The seditious practices which had been in a
great measure checked by your firm and explicit
declaration in the last session, and by the general
concurrence of my people in the same sentiments,
have of late been more openly renewed, and with
increased activity. A spirit of tumult and disorder
(the natural consequence of such practices) has shown
itself in acts of riot and insurrection, which required
the interposition of a military force in support of the
civil magistrate. The industry employed to excite discontent on various pretexts, and in different parts of
the kingdom, has appeared to proceed from a design
to attempt the destruction of our happy Constitution,
and the subversion of all order and government; and
this design has evidently been pursued in connection
and concert with persons in foreign countries."

In referring to this part of the speech, Mr. Fox made
these remarks :

" The next assertion is, that there exists at this
moment an insurrection in this kingdom. An insurrection ? Where is it ? Where has it reared its
head ? Good God ! an insurrection in Great Britain !
No wonder that the militia were called out, and Parliament assembled in the extraordinary way in which
they have been. But where is it ? Two gentlemen
have delivered sentiments in commendation and illus-
tration of the speech; and yet, though this insurrection has existed for fourteen days, they have given

us no light whatever, no clue, no information, where to find it.   *   *   *   *   *

"The honourable gentleman who seconded the motion tells us that the 'insurrections are too notorious to be described.' Such is the information which we receive from the right honourable magistrate, and the honourable gentleman, who have been selected to move and second the address. I will take upon me to say, Sir, that it is not the notoriety of the insurrections which prevents those gentlemen from communicating to us the particulars, but their non-existence."

His language on this subject hardly differs from the language of Lord Grenville to his brother, which we have already seen.

Mr. Fox, for this great cause, lost popularity, reputation, and friends; but his warm and benevolent heart told him that he had been a martyr for peace, for freedom, and the cause of nations. He had this consolation, and was comforted.

No sooner was the war begun than the great difference which existed among its supporters as to the object to be sought, and the means of seeking it, became quite obvious, and most injurious to its success. Mr. Burke, who blew the trumpet with the greatest vehemence, proclaimed aloud that he considered the war with France as a great civil war of which on our part the restoration of the old Monarchy should be the great end and object. He considered the execution of Louis XVI. a cause of war.* He could not bear to

---

* See "Letter to Duke of Portland"—Works, vol. vi.

see those who resisted the armies of the Allies treated
as prisoners of war, while the royalists were put to
death by the French tribunals as rebels. He thought
that equal justice and good policy alike required that
all prisoners taken by the Allies should be put to
death. He considered that the war should be waged
against the French Convention and its abettors in
the name of Louis XVII. the legitimate heir to the
throne, and Monsieur the lawful Regent. He would
have made the restoration of the Monarchy, and the
punishment of the rulers of France the necessary
conditions of peace. He could overlook or forgive
the proclamation of the Constitution of 1791, at
Toulon, as an adherence to its provisions might
be evaded or disavowed, but he rejoiced in the
recognition of Louis XVII., as the fit preliminary to
any negotiation, and the real standard to be raised
in war.* Happily his advice was disregarded.
Mr. Pitt took a totally different view of the nature
and objects of the war. He was ready to admit that
we had nothing to do with the internal government
of France, provided its rulers were disposed and able
to maintain friendly relations with foreign governments. He sought to confine France within her ancient
limits, to oblige her to respect established treaties,
and to renounce her conquests. He sought by expe-
ditions to the West Indies an indemnity for the
expenses of the war. In short, he treated Robespierre and Carnot as he would have treated any other

* See "Burke's Correspondence," vol. iii. and iv., and " Works," vol. vi.
and vii.

French rulers, whose ambition was to be resisted, and whose interference in the affairs of other nations was to be checked and prevented. Mr. Fox did not fail to take advantage of the discord which prevailed among his opponents. If they declaimed against the republic, he asked whether they meant to dictate to the French people the nature of their institutions, and the rules of their internal government. If they boasted of successes in the West Indies, he asked whether they meant to deprive their ally Louis XVII. of so fair a portion of his inheritance.

But although the advocates of war could make no logical reply, they could agree to carry on hostilities, leaving it to the chapter of accidents to decide on the objects and ends of the war. If Toulon opened its gates to Louis XVII., our object was the restoration of Monarchy; if we took an island in the West Indies, our object was to cripple the power of France.

Our allies acted in a manner no less inconsistent. The views of Prussia were turned more to the acquisition of Polish territory, than to the restoration of order in France, and she soon deceived the English Ministry, and abandoned the cause of Kings. Austria cared more for acquisitions in Lorraine and Alsace, than for the sacred objects of Mr. Burke's crusade ; she thought, foolishly enough, that an opportunity had arisen for weakening France, whether republican or monarchical.* Thus England, Prussia and Austria, with lofty pretensions of fighting for the cause of

* See these views and their consequences developed, in the "Mémoires tirés des Papiers d'un Homme d'Etat," especially the first and second

religion and order, had each separate and selfish objects, while the French, united and enthusiastic, fought for a mock liberty, but a real independence. With the Allies it was a war sometimes of principles, sometimes of provinces; sometimes to restore a Monarchy, sometimes to acquire Martinique. With the French the most horrible tyranny, the most systematic murder and plunder at home were accompanied by the most brilliant courage, the most scientific plans of campaign, and the most entire devotion to the glory of their country.

In the midst of this dreadful war, the course of Mr. Fox was firm and moderate. He always admitted, that we ought to require explanations from France, and that we ought to arm in order to obtain them. When the war was commenced, he moved an address in the House of Commons in these terms: " That we learn, with the utmost concern, that the Assembly, who now exercise the powers of government in France, have directed the commission of acts of hostility against the persons and property of his Majesty's subjects, and that they have actually declared war against his Majesty and the United Provinces : that we humbly beg leave to assure his Majesty, that his Majesty's faithful Commons will exert themselves with the utmost zeal in the maintenance of the honour of his Majesty's crown, and the vindication of the rights of his people ; and nothing shall be wanting on their

volumes, which are founded on materials of the highest authenticity. While Mr. Burke preached the crusade of Peter the Hermit, the Allies were intent on territory and dominion.

part that can contribute to that firm and effectual
support, which his Majesty has so much reason to
expect from a brave and loyal people, in repelling
every hostile attempt against this country, and in such
other exertions as may be necessary to induce France
to consent to such terms of pacification, as may be
consistent with the honour of his Majesty's crown, the
security of his allies, and the interests of his people."

From this time Mr. Fox found himself the leader
of a small party, who were defeated in every
division; but their masterly abilities, the vigour of
their speeches, and their devotion to Mr. Fox gave a
splendour to their light which neither power, nor
popular frenzy, nor laws against sedition could
weaken or extinguish. At no time did the energy,
the logic, the fancy of Mr. Fox appear to the world
with greater lustre; at no time did the warmth of
his heart, the sweetness of his temper, and the refinement of his taste give such tranquillity to his home.
At a period when the prospects of office nearly
vanished from his sight; when calumny loved to
paint him as a man of disordered ambition and
criminal designs, he was busy in the study of Homer
or lounging carelessly through his garden, and expressing to his beloved nephew the full sense of his
happiness and content. The trees and the flowers,
the birds, and the fresh breezes gave him an intense
enjoyment, which those who knew his former life of
politics and of pleasure could hardly have imagined.
To the capacious benevolence which longed to strike
the chains from the African slave he joined a daily

practice of all the charities of life, and a perception of the beautiful in nature, in literature, and in art, which was a source of constant enjoyment. With a simplicity of manners rare in great statesmen, he united views the most profound, and a feeling heart which calumny could not embitter, nor years make cold, nor the world harden.

We have seen in the former volumes the dissolute life in which Mr. Fox became involved. Amid the indulgences of a wandering fancy and violent passions he formed a lasting attachment. Mrs. Armitstead, who lived with him as his mistress, became his wife in the year 1795. Fortunately she was endowed with strong affection, good sense, and an unbounded devotion to Mr. Fox.

The reader of the following letters will find in them the intimate, careless, familiar communications of Mr. Fox to his nephew. Many will blame the sympathy which he shows not for the principles but for the independence of France, and condemn the harshness with which he speaks of Mr. Pitt; but none can fail to recognise a zealous love of liberty, a great and master mind, a penetrating sagacity, and a willingness to forego all objects of ambition rather than desert or surrender that which he believed to be the cause of mankind.

Even with regard to Mr. Pitt blame as strong is to be found in the writings of men who were not engaged in political strife. The celebrated Robert Hall, who had censured him most severely, wrote thus as late as 1821:—

" For the severity with which he has treated the political character of Mr. Pitt he is not disposed to apologise, because he feels the fullest conviction that the policy, foreign and domestic, of that celebrated statesman, has inflicted a more incurable wound on the Constitution, and entailed more permanent and irreparable calamities on the nation, than that of any other minister in the annals of British history. A single reflection will be sufficient to evince the unparalleled magnitude of his apostasy; which is, that the memory of the *son* of Lord Chatham, the vehement opposer of the American War, the champion of Reform, and the idol of the people, has become the rallying point of Toryism, the type and symbol of whatever is most illiberal in principle, and intolerant in practice." *

I add his praise of Mr. Fox :—

" To the honour of Mr. Fox, and the band of illustrious patriots of which he is the leader, it will however be remembered, that they stood firm against a host of opponents, when, assailed by every species of calumny and invective, they had nothing to expect but the reproaches of the present, and the admiration of all future times. If anything can rekindle the sparks of freedom it will be the flame of their eloquence ; if anything can reanimate her faded form, it will be the vigour of such minds." †

I now proceed to give the letters of Mr. Fox to Lord Holland separately. They will be followed by letters of the same period to his friends :—

---

* Hall's Works.   † Ibid.

MR. FOX TO LORD HOLLAND.*

"*June 14th*, 1793.

" I should have written to you long ago, my dearest Henry, if I had known how to direct and send my letter; but your first letter from Corunna (the only one I had received till this week) mentioned no place where you gave any direction. I have now received your letter from Bilbao; and I am afraid you are right in your conjecture, that those you wrote from Oviedo, or any other place since your landing, are lost. I had always heard that Biscay was something like Devonshire; but my notion was, that the great natural beauties were in the Asturias; and possibly this may be so, and you may have spoken of them in your last letters as having seen them in your way to Oviedo. Your account of Biscay makes it still more free than I had imagined; and I should hope, bad as these times are in some respects, that there is not much chance of its privileges being invaded. Dumouriez's defection is here so old a story that, at first, I hardly knew what you meant by the surprising news you speak of. The first impression here was, that it was likely to put an end to the whole contest; but we were soon undeceived; and the Allies, after having at first cried him up in the most excessive manner, when they found the mischief he had done to be so small, neglected him to the last degree. I do not believe his conduct was owing to any bargain;

* For the previous letters of this series see above, vol. ii. p. 363.

but only to levity and to an indignation natural
enough at the way of proceeding of the Convention.*
Your speculation, that affairs at Paris were likely to
mend, though not an unnatural one, has turned out
to be a very mistaken one ; and there is reason to
believe that Marat and Danton have forced the Convention to pass a decree of *arrét* against Brissot and
all his friends, to the number of twenty—Pethion,
Vergniaux, Barbaroux, and, in short, every man of
note in that party (except Condorcet) are of the
number : I shall not be surprised to hear they are all
either murdered or *guillotined* by a sham trial.† In
short, things at Paris have been going regularly from
bad to worse ; and yet the armies fight like heroes,
and the Allies have hitherto made no impression of
consequence. It is a strange state of things. People
here begin to be heartily tired of the war, in some
degree owing to the disgust pretty generally felt at
the scandalous conduct of the Empress and Prussia
in respect to Poland ; but chiefly to the extreme
distress which is felt at home. I do not know
whether there is not some comfort in seeing that,
while the French are doing all in their power to make
the name of liberty odious to the world, the despots

* Dumouriez, Commander-in-Chief of the French army in Flanders,
went over to the Austrians in April, 1793. The circumstances which
induced him to take this step are explained in a carefully-written article on
Dumouriez in the Supplement to the "Biographie Universelle." He passed
the latter part of his life in England, and received a pension from the
English Government. He died in 1823, and was buried in Henley
Church.

† The arrest of the Girondist leaders was decreed on the 2nd of June,
1793. Their execution took place on the 30th of October following.

are conducting themselves so as to show that tyranny is worse. I believe the love of political liberty is *not* an error ; but, if it is one, I am sure I never shall be converted from it—and I hope you never will. If it be an illusion, it is one that has brought forth more of the best qualities and exertions of the human mind than all other causes put together ; and it serves to give an interest in the affairs of the world which, without it, would be insipid ; but it is unnecessary to preach to you upon this subject. So now to myself. You will hear by others of what has been done, and is doing, for me. I may perhaps flatter myself, but I think that it is the most honourable thing that ever happened to any man. The sum which *has* been raised is such as will pay all my debts that are in any degree burthensome, and give me an income upon which I can live comfortably without contracting any more.*   I need not tell you that Mrs. A. is as happy as I am, and she says she only wants to see the young one to make her completely so. God bless you, my dearest Henry ! Pray write very often. I shall direct this to Barcelona, though I think you will be gone before it arrives. Of course you will not miss seeing Grenada. Hubiera escrito a V. M. en lengua Castellana si fuera acertado que V. M. me entendiera. He leydo in aquella lengua la Gramatica de la Academia y la mitad de Don Quixote. Yo querria que V. M. que es hoy en el pays de los refranes me dixese si sabe algun refran Castellano que responda a

---

* This alludes to the subscription which was raised by Mr. Fox's friends, in order to pay his debts.

este nuestro tan averiguado en mi ultima dichosa
ventura, *when things are at the worst they must mend.**

" Yours affectionately,

" C. J. FOX."

SAME TO SAME.

"St. Ann's Hill, *August 1st,* 1793.

" I am very much obliged to you, my dear Henry,
for your letter from Barcelona dated the 17th ult$^{mo.}$
It was very handsome of you to write as you had no
letter from me. The only letters which I had received
from you before this last were one from off Corunna,
and one from Bilbao, in which last only you told me
to direct to Barcelona, which I accordingly did, and
wrote you a long letter, which I fear will not have
reached Barcelona before you will have left it, but I
suppose they will send it after you. Bien es verdad
lo que ha dicho el buen frayle, quiero decir el de la
venta, que los consejos de nuestra corte, parece que
son los del Papa o del Rey Catholico o de algun
Principe forastero, pues por cierto se puede averiguar
que no son los del intéres de la Gran Bretaña. No
hubiera creido que mi nombre fuese conocido en
España a lo menos de los frayles, pero no tengo
muy gana que la fama de mis hazañas como dice
D. Quixote sea tan distendida accordando me de lo

---

* " I would have written to you in the Spanish language had I been sure
that you would understand me. I have read in that language the Grammar
of the Academy and half of ' Don Quixote.' I should be glad if you,
who are in the country of proverbs, would tell me if there is any Spanish
proverb which answers that one of ours, so well exemplified in my last
piece of good fortune, *when things are at the worst they must mend.*"

que dicen en este pays, *better known than trusted;*
y tambien de aquel otro, *more know Jackpudding
than Jackpudding knows.* No hay duda que hayan
refranes Castellanos que corresponden a estos Ingleses
puesto que yo no los sepa. En la otra carta que
recibi de V. S. escribiò que debia ir a Barcelona por
via de Zaragoza, pero en esta ultima no dice nada ni
di Zaragoza, ni del Ebro rio tan famoso, ni de las
alamedas tan celebres que estan alli cerca. Queria
saber si los alamos allâ son semejantes a los nuestros
o a los de la Lombardia, y si ha visto harto de aquel
esparto que aqui se nombre *Spanish broom.**

"I shall be too late for the post if I continue to write
in Spanish, so in English I must tell you a piece of
news that you have not loyalty enough to rejoice
much in ; I mean the surrender of Valenciennes.
Mentz was taken a little before, so I suppose our
Ministers and Tories of all descriptions are in high

---

* "What was said by the friar is very true—I mean him of the *venta*—
that the councils of our Court appear to be those of the Pope, or of the
King of Spain, or of some foreign Prince ; because for certain one may
affirm that they are not those of the interest of Great Britain. I should
not have thought my name would have been known in Spain, at least by
the friars ; but I have no great wish that the fame of my achievements, as
Don Quixote has it, should be so widely extended, recollecting the phrase
used in this country, *better known than trusted;* and also that other
saying, *more know Jackpudding than Jackpudding knows.* There are,
no doubt, Spanish proverbs which correspond to these English ones,
although I do not know them. In the other letter which I received from
you you wrote that you were going to Barcelona by way of Saragossa ;
but in your last you say nothing of Saragossa, nor of the Ebro, that
famous river, nor of the celebrated alamedas in that neighbourhood. I
wish to know whether the poplars (alamos) in that country are like those
of Lombardy, or like ours ; and if you have seen much of that broom
which is here called *Spanish broom.*"

glee, carrying, as they think, everything before them. Pensar que han de conquistar la Francia o de restorar al Rey Luis es pensar como se dice en lo excusado y esperar los peros del Olmo.*

" Here am I writing Spanish again without thinking of it. The internal affairs of France seem more embroiled than ever, and it is an interesting object of curiosity to see whether any and what effect is produced by the taking of Valenciennes.† Nothing can be more according to my opinion than all you say about the Polish business. There are now hopes that the two robbers may quarrel about the spoil, as it is supposed the Poles will make an offer of their whole kingdom to the Empress, and some people think that it is such a bait that she cannot resist it. However, all this I have from mere report, but you wish me to write politics, and not knowing anything authentic I must write what I hear. As to what I think upon these subjects you know all my opinions too well to make it necessary for me to repeat them, only that, whether from obstinacy or from philosophy I know not, I grow to value political liberty more and more every day. If you can get a Boccacio, read the story of the Jew who was converted to Christianity by seeing the abominations of cardinals, &c. at Rome,‡ and apply his reasoning to France and Liberty. I must finish, so God bless you.

---

* " To think they can conquer France, and restore King Louis, is thinking what is impossible, and expecting figs from thistles."

† Valenciennes surrendered to the English and Austrians, under the command of the Duke of York, on the 26th of July, 1793.

‡ Giorn. I. Nov. 2.

" I wish you would say a little more of yourself in your letters, and I should like them still better, though as they are they give me the greatest pleasure. I mean I should like to know what you do at the different towns ; whether you go to conversazioni or spectacles, and what spectacles; whether you dine alone, or with what sort of company; whether you speak Spanish as well as English, or better, &c., &c. Mrs. A. gives her love to you, and longs to see you here ; indeed, at present, that is all that is wanting to our perfect happiness.

"C. J. F."

SAME TO SAME.

" St. Ann's Hill, August 22nd, 1793.

" My dear Henry,

" It is in vain to deny it, so I must confess that I have had four letters from you since I wrote last, which by the way is only three weeks since. One of the four was dated St. Sebastian, prior to that which I last answered, one from Barcelona, and two which I received yesterday from Alicant. I am very much obliged to you indeed, my dear young one, for writing so often, and will do all I can to encourage you to continue so good a practice, by being very regular in answering you when I know your direction. I do assure you the receiving a letter from you is one of the greatest pleasures I feel even at this place where enjoyments to me are not wanting. As to your wondering at my having learnt Spanish better than you, and your methodical inquiry into the causes of it, you should remember Charles the Second's rule, that

before you wonder and investigate causes you should
first inquire whether in truth the thing you are about
to wonder at be as you suppose, and this will often
save much wonder and much inquiry; so there is a
King's saying in return for your abominable King's
precepts, of which I will say a word *by-and-by*,* as we
say in the House of Commons. The fact I believe
and hope is, that I do not know Spanish half as well
as you do, and if I were to attempt to write any now
I should probably do it worse than when I last wrote,
as I finished Don Quixote a month since, and have no
other Spanish book here. Indeed, so far am I from
having the assistances in learning which you suppose,
that I have never heard one word of Spanish spoken in
my life; except Don Quixote and an Academy grammar
(all Spanish), and a little book of the Academy upon
orthography, I have no Spanish books whatever, not
even a dictionary—and as to more time than you have
travelling, you know the life of this place enough to
know that there is no time for anything. Now pray
do not consider all this as an act of vanity to enhance
the merit of having learned what I have, but as an
excuse for not having learned more. Quisiera saber
quienes son los libros que V. M. ha traido consigo
en su viage, y principalmente si ha leido algunos
poetas, y como le *placen* (no se si esta palabra es
buena y bien escrita). En este pais si se pregunta a
algun que ha estudiado el Castellano que libros hay en

---

* It is common to say in the House of Commons, " On this part of the
subject I shall say a word by-and-by," and then to go on with the
argument in hand.

el mos estimados, se responde siempre D. Quixote
como se el jamas como se debe alabado M. Cervantes
fuese el solo autor Castellano digno de ser nombrado.
Soy yo como V. M. muy aficionado para los libros
de caballeria, y si V. M. alcancese algunos de los que
el Cura y el Barbiero no quieren que sean quemados
me haria muy gran servicio en mandarmeles. Yo
aconsejeria a V.M. de comprar la traduccion del Pastor
Fido de Guarini por el Doctor Christobal de Figueroa
y la del Aminta del Tasso por D. Juan de Xauregui, porque el mismo Cervantes que menosprecia casi todas las
traducciones, a estas dos les da alabanzas altisimas, y mi
parece a mi que se juzga mejor de una traduccion antes
de haber leido el original, porque las traducciones son
hechas para los que no entienden el idioma de donde son
traducidas, y non para otros. Si estas dos traducciones
meritan las alabanzas que han recibido han de ser muy
buenas, porque los originales lo son en extremo.*

---

* "I should like to know what are the books you carried with you on
your journey, and principally whether you have read any poets, and
whether you were pleased with them. In this country, if any one is asked
whether he has studied Spanish, and what are the books in that language
most esteemed, the answer always is, 'Don Quixote;' as if the never-
enough-praised Miguel Cervantes were the only Spanish author worth
reading. I am, as you know, very fond of books of chivalry; and if you
can find any of those which the curé and the barber did not choose
should be burnt, you would do me a great service by sending them to me.
I would advise you to buy the translation of the 'Pastor Fido' of Guarini,
by Doctor Christobal de Figueroa, and that of the 'Aminta' of Tasso, by
Don Juan de Xaureguy; because Cervantes himself, who despises nearly
all translations, gives the highest praises to these; and it seems to me
that one judges better of a translation before reading the original work
than afterwards; for translations arc intended for those who do not
understand the idiom of the language from which they are translated, and
not for others. If these two translations deserve the praises they have
received, they must be very good; for the originals are extremely so."

" I observe you say nothing in any of your letters of Montserrat; I hope you did not omit seeing it, as by the description of travellers it seems very well worth seeing, indeed next to Grenada it is the place in all Spain that I have the greatest curiosity about. Valentia you do not mention either, but I dare say if you had any great expectations about it you were disappointed, as I have always believed it to be a country something like Lombardy, flat and rich, and of course insipid to the traveller. There is nothing new of importance since the taking of Valenciennes; there were reports of the Queen's being executed, but they were unfounded, and I still hope that they will abstain from this one act of butchery.* The proceedings in Poland grow, if possible, more disgusting than ever, as you will see by the papers.† Everything in the world seems to be taking a wrong turn; and, strange as it sounds, I think the success of the wretches who now govern Paris is like to be the least evil of any that can happen. There is a notion abroad that the American States are going to quarrel with us on account of our proceedings with respect to their ships. To be sure our conduct to them, as well as to the Danes, Swedes, Duke of Tuscany, and others who wished to be neutral, has been insufferable, both for arrogance and injustice; but, on the other hand, there are some articles in the treaty between France and America that scarcely leave the latter in the state of a neutral

---

* This hope was not destined to be fulfilled. Marie Antoinette was executed about two months after the date of this letter.

† The last partition of Poland, which took place in this year, by Russia and Prussia, is here alluded to.

nation ; but these articles, as I understand, are not
the ground of quarrel, if there be one.   If Pitt is
absurd enough to bring it to one, I should think our
commerce would suffer more in this war than in any
other preceding one ; but we live in a time when
everything is so extraordinary that it is in vain to
conjecture what will happen of any political kind.
What has been doing where you are seems to exceed
everything since the expulsion of the Moriscoes, and
the story of the Imperial Consul * seems quite incredible, not because of its injustice, but because I
should have thought the Emperor would have protected his officer.   I dare say if this business is
mentioned here, Pitt will say (as about Poland) that
he disapproves it and is sorry for it.   Your contrast
of the manner in which the causes of Tyranny and
Freedom are treated here is very good, and I dare say
I shall make use of it in the House of Commons ; so
when you get the papers with the debates look sharp.
I am tired with writing, and dinner is ready, so adieu.
I will write every fortnight, or three weeks at least.

" Yours affectionately,

"C. J. F."

SAME TO SAME.

"THETFORD, 17th September, [1793.]

" PENSAR que yo pueda escriber Castellano en este
lugar sin gramatica, sin diccionario, sin libros Castellanos quienes quiera, es pensar en el excusado. Estoy
aqui para cazar y no para estudiar, para matar a las
perdices (no sè si esto es bien escrito) y no para

---

* I have not found in Lord Holland's letters the story here alluded to.

matar a mi mismo con buscar palabras y modos de hablar y sentencias en un idioma que no intiendo.

"Dicenme (escribe la Duquesa a Teresa Panza) que hay bellotas gordas en ese lugar; mandeme V. M. hasta dos docenas que los estimaré mucho por ser de su mano," y quisiera yo que V. M. me mandase bellotas ya gordas ya pequeñas de todos los generos que hay en ese pais donde esta V. M. Creo tambien que esta es la sazon para cogerlas maduras y me gustaria mucho a mi de tener bellotas de todos los robles, encinas, alcornoques se que hay en esa fertilisima España.

V. M. habra ya leído la declaracion de Milor Hood a Toulon correspondiente en todo a lo que dixo el Embaxador de Prusia. No se puede olvidar que en la constitucion de 1789, hay la destruccion de la nobilidad, de la yglesia, y que aquella constitucion y no la ultima es el sugeto de la declamacion de M. Burke. En Flandes me parece a mi que el mes de Setiembre ha de ser siempre fatal a las armadas reales como aqui a las perdices. El Duque de York no solamente ha faltado de tomar Dunquerque a los Franceses mas es aparente que está en peligro mani-fiesto. Pero no hay duda que este *asedio* (no se si es Castellano) de Dunquerque ha habido su origen aqui y no es segun el consejo del dicho Duque. Dicenme que el nuestro Tio el Duque de Richmond, *is gone out,** and that he complains much of the Admiralty, but I know this only by report.

* *" Thetford,* 17th *September,* 1793.
"To think that I can write Spanish here without Grammar, without Dictionary, and without Spanish books, is to think very unwisely. I am

"That the Admiralty have been to blame I can easily believe; and, knowing my uncle's great dislike to the Duke of York,* I do not think it impossible that he may have been so too; but, even if Ordnance and Admiralty had done all they could, the project was fundamentally absurd, dangerous to the extreme, as has appeared in the execution, and worse than useless, I think, if attained. But to besiege it, without previously enabling themselves to invest it, was a degree of madness quite unaccountable; and this I know was the general opinion of all reasonable military men before the failure; for opinions formed upon the event you know I do not give much credit to.†

here for shooting, and not for study—to kill partridges (I don't know if I have written the Spanish word rightly), and not to kill myself with looking out for words and modes of speaking and sentences in a language which I do not understand. 'They tell me,' writes the Duchess to Tereza Panza 'that there are very large acorns in that place : send me two dozen, and I shall esteem them much from your hand.' And I wish that you would send me acorns, large as well as small of all kinds that there are in that place. I believe that this is the season for gathering them ripe; and I should like much to have acorns of all the different kinds of oak and cork trees which there are to be found in fertile Spain.

"You will have read the declaration of Lord Hood, corresponding exactly to what was said by the Prussian Ambassador. One must not forget, that in the Constitution of 1789 there is the abolition of nobility and of the church, and that it is that same Constitution, and not the last, which is the subject of the declamation of Mr. Burke. In Flanders it appears that the month of September is always fatal to the royal armies, as here to the partridges. The Duke of York has not only failed in taking Dunkirk from the French, but seems to be in manifest danger himself. But there is no doubt that this siege of Dunkirk had its origin here, and not in the advice of the said Duke. It is said that our uncle the Duke of Richmond *is gone out*.

* On the enmity between the Duke of York and the Duke of Richmond, see "Lord Holland's Memoirs of the Whig Party," vol. i. p. 68.

† Soon after the capture of Valenciennes the Duke of York laid siege

" I understand from Lady Di, that Charles Beauclerk * has not received your letters, and that he
is very anxious to know whether, or not, you go to
Italy.   If you follow my advice you will; first,
because I see no use in your being here till you are
of age; secondly, because Italy is of all Europe the
most worth seeing, and if you do not see it now you
probably never will; and, thirdly, because if you do not
go to Italy you never will learn thoroughly the Italian
language, and for want of it be deprived of some of
the greatest pleasure that you who love poetry can
enjoy.   If you go to Italy, as I suppose you will, and
if affairs here turn out such as to make my absence
of no consequence, I really believe that I shall go
thither next spring.   I take it for granted that you,
as well as I, will wish to be here by the opening of
the session of Parliament which follows next summer.
A little new spirit on the right side here is very much
wanting.   Prosecutions intolerable, both here and in
Scotland, are going on every day, and nobody seems
to mind them.   The very name of Liberty is scarce
popular; but the failure of the war against France
and the calamities which the war must bring on here,
may make it so again.   The most violent Tories here,
and indeed all the world, except the Ministry and
some hot friends of mine, are for peace; but I believe,

to Dunkirk; but the attempt was unsuccessful, and he raised the siege
at the end of August.

* Topham Beauclerk, born in 1739, married, in 1768, Lady Diana
Spencer, daughter of Charles, second Duke of Marlborough.   Charles
George Beauclerk was the son of this marriage.   For an account of
Topham Beauclerk, see " Boswell's Johnson."

at the same time, that they are inconsistent enough
to be against all means of bringing about peace.
What will happen here nobody knows; but I cannot
help flattering myself that the marked incapacity of
our present Ministers for war, will produce peace in
some way or other. They appear to me to have been
much more deficient in common sense than one ought
reasonably to expect one's enemies to be. There is
no room on the paper, so adieu, my dear Nephew."

SAME TO SAME.

"*November 3rd*, 1793.

" Soon after I wrote to you last from Thetford, I
was called home by a most severe fever which had
attacked Mrs. Armitstead, but which lasted a very
little time, and from which thank God she is perfectly
recovered. I stayed with her a little more than a
fortnight, and then returned to this country to my
shooting, of which I am I think fonder than ever. I
delayed writing to you some time from being discouraged by your not receiving my letters, and to
this moment I think it unaccountable, that in
September you appeared not to have received one
which I wrote you on the first of August. Your last
letters acknowledging the receipt of mine, I have
received since I came to this part of the world, and
I have never found a moment's time to write, as the
weather has been very good, and on Sundays, the only
idle days, we have generally moved from place to
place; I say we, for Uncle Dick (now General Fitz-

patrick), has been with me till last Tuesday, when he
went to London. He shoots most deliberately as you
may suppose, and generally lets the bird go out of
shot before he has adjusted his aim. You will have
heard before this reaches you of the trial and execution
of the poor Queen, which seems to have been attended
with every circumstance that could contribute to
make the act more disgusting and detestable than
any other murder recorded in history.* Our affairs
in Flanders seem to grow worse and worse,† and I
suspect that they are not in a good state even at
Toulon.‡ The expedition to the West Indies is given
up,§ and in short everything happens that ought to
disgust everybody with the war, but whether some
persons whom I most wish to be convinced are so, I
much doubt; that the public in general wishes for
peace I have no doubt ; nor do I much fear that the
Jesuitical proclamation of last week will reconcile
them much to the war. It is a curious composition,
and I hope you will read it carefully. The only thing
clear in it is, that we are to fight till they adopt hereditary monarchy in France, disavowing at the same
time any intention of prescribing either that or any
other particular mode of government. One should

* The execution of Marie Antoinette took place in October, 1793.

† An English army, under the Duke of York, had landed at Ostend
in April, 1793. In September his army retreated from before Dunkirk ;
and the campaign ended in November, without any decisive result.

‡ Toulon had been surrendered by the Royalists to Admiral Lord
Hood, in August, 1793. The Constitution of 1791 was proclaimed.

§ The proceedings against the French in the West Indies, in 1793, are
described by Adolphus, vol. v. c. 84. Tobago, St. Pierre, and Miquelon
were taken ; but no expedition was sent from England.

think it impossible that the author of such a work could be a man of sense, and yet it is evidently Pitt's *own*.[*]

" I hope when I hear next from you, to learn whether you go to Italy or not. I gave you my advice before, and I think Charles Beauclerk's being there will tempt you. In some of your letters you seemed rather impatient at my not writing to you. You were mistaken as you now know in supposing I had not written, but if I had not, you should make some allowance for habitual indolence about writing, and never allow yourself to think for a moment that I ever can be forgetful of you, or not feel interested concerning you. Indeed, if I were to accuse myself at all upon this head, it would be rather for loving you too much, than too little. I do not mean more than you deserve, but with regard to that proportion which one ought if possible to preserve in one's affections. The truth is, that all men when they are no longer young must look forwards to something they expect to last beyond themselves. My friends whom I love most are all about my own age, and consequently, one supposes they will go off the stage about the same time as oneself. So when I have a mind to

---

[*] The "proclamation" here referred to is the "declaration sent, by his Majesty's command, to the commanders of his Majesty's fleets and armies employed against France, and to his Majesty's Ministers residing at foreign courts, Oct. 19, 1793," printed in Ann. Reg., vol. xxxv., State-papers, p. 199. It was published in the London *Gazette*, for October 26—9, in French and English. Notwithstanding Mr. Fox's opinion, it seems more probable that this Declaration should have been composed by Lord Grenville, who was Foreign Secretary at the time, than that it should have been written by Mr. Pitt. It undoubtedly expressed the views of Mr. Pitt and of his Government in entering upon the war.

build castles, and to look forward to distant times with pride and pleasure, I must think of you and only you, and I feel myself quite sure that you will not disappoint me.   Perhaps the natural disposition one has to love one's near relations, would be a more true account of the interest I take in you than all this philosophy.   Be it as it may, you are in more danger of being teazed by my affection than of ever being hurt by my neglect, and of this perhaps these last two pages may shew the probability.   I read this morning in the papers, that Lord Montague and Mr. Burdett are drowned in Switzerland;* for God's sake my dear boy take care of yourself, and do not run any unnecessary danger.   Your Uncle Harry is, as you have heard before this, in Flanders.   He was delighted with his appointment, and I was very sorry for it.   Adieu, mi querido Sobrino."†

SAME TO SAME.

"EUSTON, *Nov. 3rd.*

" THE master of this house ‡ is quite right now in politics, but I fear he will come quite alone, without either of his sons."

* The details of this unhappy occurrence may be seen in the "Annual Register" for 1793, Chron. p. 51.   George Samuel, eighth Viscount Montague, and Sedley Burdett, Esq., second son of Francis Burdett, Esq., made a rash attempt, in spite of the remonstrances of the magistrates of the place, and of their own servant, to cross the Falls of Schaffhausen in a small flat-bottomed boat, and were both lost, in October, 1793.

† My beloved nephew.

‡ Augustus Henry, third Duke of Grafton, died in 1811.   The two sons alluded to are probably George Henry, Lord Euston, afterwards fourth Duke, and Lord Charles Fitzroy.

SAME TO SAME.

"St. Ann's Hill, *November 7th*, 1793.

"Though I wrote to you no longer ago than
Sunday last, I cannot help writing two lines to thank
you for three letters which I have since received from
you, one of the 31st of August, one of the 4th, and
one of the 28th of September. They did not however
come, as you mention, by the same conveyance as
your Barcelona Journal, which Caroline* sent me a full
fortnight since. I like your fandango exceedingly, it
is a much fitter story for verse than prose, and think
you have done it very well. You will long before
this have been satisfied of the groundlessness of your
notion, that France was likely to be conquered. Since
I wrote last, the Duke of York has gained an advantage,
which *for the present* will probably make the French
retire within their own territory, and if Flanders can be
kept free from their incursions during the winter, I
believe it is as much as the most sanguine expect.
The King of Sardinia has been obliged again to leave
Savoy at their mercy, and it is reported that they
have given a considerable check to the combined
armies near Strasburg.† What a pity that a people
capable of such incredible energy, should be guilty or
rather be governed by those who are guilty of such
unheard of crimes and cruelties! I think your
parallel very good, only I cannot help belief, that the

---

* Hon. Caroline Fox, Lord Holland's sister.

† Mr. Fox refers to the advantages gained at this time by Pichegru and
Hoche over the Austrians and Prussians in that quarter.

dangers which the Jacobins announced to their countrymen were not quite so ideal as our alarm. In
none of your latter letters do you mention what your
intention is, when you get to Cadiz. I am truly
happy you gave up your American scheme, for at
Philadelphia, where you might have been as likely to
go as anywhere else, there is a fever as bad and as
mortal as the plague.

　　　" God bless you, my dear Nephew,

　　　　　　　　　　　　　　　"C. J. F."

SAME TO SAME.

　　　　　　　　　" *Dec., after Christmas,* 1793.
" My dear Henry,

　　" I have no excuse but laziness, for having been
so long without writing to you. The fact is I have been
very little away from this place, and when I am here
and the meeting of Parliament draws near, every hour
and minute of idleness grows to have a double value,
and as one knows one is so soon to have so little of it,
one likes to enjoy it while it lasts, quite pure and
unmixed. But you must not suppose that you are
not thought of when I do not write, for very seldom
indeed a day passes but you are mentioned, either by
Mrs. A. or me.

　　" You will be sorry to hear that we have almost
given up all thoughts of Italy next year. Everything
seems growing so troubled in most parts of the continent, and the animosities so violent, that I think it
wisest for a man who takes so much part as I do in
politics, to stay at home. Beside the absurd con-

structions that would be put upon one's journey, I
am not sure that I might not be in some places in an
unpleasant situation.   I am told Lord Wycombe * at
Brussels, has been insulted in the street as a Jacobin,
and as French manners seem every day gaining
ground in Europe, one does not know what might
happen.   However, I have not *quite* given up
a scheme which I was so fond of, and I will make
enquiries of such persons as have been in Germany
and Flanders this year, whether the violence I hear of
is as strong as it is represented.   I do not wonder
you saw the business of Genoa in the light you did.
It is indeed most disgraceful, and it seems as if we
were a little ashamed of it ourselves by Mr. Drake's
last note.†   Our cousin's ‡ representations in Switzerland are of the same stamp as all the rest of our
proceedings with neutral powers, only I think rather
more imprudent in that part where he says, that even
neutral nations ought to have no intercourse, direct or
indirect, with agents of the Convention. §   I wonder,

* Eldest son of the Marquis of Lansdowne.   He succeeded to the
title in 1805, and died, s. p., in 1809.

† Upon the measures of England at Genoa, in 1793, see Adolphus's
" History of George III.," vol. v., p. 508.   Mr. Adolphus states, that " in
adjusting such points with persons so predisposed, discussions took place
in which the British Ambassadors were sometimes obliged to use terms
not in exact conformity with the measured respect usually shown to
independent sovereigns."   Concerning Mr. Drake, see " Lord Holland's
Memoirs of the Whig Party," vol i., pp. 52, 59.

‡ Lord Robert Fitzgerald.   James, first Duke of Leinster, and Henry,
first Lord Holland, married daughters of Charles, second Duke of Richmond.   Lord Robert Fitzgerald was the son of the Duke of Leinster by
this marriage ; he was therefore first cousin to Mr. Fox, and first cousin,
once removed, to Henry, third Lord Holland.

§ The Note of Lord Robert Fitzgerald Minister Plenipotentiary of his

if the Swiss Minister had put him in mind of our
negotiation with Chauvelin,* what Lord Robert was
instructed to reply. In short there is such a bare-
faced contempt of principle and justice in every step
we take, that it is quite disgusting to think that it
can be endured. *France is worse* is the only answer,
and perhaps that is true in fact, for the horrors there
grow every day worse. The transactions at Lyons
seem to surpass all their former wickedness.† Do
you remember Cowper?

"Oh for a lodge in some vast wilderness!" ‡ &c.

" It is a much more natural wish now, than when it

Britannic Majesty to the Swiss Cantons, dated 30th November, 1793, with
the answer of the Swiss Republic, may be seen in the "Annual Register,"
vol. xxxv., p. 202—5. The following is the passage referred to by
Mr. Fox:—"The Minister of his Britannic Majesty will not decide
whether justice and the true interest of a State permit it to remain neuter,
against those who would again reduce it to barbarism, in a war of almost
all the powers of Europe—in a war where not only the existence of every
established government, but even that of all kind of property, is at stake.
He will only observe, that *neutrality itself will not authorize any correspondence, directly or indirectly, with the factious or their agents.* When
two legitimate powers are at war, the connection of a State with either
of them cannot injure their respective rights; but the present war being
carried on against usurpers, any correspondence with them by a neutral
State would be an acknowledgment of their authority, and consequently
an act prejudicial to the allied powers."

* Mr. Fox here refers to the correspondence between M. Chauvelin, the
French Minister in London, and Lord Grenville, the Secretary of State for
Foreign Affairs, at the end of 1792 and the beginning of 1793, which is
printed in the "Annual Register," vol. xxxv., pp. 114—28.

† The siege of Lyons by the army of the Convention, and the subsequent
devastation and massacre, took place in the autumn and winter of 1793.

‡ Mr. Fox alludes to the initial verses of the "Task," Book ii. :—

"Oh for a lodge in some vast wilderness,—
　　Some boundless contiguity of shade,—
　　Where rumour of oppression and deceit,

was uttered. If I had written yesterday, I should have said poor O'Hara! to day I am glad that he is a prisoner, as it has exempted him from being concerned in the evacuation of Toulon. We do not yet know to what number, but it is certain that thousands of poor wretches who had been deluded by our promises are now left by us to the guillotine. It must be a strong case of necessity which can justify such a proceeding, and at any rate it is fortunate for a man not to be concerned in it. That therefore which was thought a misfortune, I now esteem a great happiness for O'Hara.* I hear no certain news of Lord Moira's expedition, but I believe it is given up for the present.† So much for foreign affairs. At home we imitate the French as well as we can, and in the trials and sentences of Muir and Palmer in particular, I do not think we fall very far short of our original, excepting inasmuch as transportation to Botany Bay is less severe

> Of unsuccessful, or successful war,
> Might never reach me more ! My ear is pained,
> My soul is sick with every day's report
> Of wrong and outrage with which earth is filled."

The " Task " was first published at the beginning of 1785, in the interval between the American and French wars.

* In Sept. 1793, Toulon was garrisoned by a body of British, Spanish and Sardinian troops, and was besieged by the army of the Convention. In October, Lieut. General O'Hara arrived with a reinforcement from Gibraltar, and took the command of the garrison. Soon afterwards, General O'Hara was wounded in an attempt upon a fort, was taken prisoner, and sent to Paris. The evacuation of the town by the Royalists, and their foreign allies, speedily ensued (Dec. 1793).

† Lord Moira commanded an expedition off the coast of Brittany, in Nov. 1793 ; but he failed in effecting a junction with the Royalists, who had retreated into the interior, and after waiting a month, without landing, he returned to England. See Adolphus's " History of George III.," vol. v., p. 479.

(and to a gentleman that is not much) than death,
I do not think any of the French *soi-disant* judicial
proceedings surpass in injustice and contempt of law
those in Scotland; and yet I hear from good authority
what, till I heard it from authority, I resolutely
disbelieved, that not only these proceedings are to be
defended in Parliament, but that the sentences are to
be executed, and that *sedition*, the most vague and
loose in its description of all misdemeanours, is to be
considered as punishable, and actually to be punished
in Scotland, as a felony.   It is evident that those who
execute the supposed law in Scotland must *wish* it
were law here too, and such are the times that what
they wish they may easily obtain if they have the
courage to ask it.*   You will easily believe I shall not
acquiesce in this tyranny without an effort, but I am
far from sanguine as to success.   We live in times of
violence and of extremes, and all those who are for
creating or even for retaining checks upon power are
considered as enemies to order.   However, one must
do one's duty, and one must endeavour to do it
without passion, but everything in Europe appears to
my ideas so monstrous that it is difficult to think of
things calmly even alone, much more to discuss them
so, when heated by dispute.   Good God ! that a man

---

* Mr. Thomas Muir, an advocate, was tried at Edinburgh, in August,
1793, for sedition, and Mr. Thomas Fyshe Palmer, was tried at Perth, in
September, for the same offence. Both were sentenced to transportation for
fourteen years. See Howell's "State Trials," vol. xxiii., and Adolphus's
"History of George III.," vol. v., pp. 538—41. Mr. Adam called the attention of the House of Commons to the legality and propriety of these
sentences, on the 10th of March, 1794, on which occasion the conduct of
the Scotch judges was severely censured by Mr. Fox.

should be sent to Botany Bay for advising another to read Paine's book, or for reading the Irish address at a public meeting! for these are the *charges* against Muir, and the first of them is I think not satisfactorily proved.

"On tremble en comparant l'offense et le supplice."

" You will perceive by this long letter that I am not very sanguine about the events of this winter ; I am not indeed ; I feel it at the same time to be a most critical period, for if all these horrors abroad and at home can be endured with the bad success of the war, what will, or rather what will not be the power of the crown if chance should ever make us prosperous ?   It is true indeed that in the way in which we proceed this is not very likely to happen.

" God bless you, my dear Henry."

MR. GRENVILLE TO C. J. FOX.*

"Taplow, *December 29th,* 1793.

" Dear Charles,

" I sit down to write to you with an impression of greater uneasiness and anxiety, than has ever yet belonged to any letter from me to you : that impression is too the more hopeless because it arises not out of any new event, or alteration of any opinions which I have been used to entertain, but out of a conviction daily increasing in my mind, that the opinions which I hold are such as I cannot change, and

---

* This Letter is inserted here, as it tends to the explanation of those which follow.

yet are such as are likely to be most at variance with yours, in very many of the most probable subjects of public business, perhaps in the greater part of those which are at present easy to be foreseen. The main points of difference between us are two ; the one is respecting the war with France, which you condemn and oppose, while I think it the greatest of all duties to support and maintain it to the utmost : the other respects an apprehension which I entertain of those principles, and designs in this country adverse to the constitution of it, which makes me feel it to be my duty to resist whatever can give to such designs either strength, opportunity, or countenance ; while you on the other hand, believe in no such designs, and believe the danger to arise from there being too little spirit of free inquiry and resistance, in the minds of the people of this country. Either of these subjects of difference existing between us would tell much in public conduct, but both united extend very widely indeed, and must in their direct course, or at least in their bearings and consequences, pervade almost all measures of public discussion. I do not write to go into the arguments of these questions ; there is nothing new to be stated about them ; nor to any detail of new measures which would seem to call for any explanation ; I have none in view, other than a more direct and manifest assertion of those opinions which the pressure of the time seems to make necessary, and which it would be neither manly nor honorable, nor useful in me to disguise or suppress; if I write to you then at this moment, it is rather to anticipate the pain which I am to feel out of this miserable shape of things, and, bad philosophy as it may be to force both into your view and mine all this scene of uneasiness three weeks earlier than it need come, I have not been able to resist doing so. Perhaps that it is so unpleasant to me to write this letter, has been the temptation to me to do so: if I have any other motive it is only the honest one of making myself sure that you should know my thoughts and feelings to the same extent to which I know them myself. I know no other happiness in life, than that of being persuaded that I do right whatever may be the consequences, and sure I am that in this instance, I need not tell you what it was to me to do so.

> " Ever, my dear Charles,
>> " Very truly and affectionately yours,
>>> "THOMAS GRENVILLE."

MR. FOX TO LORD HOLLAND.

" *March 9th,* 1794.

" MY DEAR HENRY,

" I am quite ashamed when I think of my not having written you one line since the meeting of Parliament, but for some time you know your direction was uncertain: you will perceive from the newspapers to what numbers we are reduced, though small as they are, they are better than I expected. I mean the 59 upon the first day; * for the smallness of our divisions since

---

* Parliament met on the 21st of January, 1794. An amendment to the address, advising the Crown to treat with France for peace, was moved; but the original address was carried by 277 to 59 votes.

is owing to want of exertion for attendance, not to any defection. The Duke of P. (Portland), Fitzwilliam,* and Grenville † all came, or wrote to me some days before the meeting of Parliament, to tell me, with the strongest expressions at the same time of personal friendship and esteem, that they felt it necessary to take a more decided line than they had hitherto done, in support of the administration, in short to declare formally the separation, or rather the dissolution, of the Whig party. Many from this supposed that they meant to join Ministry by taking offices. I did not, and I now think it is clear that I was right. However they all voted for the address, and persuaded the Duke of Devonshire to do the same, and the Cavendishes in the House of Commons to stay away, for they could not be brought to vote with Pitt, or for the war. You will easily imagine how much I felt the separation from persons with whom I had so long been in the habit of agreeing; it seemed some way as if I had the world to begin anew, and if I could have done it with honour, what I should best have liked would have been to retire from politics altogether, but this could not be done, and therefore there remains nothing but to get together the remains of our party, and begin, like Sisyphus, to roll up the stone again,

---

* Earl Fitzwilliam, born 1748; died 1833.

† Mr. Thomas Grenville, second son of Mr. George Grenville, and brother to Lord Temple, afterwards Marquis of Buckingham, the writer of the preceding letter. His mission to Paris, in 1782, is described in the first volume of these Memoirs. For an account of Mr. Fox's friends who at this time joined the Government, see " Lord Holland's Memoirs of the Whig Party," vol. i. p. 73.

which long before it reaches the summit, may probably roll down again. Even in our small party all is not quite in harmony, but I rather think that the necessity of concert begins to be more felt, and that we may soon become something like a party. In the House of Commons we are weak in numbers, but not in argument, nor I think in credit, for notwithstanding Pitt's great majorities it is evident that the House is very far from sanguine about the war, if not altogether disgusted with it. Every thing we say against it is heard with great attention, and though Pitt has spoken two or three times extremely well, the House does not appear to be responsive to him. I must except from his good speaking this year, his first speech, and that of last Thursday, both of which, were uncommonly feeble and bad.* Burke has not appeared much this year, and Windham † has made a miserable figure. Your friend Jenkinson ‡ trains off, and I think Ryder § and Mornington ‖ rather come on. Of Canning ¶ I say nothing, because I cannot honestly

* The speeches of Mr. Pitt here alluded to are that on the debate on the address, January 21st, and that on Mr. Whitbread's motion, for a separate peace with France, March 6th, 1794.

† Right Hon. William Windham, born in 1750. He was first elected to Parliament, for the county of Norfolk, in 1784. His death took place in 1810, in consequence of an injury he received in assisting to extinguish a street fire.

‡ Robert Banks Jenkinson, second Earl of Liverpool, First Lord of the Treasury from 1820 to 1827; born 1770, died 1827. His father, Charles Jenkinson, was created Baron Hawkesbury in 1786, and Earl of Liverpool in 1796.

§ Dudley Ryder, succeeded to the title of Baron Harrowby in 1803, afterwards created Earl of Harrowby, died in 1847.

‖ Richard Wellesley, Earl of Mornington, in the Irish peerage, afterwards Marquis Wellesley, born 1760, died 1842.

¶ Right Hon. George Canning, born 1770, died 1827.

say anything a friend would like to hear.   On our side Grey I think is the person most improved. Sheridan has spoken admirably; but that is not new. Whitbread did very well indeed last Thursday,* which was the first time he has done so since the Russian business, which raised my expectations of him so much.   In the House of Lords, Lord Guilford † has raised himself very high in all people's opinions, and Lord Albemarle is very promising indeed.‡   The Duke of Bedford § spoke, as I hear from everybody, excessively well; which, on every account, I am very happy at.   His steadiness and zeal have been of the greatest use; and I think he is a man that, having begun, is sure to go on.   I look upon him to be one of the main pillars of the Party. You know I am one who think both property and rank of great importance in this country in a party view; and, in addition to these, the Duke of Bedford has a very good understanding; I wish I could add popular manners.   Lauderdale ‖ and Derby ¶ you know; in short, there is quite enough in the House of Lords to make it a very troublesome place to Ministers,

---

* In the motion for peace already mentioned.

† George Augustus, third Earl of Guilford.   His father, Frederick, second Earl (better known as Lord North), had died in 1792.   For a character of George Lord Guilford, see Lord Holland's "Memoirs of the Whig Party," vol i. p. 86.

‡ William Charles Keppel, fourth Earl of Albemarle, born 1772, died 1851.

§ Francis, fifth Duke of Bedford, born 1765, died, unmarried, 1802.

‖ James, eighth Earl of Lauderdale, born 1759, died 1839.

¶ Edward, twelfth Earl of Derby, born 1752, died 1834.   Characters of Lord Lauderdale and Lord Derby are given by Lord Holland, " Memoirs of the Whig Party," vol. i. p. 32.

and to give you an opportunity of debating when you
come.   When will that be ?   I do long to see you,
I own ; and when you have seen Italy I do not know
what should stop you.   At Naples there is a great deal
to see, particularly antiquities ; some of which are not
so much worth seeing for themselves, as for the very
pretty places you see in going to them.   The temples
at Pæstum are more curious than beautiful, but the
road thither is very well worth seeing, especially about
Salerno, which seems to be the country Salvator Rosa
most studied.

" I hope you have a good Italian master at Naples;
when I was there there was none, so I taught myself.
But when you get to Florence, where I advise you to
stay some time if you can, I advise you to have a
master, and to read with him ' Dante ' and other
difficult books ;   particularly, if you have time, read
the ' Tancia ' of Buonarotti.*   You cannot read it
without a master ;   and, indeed, scarcely with any
master who is not a Florentine.   God bless you, and
good bye, for I have written an enormous letter.
Pray go and see Lady Bessborough, and remember
me to her, and assure her of the pleasure with which
I hear, from the Duchess of D. (Devonshire), of her
growing better.   Tell her I have not yet been able to
execute her commission (she will understand you) ;
but that I beg she will always write to me whenever
she has anything to be done for her in England of
any sort."

* The ' Tancia ' of Michel Angelo Buonarotti, nephew of the great
artist, is a rustic comedy in *ottava rima*, written in the language of the
Tuscan peasants.   He was born in 1568, and died in 1646.

SAME TO SAME.

"SOUTH STREET, *9th March.*

"YOUR Uncle Dick is to move an address to-morrow se'nnight to desire the King to intercede for La Fayette.* If you were here, and of age, you would move a similar one in the House of Lords, would not you?"

SAME TO SAME.

"SOUTH STREET, 18*th March,* 1794.

"THOUGH I wrote to you so very lately I must write you one line to-day to tell you that Uncle Dick made one of the best speeches yesterday that I ever heard in Parliament. It was universally allowed to be so; and even Pitt, who is, as we all ought to be (according to poor Jack Lee's phrase) very *abstemious* in praising his enemies, could not refrain from complimenting him. We made a miserable division, considering the question, only forty-six, though your Uncle Ossory and a few other supporters of Ministry voted with us.† There is nothing new here of importance. Foolish people are sanguine about the scarcity of provisions in France, and others are waiting with great curiosity to know whether the King of Prussia will take or refuse the millions we

---

* Richard Fitzpatrick, second son of the first Earl of Upper Ossory; his sister, Lady Mary Fitzpatrick, was married to Stephen, second Lord Holland.

† The motion of General Fitzpatrick, relative to the detention of La Fayette, was made on March 17th, 1794. The motion was rejected by 153 to 46 votes.

are offering to him. Pitt tried last night to explain away Lord Hood's declaration in favour of the Constitution of 1789, but succeeded very ill even (as I should think) in his own opinion.* The country here are violent, and like to continue so. Our old Whig friends are many of them worse Tories than even those whom they have joined. Grenville maintained the right of the King to introduce foreign troops in time of war,† which his brother ‡ had nearly given up in the House of Lords. Windham defended the judgment upon Muir and Palmer, and more than insinuated that he wished the law of England was similar in those cases to what he supposed to be the law of Scotland.§ Arguments against the war and our alliances are heard favourably in the House of Commons, though they do not get us a vote; but sentiments of liberty and complaints of oppression are very little attended to, however well founded. In short, liberty is not popular; and of those who are attached to it, there are too many who have wild and impracticable schemes of government to which the miserable state we are in, both in regard to foreign affairs and our constitution, gives more plausibility and credit than they are by their own merit entitled to. The country seems divided (very unequally indeed) between the majority, who are subdued by fears or corrupted by hopes, and the minority, who are waiting sulkily for opportunities for violent

* In his speech on General Fitzpatrick's motion.
† Mr. Grenville, in the House of Commons, March 14th, 1794.
‡ Lord Grenville.
§ On Mr. Adam's motion, in the House of Commons, March 10th, 1794.

remedies. The few who are neither subdued enough to be silent through fear, nor desperate enough to give up regular opposition, in expectation of more violent measures, are weak both in number and weight; but, though weak, we are right, and that must be our comfort.

" Adieu, yours ever,

"C. J. F."

SAME TO SAME.

"St. Ann's Hill, *April 25th,* 1794.

" It is longer since I heard from you than it has ever been since you left England; but I hear from Ossory that you are very well. I have written you two letters since you came to Italy, one by Fabiani, a messenger who went with your chaise, and one by the post. In the first I gave you an account, at length, of politics, particularly as far as concerned myself. They go on, according to the Irish translation of *semper eadem,* worse and worse. I am heartily tired of them, but one must do one's duty. In the course of the debates upon the last measure of enlisting the Emigrants, it seemed to be avowed that the restitution of the old Government of France is *now* the object of the war, and that the re-instatement of the Emigrants in their possessions is to be a *sine quá non* of peace. Surely this is madness, or I am mad. Here am I passing a most comfortable week of holidays, the weather delicious, and the place looking beautiful beyond description, and the nightingales singing, and Mrs. A. as happy as the day is long; all which circumstances enable me to bear public calamities with wonderful philosophy; but yet I cannot help thinking now and then of the dreadful state of things in Europe, and the real danger which exists, in my opinion, of the total extinction of liberty, and possibly of civilization too, if this war is to go on upon the principles which are held out. We hear of a great struggle in Poland, but I do not like to indulge myself in hopes for the poor Poles, lest it should be all noise and end in a disappointment. I suppose I shall soon hear from you, and when I do I will write to you again, and, when I know where you are, put you in mind of something which you must not miss seeing. Pray, when you are at Florence, make an excursion to Camaldoli, Vallombrosa, and the country about Bibiena; I am sure you will be pleased with it, especially with Vallombrosa. I should like to have some notion when you are likely to come home; I suppose time enough for the next Session.

SAME TO SAME.

"MANAGER'S BOX, WESTMINSTER HALL,
"*April 29th*, 1794.

"HERE we are in this cursed place, very different from St. Ann's or from Tivoli, where perhaps you now are; and it begins to be doubtful whether we shall even finish this Session, though I hope we shall.*

"Pitt brought the message relative to the Prussian Treaty yesterday, and we are to vote the money to-morrow, 1,800,000*l.* for this year, and 1,400,000*l.*

---

* The impeachment of Mr. Hastings lasted from 1788 to 1795.

per annum for the future years of the war, exclusive
of what the Dutch are to pay ; and it will be borne here
with perfect patience, though I believe not *liked*.* I
like your politics very much, though I have not now
time to discuss them.   I do assure you the turn you
take upon these subjects is one of the most real satis-
factions that I enjoy ; perhaps it is in some degree an
enjoyment of pride and selfishness, but a most solid
enjoyment it is.

"I am sorry your schemes of travelling seem to put
off your return farther than I had hoped, but I think
you are in the right, and I most heartily wish I was
with you. If you go from Bologna to Venice pray do not
forget to go to Cento, where there are several beautiful pictures of Guercino ; † but one in particular, of
Christ in the Garden, which I think is the first of his
pictures, and perhaps the most *pleasing* picture in the
world.   I hope you like him very much, though he is
what is called a *mannerist*.   Avrà già veduto con
istupore le opere di Rafaelle nel Vaticano e principalmente la scuola d'Atene ed il sacramento.   Che vi
pare del San Girolamo del Dominichino?

"We expect, every day, news from Flanders. Your
Uncle Harry ‡ writes me word that he thinks a
general engagement likely to take place soon."

---

* The message from the Crown relative to the Prussian subsidy was
delivered to the House of Commons on the 28th of April, 1794, and taken
into consideration on the 30th, when Mr. Fox's amendment, for a vote of
1,150,000*l.*, instead of 2,500,000*l.*, as proposed by Mr. Pitt, was negatived
by 134 to 33 votes.

† Francesco Barbieri, called Guercino da Cento ; Guercino from his
squinting, and Cento from his birthplace.

‡ General Fox, brother of Mr. Fox.

SAME TO SAME.

"St. Ann's, *June 23rd,* 1794.

" I was very happy indeed, my dear Henry, to receive your last letter dated Venice, for I began to think it a long time since I had heard from you, or indeed of you, for Caroline has been gone to Bowood some time, and Rolleston said he had no directions from you about letters. I will keep your books for you, nor do I know that there are any, except perhaps the Parnaso,* that I shall beg of you. I have hitherto looked very little into them. I read one novel, ' El cochero honroso,' which I thought very poor, one thing in Cadalso, ' la Violeta,' † or some such name, which I like exceedingly, and ' Galatea,' in which there are many pretty things but not much genius. ‡ Cervantes's style in this, and I think in some other things, appears to me to be formed entirely upon Boccacio, whom by the way I do not know that he anywhere mentions, and it appears to me, to be forcible or affecting, or descriptive, precisely in proportion as it resembles its original. The poetry in ' Galatea ' is I think generally rather flat, though in some places, particularly where he imitates the manner of Ariosto, pleasant and easy. By the way that long speech of Calliope, in stanzas, is in the manner of it a

---

* "The Parnaso Español," a selection of Spanish poetry in several volumes.

† Don Joseph Cadalso wrote some poems, and a prose satire, entitled "Las Eruditos a la Violeta," which appeared in 1772. He wrote also "Las Cartas Marruecas," a very amusing work. He was killed at the siege of Gibraltar, in 1782.

‡ "The Galatea," a pastoral novel, by Cervantes.

most direct imitation of Ariosto, in those parts of his poem which we his admirers admire the least, and which his detractors are fondest of quoting ; so that I think the little slur which he throws upon him in ' Don Quixote,' might as well have been omitted. I have a great notion that ' Persiles ' will be more to my taste, though I have only looked at the first page of it.*   From what I once read in a translation of some works of Feyjoo,† I should think as you seem to do about him, but I will look into his works, because I heard the Bishop of Salisbury ‡ speak very highly of them the other day, and you know I have a great opinion of him.   So much for Spanish, only you have never said anything of Lope de Vega or Calderon, nor do I see any of their works among these books. I do not wonder at your admiring the Bolognese school and Guercino particularly, but Mrs. A. will never forgive you, if you have not taken particular notice of his picture of Christ in the Garden, at Cento, which probably you saw in your way from Bologna to Venice, though you do not mention it.   I think it by far the most pleasing of his works.   I have been always partial to the Venetian painters Titian and Tintoret, and I doubt whether there is any one picture upon the whole superior to the Martyrdom of St. Peter

* "Persiles and Sigismunda," a novel, by Cervantes.

† Feyjoo, a Spanish writer of celebrity, the author of numerous critical pieces, born 1701, died 1764.

‡ Dr. John Douglas, canon of St. Paul's, was Bishop of Carlisle in 1787, and was translated from Carlisle to Salisbury in 1791.   He died Bishop of Salisbury in 1807.   He is celebrated in Goldsmith's poem of " Retaliation" for his exposure of literary impostures.   See " Boswell's Johnson."

the Hermit.* Titian has not in general that greatness of manner (which there is however in this picture), nor that ideal beauty which some others have, but then I think he compensates for this by his exact representations of nature. I hope you admired properly the Martyrdom of St. Agnes by Domenichino at Bologna, which I think the finest there. Non mi piace molto quella Santa Cecilia di Raffaelle.† If you have time while you are at Florence go and see Vallombrosa and Camaldoli. I am sure they will answer ; but do not see so many things as not to give you time to come over in November, when I suppose Parliament will meet, and I should think you would not like to be absent the first day, which in times like these, is sure to be an important one. Many things have happened since I wrote to you last, but the state of things is essentially the same. We have had warm and good debates in Parliament, in which if my partiality does not deceive me, our advantage in speaking has been as great as that of the enemy in voting, especially upon the suspension of the Habeas Corpus, and on my motion for peace.‡ I believe the country is heartily tired of the war, but men dare not

---

* Mr. Fox appears to mean Titian's celebrated picture of Peter Martyr, in the church of San Giovanni e Paolo, at Venice. See " Murray's Handbook for Northern Italy," p. 348. Peter Martyr was killed in 1252 ; whereas Peter the Hermit died in 1115.

† The " St. Cecilia" of Raphael is in the Academia at Bologna.

‡ Mr. Fox moved fourteen resolutions, in the House of Commons, for terminating the war with France, on May 30th, 1794. There were 208 votes for the previous question, and 55 against it. The suspension of the Habeas Corpus was moved by Mr. Pitt on the 16th of May. This bill was carried by a large majority.

shew themselves. I think, of all the measures of
Government, this last nonsense about conspiracy is
the most mischievous and at the same time the most
foolish. How truly have they made good that parallel
you drew between the Jacobins of France and the
Crown party here! If they succeed in committing and
hanging any of these fellows whom they have taken up,
it will be considered as a corroboration of the conspiracy, and a pretence for more extraordinary powers;
if they fail, as I rather think they will, then, the consequence that always belongs to men who have been
falsely accused and acquitted will attach upon Horne
Tooke, Thelwall,* and others like them, and possibly
that danger which was only imaginary may in time
become real by these wise manœuvres, which unac-
countably to me, my old friends think calculated to
dispel it. Jay is come from America, and it is supposed everything will be settled amicably, but I own
I doubt it, from the disrepute in which everything
like moderation seems to be held in our councils at
present.† It is a great comfort to me to reflect how
steadily I have opposed this war, for the miseries it
seems likely to produce are without end. They say

---

* Horne Tooke and Thelwall were arrested on a charge of high treason,
and committed to the Tower in May, 1794. The trials of Hardy, Tooke, and
Thelwall took place in the following November, and in each case ended in
an acquittal.

† John Jay, born 1745, was one of the commissioners who negotiated the
treaty of Paris with England in 1782-3; and subsequently, as American
Minister to Great Britain, he signed the Commercial Treaty of 1784.
In 1794 he was sent on a special mission to Great Britain to complain of
captures and condemnations of American vessels during the French war.
See his letter to Lord Grenville on this subject, and Lord Grenville's
answer, in "Annual Register," vol. xxxvi. State-papers, pp. 247-50.

indeed, that the savage decree of the Convention forbidding quarter to the British and Hanoverians is repealed;* but I do not know upon what authority this is said, and its having existed even on paper, and for a short time, must have the worst effect in hardening the hearts of mankind, which God knows are hardened enough already. However in these bad times, here am I with Liz, enjoying the fine weather, the beauty and (not its least beauty) the idleness of this place, as much as if these horrors were not going on. When one has done all one can, as I think I have, to prevent mischief, one has a right I think to forget its existence if one is happily situated, so as not to be within its reach; and indeed I could not name any time of my life when I was happier than I am now, but I do not believe I should be so, if I had acted otherwise than I have done. This is quite such weather as you would like, warm enough to sit under a tree, and do nothing all day, or as Ariosto says :—

> 'All' ombra de'poggetti
> Legger d'antichi gli amorosi detti.'

I wish you were here to enjoy it with us, and faith for myself, that is almost the only wish I have. There is your picture on the other side of the room ready to say, I *say* my Uncle, and I do assure you that Mrs. A. looks at it with almost if not quite as much pleasure

---

* A decree of the Convention, prohibiting quarter to the English and Hanoverians, was passed upon a speech of Barrère, May 26th, 1794. It is stated in the "Annual Register," vol. xxxvi. p. 145, that the French armies never carried this decree into execution. The decree itself is printed in Marten's "Recueil des Traités," vol. v. p. 374.

as I do. Addio carissimo, this is a very long letter
considering the weather and the idleness which it
produces. I suppose you will not go to Venice again,
but if you do, pray see Sig. Gazzaniga, a composer,
and give him Mrs. A's. compliments and mine, and
desire him to send her some new airs, easy and pretty,
e su'l gusto Veneziano il piu che sia possibile."

SAME TO SAME.

"St. Ann's Hill, *August* 18*th*, 1794.

" It is so long since I wrote to you last that I think
I must write now, or you will fancy (which is very far
indeed from being the case) that I have forgot you.
The truth is I never had so great a dislike to writing
or talking about any event that ever happened as
about those which took place in the beginning of last
month. I have nothing to say for my old friends, nor
indeed as *politicians* have they any right to any
tenderness from me, but I cannot forget how long
I have lived in friendship with them, nor can I avoid
feeling the most severe mortification, when I recollect
the certainty I used to entertain that they never would
disgrace themselves as I think they have done. I
cannot forget that ever since I was a child Fitzwilliam
has been, in all situations, my warmest and most
affectionate friend, and the person in the world of
whom decidedly I have the best opinion, and so in
most respects I have still, but as a politician, I cannot
reconcile his conduct with what I, (who have known

him for more than five-and-thirty years,) have always thought to be his character. There is a sentiment in a writer from whom one would not expect much sentiment (I mean Lord Rochester) that I have always much admired and which I feel the truth of very forcibly upon this occasion : it is this—

" To be ill-used by those on whom we have bestowed favours is so much in the course of things, and ingratitude is so common, that a wise man can feel neither much surprise or pain when he experiences it; but to be ill-used by those to whom we owe obligations which we can never forget and towards whom we must continue to feel affection and gratitude is indeed a most painful sensation.'—I do not believe these are the words, but I know they are the sense of the passage I allude to. I think they have all behaved very ill to me, and for most of them, who certainly owe much more to me, than I do to them, I feel nothing but contempt, and do not trouble myself about them ; but Fitzwilliam is an exception indeed, and to my feelings for him everything Lord Rochester says, applies very strongly indeed. But I will not say any more upon this unpleasant subject, only that I do not think we shall be much weaker as an opposition, on account of what has happened, and one would think if anything happened as it used to do, that the events of this campaign must make us stronger. I hope you will come home soon, and if you make the figure I cannot help thinking that you will, it will make amends to me for everything, and make me feel alive again about politics ; which I am now quite sick of, and attend to only because I think it a duty to do so, and feel that it would be unbecoming my character to quit them at such a moment. Here I am perfectly happy. Idleness, fine weather, Ariosto, a little Spanish, and the constant company of a person whom I love, I think, more and more every day and every hour, make me as happy as I am capable of being, and much more so than I could hope to be if politics took a different turn. Though the death of Robespierre took place on the 28th of last month, we have yet no regular account of it here.* I own I think it a very good event in one view, that it will serve to destroy an opinion which was gaining ground that extreme severity and cruelty are the means of safety and success to those who practise them. Whoever comes in Robespierre's place, cannot be worse than he was in these respects, and I am afraid too, that they are not likely to be much better. As to the mischief this event may do by encouraging our ministry to go on with the war, I do not think of that at all, because I am persuaded they were determined on this point before. I hope you are diverted with the solemn recognition we have made in the Corsican business, of the sovereignty of the people, and of their right to *cashier* Kings, even without the pretence of misconduct; and to *elect* new ones.† The serious mischief

---

* Robespierre was guillotined on the 10th Thermidor, or 28th of July, 1794.

† In May, 1793, Bastia surrendered to the English fleet under Admiral Hood. The crown of Corsica was afterwards offered by Paoli and a deputation of the Corsican Provisional Government to the King of England. The offer was accepted, and Sir Gilbert Elliot went to Corsica

attending this nonsense, however, is, that it may be the means of throwing additional difficulty in the way of peace whenever we come enough to our senses to desire it. I have received two letters from you since I wrote last, the last from Bologna dated the 5th of July; you were near losing all credit with the Lady of the Hill for speaking so coldly about the Correggio at Parma;* but you recovered it a little by admiring so much that at the Caprara Palace, which was the first of the master she ever saw, and which she was wild about. I do not agree with you about your preference of Guido to all painters, but I have not time to discuss it now ; I like, however, the Massacre of the Innocents extremely, and think it a very good subject, and cannot think that the two old apostles, though most capitally executed I allow, can be considered as a remarkable instance of a painter's superiority in choosing subjects. You do not mention Domenichino, whom in some of his works I prefer to Guido. The Death of St. Jerome and the chapel of St. Cecilia in the Church of St. Louis at Rome, and the St. Agnes at Bologna are in my mind far superior to anything of Guido's.† Mrs. A. does not recollect

as Viceroy. Mr. Fox alludes to Burke's strictures, in his " Reflections on the French Revolution," on the doctrine of the Revolution Society, as to the " right of cashiering governors for misconduct."

* The picture called the "St. Jerome," now in the Galleria Arcidacale, at Parma, is probably alluded to.

† "The Death of St. Jerome," commonly called " The Communion of St. Jerome," considered the masterpiece of Domenichino, is in the Vatican. See "Murray's Handbook for Central Italy," p. 457. The chapel in the Church of S. Luigi, at Rome, contains several pictures by the same painter, ib. p. 423. " The Martyrdom of St. Agnes," by Domenichino, is

any more than I any fine Guercinos at Modena, but
we suppose you mean Guidos, of which I remember
two very fine ones I think.   I am sorry you have not
made more progress in Italian ; you ought to have
learnt it here, and then you would have easily perfected
yourself in it in Italy by hearing it spoke and speaking
it.   God bless you my dear Henry, and believe me.
            " Most affectionately yours,
                                    " C. J. F.

    " Lady Bessborough is not yet (I believe) come,
though she has been some time at Helvoet or Flushing,
I do not know which.
    " I like Persiles and Sigismonda very much, but I
have not yet finished it ; I have dipped into Mariana,
and like him much ; there is a very good passage
about the deposal of Henry IV. of Castile at Avila,
the gravity of which has a very good effect.   Come,
I must finish, for my pen would not write more if
I would.   I am not otherwise surprised at Ossory's
peerage than that I cannot conceive why he wished it."

                    SAME TO SAME.
                                " *August* 21*st*, 1794.
    " MY DEAR HENRY,
        " I wrote you so long a letter last Monday that
I only write now to thank you kindly for that which
I have received from you from Florence by a private
hand, I suppose by Mr. Newton.   Whether what you
say will ever be of use to me or not I cannot tell, but

---

in the Academia at Bologna, *ib*. p. 34.   The Massacre of the Innocents, by
Guido, is at Bologna.

at any rate I am equally obliged to you for the communication. What we have heard since I wrote last from Paris confirms me in my opinion that the destruction of Robespierre will make no considerable difference in the state of things; however, I still think it a good event in the view in which I mentioned it in my last letter. I believe I only spoke in my last of the ridiculousness and inconsistency of our behaviour in regard to Corsica, but I perfectly agree with you in the more serious objections which you feel to the proceeding, many of which indeed have already occurred to me.* I have had a letter from Jem Hare from Guadaloupe, with a long and melancholy account of the transactions there, which, however, does not differ materially from the official accounts published in the Gazette, only he speaks more particularly of the incredible bravery and *acharnement* with which the French fought in some of the actions.† If the French should be able to make head against us in the West Indies by sending out reinforcements (for without them I think they cannot), the figure Britain will have made in this war will be indeed most complete. It is, as you say, a great comfort indeed, to reflect that one is wholly innocent of all the national disgrace, and more extended calamity and misery which have already arisen, and will still increase, from the rashness and violence of our Ministers. When it will end or how it can end is

---

* See above, p. 83, n. †.

† Guadaloupe was taken by the English in the spring of 1794; but was afterwards retaken by a force of 2000 French, who sailed from Brest.

more than I can foresee. I am convinced our Government is as determined as ever to make no peace without Monarchy in France, which appears to be, if possible, more out of the chances than ever.

There was a report here some time ago that St. Just was Robespierre's chief rival and competitor. His falling with Robespierre seems to prove this idea to have been false,* and serves to show, among other instances, what erroneous accounts we have of things at Paris. I should not, therefore, have been sorry to have seen Mr. Smith, who, if he gives a candid account of France, is quite singular in so doing, for nothing can be so exaggerated as the accounts given by most of his countrymen who come from thence, who represent it as the most flourishing and happy part of Europe.

Notwithstanding all they talk of idleness, I have not had time to read five pages of Persiles these three days.

> " How various his employments whom the world
> Calls idle ! "

is my motto, which I have half a mind to have written upon the front of the house here. I have not seen your Uncle Dick since we were at Woburn together about a month ago. We had a very pleasant party there, but I am sorry to tell you that the Duke has overtaken me at tennis, and beat me even; last year I gave him near fifteen. We have a kind of annual party there, and next year when you are there the great pond is to be dragged, which has been kept for you. He takes much to politics, and will I have

---

* St. Just was beheaded with Robespierre, in 1794.

no doubt be steady. I believe I told you in my former letters not to omit seeing Vallombrosa, and Camaldoli, with both of which I am sure you will be delighted. Pray in the Palazzo Pitti (I think it is there) take notice of Titian's portrait of Paul the Third.* It is by far the finest portrait in the world to my thinking, and I have not yet heard you speak of Titian with the praise he deserves. There is a S. Mark by Fra Bartolomeo there too, which is a wonderful fine thing, and as grand as anything of M. Angelo. Dinner is on table, and indeed if it were not, I have nothing more to say, so God bless you and write me good long letters and come home as soon as you can."

SAME TO SAME.

"HOLKHAM, *October 5th*, 1794.

" I RECEIVED yesterday two letters from you, the last dated the 15th of September, and I have besides one which I received the very day after I last wrote to you, in answer to that which came by a private hand, so that I have three letters unanswered. As to the first, our tastes are certainly not very like in painting, for to doubt about Correggio, seems to me just as if a man were to doubt about Homer, or Shakspeare, or Ariosto ; and as to his imitators whom you dislike so, who are they ? Do you reckon Parmegiano one, and do you dislike him ? His other principal imitators that I know are, Schidone,

---

* The portrait of Paul III., in the Pitti Palace, is attributed, in " Murray's Handbook," to Paris Bordone.

Baroccio, and Sir Joshua Reynolds, all of them I think very excellent painters. You seem to think, (and in that I agree) that expression adapted to the subject is the first merit of a painter, and yet by some strange difference of seeing I suppose from me, you prefer Guido to Domenichino, who, of all painters excepting only Raphael, has this merit to the greatest degree. I did not mention his St. Agnes as his best, I think the St. Jerome, at Rome, and his frescoes in San Luigi,* much superior; but I mentioned it because being at Bologna, you might more easily compare it to the works of the other Bolognese painters. As to the St. Cecilia at Bologna, I am not ashamed of my opinion, and think, as Annibal Caracci said of it, after he had seen the Correggio at Parma, " Quella Santa Cecilia di Raffaelle mi pare una cosa di legno, così dura è e tagliente." But I have seen Charles Beauclerk, and I perceive that you have been encouraging one another in these heretical opinions so much, that there is no persuading you out of them. That Rubens is a greater genius than Paul Veronese (though by the way it was not quite fair to compare the first of the Flemish School with the second or third of the Venetian) I readily admit, but in point of that propriety of expression which I mentioned above, he is far his inferior. I do not know whether you were struck with the expression of countenance of a Pope in one of P. V.'s large pictures, I believe

---

* S. Luigi dei Francesi. The second chapel on the right contains two brilliant frescoes by Domenichino. See "Murray's Handbook—Central Italy and Rome."

that at Vicenza. He is listening I think to our Saviour, who is supping with him in the habit of a Pilgrim, and in point of grave and sedate expression, it is equal almost to anything in the school of Athens itself. I cannot conclude this subject of pictures without observing that, from questioning Charles Beauclerk, and from saying nothing about it, I conclude that neither of you saw when you were at Venice Titian's Martyrdom of Peter the Hermit,* which is by far his first work, and in grandness of style which is not usually his excellence, would not shame M. Angelo himself. By the way, in what you say of him (M. A.) I do most exactly agree with you, and here ends this discussion of pictures. I should be much more sorry if we should have any difference of opinion about politics, nor do I think it at all likely, except perhaps in the degree of utility which belongs to the system of party. I do not wonder that the late events lead you to doubt the wisdom of that system. I believe they have shaken everybody; and, if instead of doubting the wisdom of the system, you had said that they shewed you the *imperfection* of the system, I should entirely agree with you; so far I go, but no further. I remain of opinion, I hope not from mere obstinacy, that party is by far the best system, if not the only one, for supporting the cause of liberty in this country; and I fear the services it has done, will appear but too plainly from the mischiefs which are likely to follow its destruction, if indeed it be quite destroyed. I am

* See above, p. 77, n. §.

convinced that this system, and this alone, has prevented Great Britain from falling into what Hume*
calls, its euthanasia of absolute monarchy; and that,
therefore, it is my duty, and that of those who think
like me, to use the utmost endeavours to preserve
together what little remains of this system, or to
revive it if it is supposed to be quite extinct. The
master of this House,† the Duke of Bedford, Guilford,
and Derby, and some others, with myself, make undoubtedly a small basis, but then how glorious it
would be from such small beginnings to grow into a
real strong party, such as we once were. The times
are, in some respects, favourable to such an attempt;
at the commencement of the American war, though
we had a greater number of splendid names, we were
not much more numerous in Parliament, and we grew
to what we afterwards were by events. This war
must grow to be disliked by all classes of people, as
much, or more than the American war, and we may
profit, as a party, by such an opinion becoming prevalent. You may say, that when we are again
become strong other men may act as the Duke of P.
(Portland), &c., have done, and again reduce us;—they
may;—but this is an objection to all systems, for in

---

* Hume, Essay vii., on the question, "Whether the British Government
inclines more to absolute monarchy or to a republic," contemplates the case
in which the House of Commons will be the sole governing body in the
State. He then proceeds to say, "As such a violent government cannot long
subsist, we shall, at last, after many convulsions and civil wars, find repose
in absolute monarchy, which it would have been happier for us to have
established peaceably from the beginning. Absolute monarchy, therefore,
is the easiest death, the true euthanasia of the British Constitution."

† Mr. Coke afterwards Earl of Leicester.

all systems men must be the actors and the means,
and men are always liable to act both corruptly and
absurdly. The question upon the solution of which,
in my opinion, principally depends the utility of
party, is, in what situations are men most or least
likely to act corruptly—in a party, or insulated ? and
of this I think there can be no doubt. There is no
man so pure who is not more or less influenced, in a
doubtful case, by the interests of his fortune or his
ambition. If, therefore, upon every new question a
man has to decide, this influence will have so many
frequent opportunities of exerting itself that it will in
most cases ultimately prevail ; whereas, if a man has
once engaged in a party the occasions for new decisions are more rare, and consequently these corrupt
influences operate less. This reasoning is much
strengthened when you consider that many men's
minds are so framed that, in a question at all dubious,
they are incapable of any decision ; some, from nar-
rowness of understanding, not seeing the point of the
question at all ; others, from refinement, seeing so
much on both sides, that they do not know how to
balance the account. Such persons will, in nine cases
out of ten, be influenced by interest, even without
their being conscious of their corruption. In short,
it appears to me that a party spirit is the only sub-
stitute that has been found, or can be found, for
public virtue and comprehensive understanding ;
neither of which can be reasonably expected to be
found in a very great number of people. Over and
above all this, it appears to me to be a constant

incitement to everything that is right; for, if a party spirit prevails, all power, aye, and all rank too, in the liberal sense of the word, is in a great measure elective. To be at the head of a party, or even high in it, you must have the confidence of the party; and confidence is not to be procured by abilities alone. In an Epitaph upon Lord Rockingham, written I believe by Burke, it is said, " *his virtues were his means ;* "* and very truly; and so, more or less, it must be with every party man. Whatever teaches men to depend upon one another, and to feel the necessity of conciliating the good opinion of those with whom they live, is surely of the highest advantage to the morals and happinesss of mankind; and what does this so much as party ? Many of these which I have mentioned are only collateral advantages, as it were, belonging to this system; but the decisive argument upon this subject appears to me to be this: Is there any other mode or plan in this country by which a rational man can hope to stem the power and influence of the Crown? I am sure that neither experience nor any well-reasoned theory has ever shown any other. Is there any other plan which is likely to make so great a number of persons resist the temptations of titles and emoluments ? And if these things are so, ought we to abandon a system from which so much good has been derived, because some men have acted inconsistently, or because, from the circumstances

---

* This inscription is printed in Lord Albemarle's " Memoirs of the Marquis of Rockingham," vol. ii. p. 46. It is to be seen in a mausoleum at Wentworth Woodhouse. The words of the inscription are : " His virtues were his arts."

of the moment, we are not likely to act with much
effect ? I had no idea of going on so far when I
began, or I would have endeavoured to have written
a little more regularly and systematically upon a subject which I have certainly thought much of, but not
with a view of discussing it in a regular way ; but
when we meet, which I hope will now be soon, I will
talk it over with you till you are tired. I am much
obliged to you for your account of what has passed
with respect to Tuscany and Corsica, many particulars
of which are entirely new to me. I depend upon
your being in England before the 21st of next month ;
and, as Parliament is now prorogued till the 25th, you
may let me know before the meeting how far some of
the facts you mention can be stated as certain, because
they appear to me to be very important. This last
prorogation will enable you to take your seat the first
day of the session, which I suppose you will do. I
do not wonder at all at your suspecting that there is
an inclination to take a pretence for treating with the
French Republic ; but I have reason to think that
there is none ; but, on the contrary, that in conversation it is pretty openly avowed, " *No peace without
monarchy in France.*" It appears to be madness ; but
the American war went on long after all hope of
success was at an end ; and this will still longer,
because *then* there was a strong party against the
Ministry, and now there is a weak one, or none.
Affairs in the Low Countries go on from bad to worse ;
and I begin to think that Holland will fall ; and only
hope that Burke was not quite correct in saying

the banks of Amsterdam and London were one
and the same, though I know they are very nearly
connected.*

"What a length of a letter; you need not read it
through at one sitting.   Adieu.

"Yours most affectionately,

"C. J. FOX."

SAME TO SAME.

St. Ann's Hill, 15th December, 1794.

"THERE are many reasons besides the mere desire of
seeing you, (which perhaps however may have its
weight even more than one perceives), which make
me wish you very earnestly to come home.   The
argument which may possibly weigh most with you,
is, that which without affectation I feel the least, I
mean the credit and even to a certain degree, the
strength which at a moment so peculiarly critical to
me as well as to the country, I should derive in my
political situation from your taking a part at this
particular juncture.   That there is something in this
I admit, but the degree of strength, or power, or even
credit which I may have in the country, is grown to
me an object of much more indifference than it used
to be, or may be than it ought to be; and what I
have left of ambition is much more for others than
myself.   But my principal reason for wishing so
anxiously for your coming is, that I think you *ought*

---

* This must allude to some passage in a speech of Mr. Burke's, when
the policy of defending Holland was in question.

to come. With the opinions which you entertain of
public affairs, and in your station of life it is a duty
to support those opinions, in the manner that may be
most useful to the cause, and the declaration of one
young man in favour of it at a time when it has so
few supporters may be more serviceable to it, than of
ten at another time, not to mention how much more
honourable and satisfactory it is to have declared
against a system in the time of its strength, than to
appear to join in the cry against it when it is falling.
Whether even if you stay away this whole session,
you will have lost the opportunity of joining us in our
weak state I do not know; I rather think not, but I
do not like that you should risk it. I am sure if you
will reflect, and take into consideration, the extraordinary importance of the present times, you will
think you ought to come home. At least I think so
so strongly that I am very anxious indeed that you
should.

"I have not time to day to write to you upon half
the things that I had intended, so will only say one
word in answer to what you say in your last about
party. You conceive the influence of the Crown,
which you admit party to be good for counteracting,
to be all abuse, and that it may be destroyed; and in
this in my opinion consists your principal error.
How is it possible that the Executive Government of
such an empire as ours, should not have a great
patronage, which must always be liable to be abused
for the purpose of improper influence? The defence of
such extensive possessions, and the collection of so

large a revenue must always in our form of government be attended with an influence of the Crown, to
counteract which, party (even according to your
notions of it) is necessary, and I am so far from
thinking as you do that this influence may be destroyed, that I am at a loss for any plan by which it
can be in any considerable degree diminished, and
perhaps the more you think upon this subject practically and in detail, the more difficulties you will find;
however let anything be tried that affords any rational
hope of success, though I may not be sanguine in it.
You will perceive I am always speaking upon the
supposition of the form of government remaining
unaltered, but even in the case of republics, I think I
could equally shew the necessity of party principles
and parties, but as I believe we thoroughly agree in
wishing the form of government to continue, that
argument would be foreign to our present purpose.
However of all these things I shall have great pleasure
in conversing with you, at leisure, and more perhaps
than you will like. Adieu; I must finish, though I
have a thousand things to say. I have no doubt but
you rejoiced as I have done upon all these acquittals,*
about which I was very anxious indeed. It is a good
thing that the criminal justice of the country, is not
quite in the hands of the Crown. I thought as you
did, that the Emperor was thinking of peace, but as
it is now public that we are to lend him or to be
collateral security for him, for six millions sterling,

---

* The acquittals of Hardy, Horne Tooke, &c., which did so much
honour to the honesty of our juries and the eloquence of our bar.

I take it for granted that he is to go on with the war.
The Duke of York it is supposed is not to go back, and
the Duke of Brunswick is to be solicited to command.
There is a talk of an expedition to France. In short
everything that is mad and desperate is *à l'ordre du
jour*.

"God bless you my dearest Henry. Pray write, and
if you come yourself with your letter, so much the
better."

SAME TO SAME.

"St. Ann's Hill, December 25th, 1794.

"I SHALL defer any more argument upon the
subject of party till we meet and are at leisure,
because whatever may be our opinions upon that
question, our conduct at *present* would be the same ;
but I think you quite right in considering the subject
over again, and not shutting your ears to the arguments on either side of the question, for, on each side
there are many, though I confess I am very clear as to
the result of a fair comparison of them. It is singular
enough that while we have been arguing this point,
Lauderdale, in his pamphlet which is just published,
and which I wish you very much to see, has dilated
upon it very considerably, and has argued it (on my
side), as I think, very ably. I wish I may find an
opportunity of sending you his book, not more though
for the sake of this part of it than of others, for it
really is an excellent pamphlet; I mean in point of
matter, for as to style it is very uncouth indeed, and
in many parts not more English or grammatical than

his speeches.* I thank you for your intelligence about the Emperor. The loan for him here had made us conjecture matters to be as you state them, but there are circumstances in what you mention of which I was wholly ignorant; and, in general, pray do not neglect sending me information, from a supposition that it may be stale, for you have no conception how mainly ignorant we are here with respect to what passes in far the greater part of Europe. There is a point upon which I am very anxious indeed, and upon which you are I dare say still more so, I mean Lafayette's escape and supposed recapture, but even upon this I can give you no information. That he escaped is, I believe, certain ; that he was retaken has been asserted and contradicted with almost equal confidence, but I own that his safety not having yet been authentically made known by *himself* to his friends here makes me incline to fear that it is not true.† The papers today are full of negotiations for peace between France and Holland, but whatever may be the issue of them, I do not think they have any tendency to bring about a *general* peace. If the French

---

* Mr. Fox appears to allude to a pamphlet published by Lord Lauderdale, in 1794, entitled " Letters to the Peers of Scotland."

† La Fayette having left France in August, 1792, fell into the hands of the Austrians, and, after being detained in several places of imprisonment, was ultimately transferred to Olmütz. In October, 1794, La Fayette, with the assistance of a Dr. Bollmann and a young American named Huger, made an attempt at escape from Olmütz ; but was retaken at a distance of only eight leagues, and brought back to his prison. This is the circumstance to which Mr. Fox alludes. He was ultimately liberated, in consequence of the negotiations at Leoben, in September, 1797. An interesting account of this attempt, with full details, is given in the Conversations-Lexicon, art. Bollmann.

should make a separate peace with the Dutch upon the terms of the *status quo ante bellum*, as it is reported, their enemies will probably consider it as a symptom of weakness. I shall consider it as the strongest instance in history of a nation preferring the principles of justice to the *apparent* dictates of policy, and I have so strong a *desire* to think the exercise of justice always prudent upon a large scale, that I generally do so. And even in this case, I rather think that the advantage the French will gain in point of reputation, if they act as it is supposed, will compensate for the advantages they evidently sacrifice in the mode of carrying on the war. However, all this is speculation upon an hypothesis which I do not believe to be founded. At any rate the general conduct of the French since Robespierre's death appears to be extremely good, and has reconciled me to them wonderfully. But they ought still to go farther than they have done, and especially with regard to that description of Emigrants who became such from the danger they were exposed to by the system of tyranny which is now so universally condemned.* * * Parliament meets Tuesday. I do not know of any accessions in the House of Commons, but I think it impossible we should not have some before the end of the session. In the House of Lords we have hopes of Thurlow and the Duke of Leeds, and some talk of the Duke of Richmond, ma io non lo credo. However, the circumstances of the times must bring these, and many more soon.

"Adieu! yours most affectionately,

"C. J. F."

SAME TO SAME.

"SOUTH STREET, *February 24th,* 1795.

" I DO not believe the Ministry are doing anything towards peace, and yet this is to suppose them mad, for there is every reason to suppose the French are inclined to peace if it can be had on just terms.—Every day things will grow worse. Guadaloupe is gone, St. Domingo is nearly gone, and must be quite so in a short time, and our own islands of Antigua and Dominica must fall if the French know what they are about, which they generally do.

" P.S.—I have just heard that orders are sent to Ireland to Lord Fitzwilliam to replace all the people whom he has turned out; I do not believe it, but if true I think it impossible that Fitz can submit to it, and that there must be a break up."*

SAME TO SAME.

"*March, 6th,* 1795.

" THOUGH I have no time to write you more than a few lines, I must not let the post of to-day go without telling you how very much delighted I am with your verses to Mrs. A., which I received together

* Lord Fitzwilliam was appointed Lord Lieutenant of Ireland in December, 1794, and recalled in March, 1795. His recall was produced by a difference with the English Ministry respecting a motion in the Irish Parliament for the relief of Roman Catholics. See Lord Holland's "Memoirs of the Whig Party," voi. i. p. 75. See also Adolphus's "History of the Reign of George III."

with another letter from you dated the 24th of January this morning. I do not know that the verses, as such, are particularly good, but there is a kindness in them and something altogether that made me quite happy when I read them, and indeed you are right, for I believe if ever there was a place that might be called the seat of true happiness, St. Ann's is that place.

"In a postscript to the last letter I wrote you, I told you a report of the Ministry here having disavowed Fitzwilliam ; I did not then believe it, but it is turned out to be true, to a greater extent even than the report. He is to come home immediately, and states himself publicly to have been betrayed and deserted not only by Pitt, but by the Duke of Portland.* The business will I hope be made public soon in all its parts. At present it is very unintelligible, but I feel myself quite sure that Fitzwilliam will turn out to be as much in the right in all its points, as he is clearly so in my judgment, with respect to the measures about which the difference between him and the Ministry is said to be the widest. I am told they gave out that the Catholic Bill is the real cause of his recall and that the question of Beresford Attorney General, &c., is comparatively of no consequence. Now as to the Catholic Bill, it is not only right in principle, but after all that was given to the Catholics two years ago,† it seems little short of madness to

* The Duke of Portland, who had been First Lord of the Treasury in the Coalition Ministry, was now Secretary of State for the Home Department, having been appointed to that office in July, 1794.

† Mr. Fox alludes to the 33 Geo. III. c. 21 (Irish), by which various

dispute (and at such a time as this) about the very little which remains to be given them. To suppose it possible that now that they are electors they will long submit to be ineligible to Parliament, appears to me to be absurd beyond measure, but common sense seems to be totally lost out of the councils of this devoted country. In Ireland there is, as you may suppose, the greatest agitation; addresses from all parts marking respect and attachment to Fitzwilliam and his system, and implying of course the contrary to his successor, whoever he may be, and to the old system which he is to revive. I think this business has made great impression here, but whether it will have any effect God knows. Adieu, my dear Nephew, I have no time to write more at present.

" Yours most affectionately."

SAME TO SAME.

" House of Commons, *March 6th.*

" I HAVE just been at the House of Lords, where Lord Loughborough has been speaking against Hastings upon the Benares charge. I left Thurlow defending him, very lamely indeed, but yet as it is supposed successfully."

SAME TO SAME.

" *April 12th,* 1795.

" Mrs. A. tells me that it is a long time since I

disabilities of the Irish Roman Catholics, and, among others, the disqualification to vote at elections of members of Parliament or municipal officers, were repealed.

wrote to you; I thought not, but yet I recollect that
when I wrote last, I was in the ninth book of the
Odyssey, which I have since finished and read eighteen
books of the Iliad, so that it must be a good while
since. I think the superiority of the Iliad is greater
than I had imagined, or than I believe is generally
allowed, and more than makes up for the fable being
so much less entertaining. To be sure the battles are
too long, and the wounds too minutely described,
but there is a charm in it which makes one read on
with eagerness, and a rapidity and fire and freedom
in the manner that surpasses all other poets; and I
mean this of his style in general, exclusive of the
passages (of which there are so many) containing
anything particularly sublime or affecting. In short
the more I read the more I admire him. There are
parts of Virgil (and among those too imitated from
Homer) which I think fully equal to Homer, but then
he has not in any degree approaching to his master
that freedom of manner, which I prize so much; and
Milton, who has some passages as sublime as possible,
is in this respect still more deficient, or rather he has
no degree of it whatever. Ariosto has more of it than
any other poet, even so as to vie in this particular
merit with Homer himself, and possibly it may be that
my excessive delight in him, is owing to my holding
in higher estimation than others do, the merit of
freedom and rapidity. My mind is so full of poetry
just now that I could not help giving you the *sec-
caggine* of this long intrusion, though I suspect you are
quite out of the habit of reading poetry, as you never

say a word either of Ariosto or Dante, or Tasso, or
indeed of any poet at all; and yet you write some, and
I think your translation of Medea to Jason one of the
best things you ever did in that way.   You have done
Dos ubi sit quæris and what follows,* remarkably well,
but you have failed very much in these two beautiful
lines :—

> ' Jussa domo cessi, natis comitata duobus,
> Et qui me sequitur semper, amore tui.' †

" Now for politics. The French answer to our propositions is come, and all hopes of peace are at an
end. ‡ From the circumstances attending our proposition, and the delay in making it, they were fully
justified in suspecting our sincerity; but, even upon
that supposition, I do not think their answer judicious.
As yet I do not perfectly understand it, because till
I have examined, or got examined by others, their
public Acts, I cannot say precisely what countries
they consider themselves by the Constitution as forbidden to alienate. The Ministers give out that they
mean *all* the countries conquered in Europe; I am convinced they do not mean this; but I suspect they do
mean quite enough to make their answer very high,
if not insolent. Pitt does not mean to lay the papers
before Parliament; but I think we must have some

---

* Ovid, " Heroid." xii. 199.   † Ibid, v. 135.

‡ I do not know what propositions are here alluded to. In the debate
on the address, October 29th, 1795, Ministers are reproached by Mr. Fox
with not having, up to that time, consented to negotiate with France;
while " Prussia had made peace with her, many of the States of Germany
had made peace with her, and, among others, the Elector of Hanover had
made peace."—" Fox's Speeches," vol. v. p. 497.

discussion upon them, which I fear cannot be so managed as not to give him some advantage in representing us to the Country as men who are inclined to make peace upon too low terms. It is an awkward thing for us to say, but the true inference to be drawn from the late transaction is, that it is impossible for a Ministry who have made war upon the principles upon which these Ministers have made it, to make any peace except by unconditional submission on one side or other. This was thought to be true in the American War, and in every other case that has any similarity to it, and will be found to be true in the present instance also; so that how long this war will continue God knows. The state of finance here is very bad indeed, and what Pitt intends to do next Monday to remedy the present *temporary* scarcity of money, as he calls it, I know not. Nothing effectual can be done, I believe; and I fear that in a very short time (maybe in a few years) our finances will be in such a state as to be wholly incapable of remedy from any Minister whatever. I do not think that even peace would prevent our experiencing great difficulties, nay, perhaps it might accelerate them; but the continuation of the war, on the other hand, must make every remedy more difficult, and consequently the ruin more certain. I forget whether my last letter to you was before or after Grey made his excellent speech upon this subject.* He is improved to the greatest degree; and would, if the country were in a state to admit of being saved, be as likely to

---

* On the 26th of February, 1795, in the House of Commons.

save it as any man I ever knew. As to myself, I grow every day to think less of public affairs ; possibly your coming home and taking a part in them might make me again more alive about them ; but I doubt even that. The Bills of this year appear to me to be a finishing stroke to everything like a spirit of liberty ; and though the country did show some spirit while they were depending, yet I fear it was only a temporary feeling, which they have quite forgotten. I wish I could be persuaded that it was right to quit public business, for I should like it to a degree that I cannot express ; but I cannot yet think that it is not a duty to persevere. One may be of opinion that persevering is of no use ; but ought a man who has engaged himself to the Public to trust so entirely to a speculation of this sort as to go out of the common road and to desert (for so it would be called) the public service ? Would it not be said, with more colour than ever, that my object was all along personal power ; and that, finding that unattainable, I gave up all exertion for the Public ? I know there is another view of this question, and that it may be said with some truth, that by persevering we are assisting the imposture which is putting upon the people, that the government is still a free one. But, though some would put a candid construction upon secession, yet, as I do not think the people are in a disposition to interpret favourably the conduct of public men, I fear the general opinion would be what I mentioned before ; that, having lost all hope of place, we left the country to take care of itself. Homer makes Ulysses say,—

'Αλλὰ τίη μοι ταῦτα φίλος διελέξατο θυμός ;
οἶδα γὰρ ὅττι κακοὶ μὲν ἀποίχονται πᢐλέμοιο ; *

and I cannot help feeling something like the same
sentiment ; I am so sure that secession is the measure a
shabby fellow would take in our circumstances, that
I think it can scarcely be right for us. But as for
wishes, no man ever wished anything more. I am
perfectly happy in the country. I have quite resources
enough to employ my mind ; and the great resource
of all, literature, I am fonder of every day ; and then
the Lady of the Hill is one continual source of happiness to me. I believe few men, indeed, ever were
so happy in that respect as I. Besides, with my
limited income, it would be far easier to us to keep
out of debt, if I were not obliged to have a house in
town. In short, every reason that relates to my own
interest or happiness is on the side of giving up the
thing, and perhaps this makes me suspect the argument on that side of the question. However events
and circumstances may happen which may make that
right which I am sure would be pleasant, and I think
it not unlikely but they may. God bless you. I do
not make any apology for all this about myself,
because I know it interests you ; and I wish it may
be an example to you to talk to me a little about yourself, which you never do. Mrs. A. desires her love to
you kindly, but she quite despairs of ever seeing
you."

---

* Yet wherefore doubtful ? let this truth suffice ;
The brave meets danger, and the coward flies.
"Iliad," xi. 407-8.—Pope's Translation.

SAME TO SAME.

"ST. ANNS, *May* 17*th*, 1795.

" I HAVE so many unanswered letters of yours, that to answer them is quite out of the question ; and I can only thank you very heartily for them, and assure you that, besides the pleasure which hearing from you always gives me, a great many of them have given me a great deal of information upon points about which we were here very much in the dark. I am very glad to find by your last, first, that we agree so exactly in our sentiments about France ; and next, that you are so well pleased with my speech upon the state of the nation.* I exactly agree with you, that for France alone Robespierre is worse than any other despotism ; but that, for the general good, considering the diabolical principle of the present war, even his government, or a worse, if worse can be, is better than the restoration of the Bourbons. This last many persons here think not an unlikely event, and certainly this is the opinion of many individuals who have lately come from France ; but I cannot believe it, and most sincerely do I deprecate it. Even the opinion of its probability does great mischief, as it encourages many people in thinking, that by waiting for such an event we may have a more honourable peace. However, I believe the general opinion is very strongly for immediate peace ; but there is a slackness about expressing it, and a general torpor that is quite incredible, and would be very disheartening to me, if I did not deter-

* In the House of Commons, March 24th, 1795.

mine that nothing upon earth shall ever have that effect.   I believe I did speak very well upon the state of the nation, and yet I am very much surprised it should have been so ; for my mind had been for some time in a state of great uneasiness, and I never felt less inclined to speak in my life ; however, all my friends flattered me about it, and even as it is taken down in the newspapers you seem satisfied with it : how it so happened is one of those paradoxes about the human mind which I am sure I cannot explain. At present, the Prince's establishment and debts are the subjects which occupy most attention.   I voted in the majority on Thursday, and made a speech which may possibly be nearly equally displeasing to all parties and persons.   However, it seemed very well received by the House ; and some people think Pitt will adopt my ideas, and be kind enough to let me act as Minister upon this agreeable occasion, which I shall not know how to avoid.*   Wilberforce is to make a motion for peace next Thursday ; and he I am told, and others are very sanguine about the division ; I am not, though I am convinced there are not twenty members in the house who are not really with us in opinion ; but the system of confidence has outrun all bounds and all former example, with this new circumstance, that it is now confidence without the basis of good opinion, and without the pretence of success."†

* Mr. Fox alludes to the debate, on the 14th of May, respecting the settlement of the revenue of the Prince of Wales, and the payment of his debts, upon his marriage with the Princess Caroline of Brunswick.

† Mr. Wilberforce's motion in favour of a peace with France was made

"South Street, *May 19th.*

" I BEGAN this at St. Ann's and meant to finish it here, but I have not had a moment's time, I will write by next post or at least next week."

SAME TO SAME.

"South Street, *Sunday, June 14th,* 1795.

" My dear Henry,

" When I sent my last I told you I would write again in a few days, and it is now I believe above three weeks since and I have not written a line, I was always till this last week either in the House of Commons or going backward and forward to St. Ann's, where I sometimes stayed only a day and of course liked to have it a complete holiday. The Prince's business turned out as I foretold you; Pitt adopted my plan, for which though I believe the King and Prince are a good deal displeased at him, they are not more pleased with me. However, I could not do otherwise than I have done, and I am sure it is the best plan for the Prince's real interests, and the only one which can operate to soften in any degree the general odium against him. I believe it is since I wrote to you, that the news of the insurrection at Paris and Toulon arrived.* The foolish sanguineness

on May 27th. The House decided in favour of proceeding to the orders of the day, by 209 to 86 votes.

* This allusion is to a body of insurgents, who broke into the hall of the Convention, and demanded bread and the Constitution of 1793, on the 1st of April, 1795. About the same time the insurgents obtained possession of Toulon; but, on marching to Marseilles, they were met by a considerable force of the troops of the Convention, and were defeated.

of Ministers upon these events is beyond all description, and all of them believed for a time, and for aught I know still believe, that Royalty is sure to be re-established in France in a few weeks. Report says, that we are at last going to send an expedition to the western parts of France; but I doubt it, and indeed do not think it will take place unless some much more certain accounts of the force of the Chouans should come, than any which have been yet received.* On the day of Wilberforce's motion, we had what I reckon a pretty good division; Pitt made a good speech, in which he plainly showed how very sanguine he was, and Windham made the most ridiculous and absurd one that I ever heard, and indeed it was most universally so considered. The Austrian Loan has been voted by small majorities, and evidently I think against the grain. Indeed, it is the most impudent measure all things considered, that ever was carried through.† The Prince's business has since been the chief business, which is much too complex to explain to you, and which perhaps you will scarcely understand from the newspapers. To-morrow it comes on again, I hope for the last time, for I am heartily tired of it, and of the Session too, and do very much long for St. Ann's, and quiet. Mrs. A. and I had each a letter from you

* The disastrous expedition to Quiberon sailed in the beginning of June in this year.

† This measure was the guarantee of a loan of 4,600,000*l.* to the Emperor, for defraying the expenses of the war with France. The message from the Crown, on which it was founded, was brought down by Mr. Pitt on the 4th of February. The convention between the Emperor and the King of England, by which the interest of the loan was guaranteed, is in Martens, "Recueil des Traités," vol. vi. p. 508.

last week, I need not say how much pleasure your letter to her gave me. You were never more right than in what you say of my happiness derived from her; I declare I think my affection for her increases every day. She is a comfort to me in every misfortune, and makes me enjoy doubly every pleasant circumstance of life; there is to me a charm and a delight in her society, which time does not in the least wear off, and for real goodness of heart if she ever had an equal, she certainly never had a superior.

" I am very much obliged to you for your account of the different language, held at different periods by our Court to Austria. It is very curious, but the inference which you naturally enough draw from it, that we are inclined to negotiate, is certainly not the fact. I do not think it would have been so even without the late events, and the distress for bread in France; but as it is, it is totally out of the question, as our Ministers say (and I believe think too), that by waiting a few months they shall have peace their own way. This appears to me to be madness, but so it is; as far as I can judge the country does not join with them in this delusion, but yet it is not yet ready to speak vigorously against Ministry, and till it does, the effect of public opinion will not be what it ought to be. As the post does not go till Thursday, I will finish this letter another time."

"*Tuesday, June 16th,* 1795.

" SINCE I began my letter, news is come of the taking
of Luxembourg,* and of the death of the young Capet.†
The first of these events puts out of the question all
attacks upon France in her northern frontier, and the
second I think will tend very much to damp the
spirit of royalism if any such exists in France, as
Monsieur ‡ is very generally and justly odious and
contemptible; and besides the cause of monarchy is
never tried to so much advantage, as when the person
who is to exercise it is unknown. The Chouans seem
to be alive again; but the report which has been
spread here of their being masters of L'Orient, does
not appear to be founded.

" In regard to what you say about any intimate
connexion between Lansdowne§ and me, I agree
almost entirely with you, except perhaps that I do not
give him the credit for sincerity in any system which
you seem to do. I never can have a good opinion of
him, and still less a great one. However, we are
upon terms of the greatest civility, and it must be
confessed that his conduct for these last three years
has had an openness and consistency, which entitles
him to every outward mark of respect, from those

* This fortress, defended by General Bender, surrendered to the French
on the 7th of June.

† The son of Louis XVI. died on the 9th of June, in the twelfth year
of his age. A very interesting work, showing the brutal treatment of this
unhappy child, has been lately published.

‡ Afterwards Louis XVIII.

§ William, second Earl of Shelburne, formerly Secretary of State, and
Prime Minister, was created Marquis of Lansdowne in 1784, and died in
1805.

who think as we do. I have dined with him once,
and may probably do so oftener next year, and we
have so far explained ourselves to one another, that
we agreed that if any opening came from the Court
to either of us, that we would mutually communicate
and consult. I own I think this is no more than
what his conduct has entitled him to, and if there
were a change I cannot think that he ought to be left
out of any new arrangement, however impossible I
may feel it really to confide in him. I think it would
not be right for our characters that he should be left
out, and the events of these last years not only make
one less nice about one's associates; but make it
impossible that any system should be formed without
some exceptionable members forming a part of it ; and,
among those who are objectionable, I confess I feel
less repugnance to those whose life has been mostly spent
in opposition, than to those whose habits are all courtly,
and whose prejudices are always of the Tory side.   I
think any overture from the Court so improbable, that
perhaps all this discussion is very unimportant ; but I
felt (and I believe Lansdowne felt so too), that some
explanation was necessary or at least desirable, for the
purpose of going on pleasantly in opposition.   By
the way he has had very bad health this year, and
looks I think very ill indeed.

"I suppose by your staying so long at Florence,
that you will become a complete master of the Lingua
Fiorentina, for that is held to be the true name of the
language, not Toscana, and far less Italiana ; and with
your love of poetry, you must own that it is a treasure

indeed. I have no doubt of your liking Ariosto, and Boccaccio, as much as I do, and I am sure you will admire Dante, if you take the trouble (for it is some) to read him. Aminta, and Pastor Fido, everybody will recommend to you, and parts of them are charming; but, if you can get a tolerable master, I wish very much you would read with him (for it can hardly be managed without), Buonarroti's 'Tancia,' which I think the best specimen in any language of what Pastoral ought to be, but I believe I have said this to you before.

" Adieu, my dear nephew."

" I forgot to tell you that there is much talk of a triple alliance of Great Britain and Russia and Austria, which is to bring on a war with Prussia, possibly with Sweden and Denmark, and probably with Turkey, and so involve all Europe, and this some people approve. What a truly diabolical character we are taking up! for it is certain that if we were to let them alone, all the world would be at peace, and for what a purpose are we instigating them all to war? However, I understand that in all foreign countries we are hated as much as we deserve; more cannot be."

SAME TO SAME.

"St. Ann's Hill, July 28th, 1795.

" ALL that you tell me about Spain is quite new here. Nobody here had heard of the sickness which you mention as being so fatal, nor was it suspected

here that the French had insisted upon keeping their
conquests, and indeed it seems very extraordinary
that they should, at a time when they seem so very
eager for peace and are (very imprudently, in my
opinion) promising it daily to their people. To
declare to the world your own readiness and even
eagerness for peace is seldom, if ever (according to my
system) dangerous or improper, but to flatter the
people with false hopes of the enemy's being in the
same disposition is, in my opinion, a great symptom
of weakness, and may, when those hopes are disappointed, cause much mischief.   I agree with you that
the moderate Government of France is very inferior
in point of ability and energy to the tyrannical one,
and I am very much grieved that it is so, for I know
the inference which the admirers of tyranny and
violence (who are many more in the world than one
should imagine) will draw from the comparison.   In
our own history the example in favour of tyranny is
so strong that it frightens me when I apply it to the
present affairs of France, and if there should be a
second example of the same kind, alas, for poor
liberty ! and for all moderate notions of government.
While Cromwell's tyranny lasted, the royal cause
seemed desperate ; England was great abroad, splendid at home ; Waller and Dryden sung his triumphs,
&c., &c.   When he was gone and his son deposed,
and the rump Parliament took the government, among
whom were many considerable men, and who never
were accused, even by their enemies, of intending to
overthrow the Republic, or of violence of any kind,

you know the consequence, and what is very strange, the name of the rump Parliament became more odious than that of Cromwell, or the Regicides, or any other. I hope we shall not have to make the application, and indeed I think we shall not; but as the alarmists say, the magnitude of an evil must be taken into consideration as well as the probability of its befalling us, and a greater evil than the restoration of the Bourbons to the world in general, and England in particular, can hardly happen. You will be happy, as I am, to hear of the ill success of the Emigrants,* but you will be astonished to hear that Ministers are so far from being discouraged by it that they are more sanguine than ever in their hopes of re-establishing Louis XVIII. Lord Moira is gone or going immediately with a considerable army,† and a greater is to follow them, and in short they are in the greatest *hopes* of a complete civil war in France, which, if it is not decided immediately one way or the other, may, by giving us opportunities of assisting the Royalists, make the present war as long as that with America. Is the folly or the wickedness of these projects the most striking? I am glad you think I did right about the Prince's business; indeed, I had no doubt myself. As to the Prince he has been abused much more than he deserves . . . . . We have had a bad wet summer, and harvest will be very late, which, in the present state of provisions, is a great misfortune.

---

* The expedition to Quiberon is here alluded to. The successful attack by Hoche on the camp of the emigrants was made on the night of the 20th of July.

† No expedition, under Lord Moira, was sent in this year.

What used to be a 6d. loaf is now 12$\frac{1}{2}d$., and
what is worse is that it is very doubtful whether
there is corn enough to supply the consumption till
the harvest. There have been some riots, not very
serious ones. Surely the people of this country have
the merit of patience beyond all the world, when, in
the present state of things, they can see quietly provisions and stores of all sorts sent out of the country
to fleets and armies for the purpose of restoring monarchy to France. The Austrians are much complained
of, and are supposed hitherto to have done nothing, nor
to be likely to do much. Pray take some opportunity
of expressing my thanks to M. Manfredini for enabling
you to give me the information which you have sent
me, and of telling him how much I admire the
prudence with which he has managed the affairs of
Tuscany in this difficult crisis.* To be allowed to
have had no other view in one's politics than the
good of the people governed, is in these times no
small nor common praise, and that this has been the
character of the Grand Duke's government cannot be
denied.

" Adieu ! yours affectionately,

" C. J. F."

" From your never saying anything about Italian
poets, it runs in my head that you have not made all

---

* The Marchese Federigo Manfredini, was born in 1743, and died in 1829.
He was First Minister of Tuscany, from 1790 to 1799. A life of him is in
the Supplement to the "Biographie Universelle." I remember meeting
him at Padua, in the year 1815, and being struck with his lively and
intelligent remarks on the position of Napoleon, then at Paris.

the use you might of the opportunities you have had of studying the language; if so, you are very wrong, I have been reading Ariosto again, and I declare I like him better than ever. If I were to know but one language besides my own, it should be Italian."

"I told you, I believe, in my last, how very much Mrs. A. admires the ring you sent her. She desires me to tell you that the hours here, which always used to be too short, grow shorter than ever, and that we improve in laziness, which however as to me is a false accusation, for, so far from being idle, I hardly have time for anything, though what the time is taken up with is a little difficult to say."

SAME TO SAME.

"St. Ann's Hill, *August 7th*, 1795.

" MY DEAR HENRY,

"Since I last wrote to you, the account is come of the peace between France and Spain,* and the very day after came your letter of the fifth of July, in which you speculate upon the subject but conclude with an opinion that such a peace would take place. It seems to me a very reasonable peace for both parties. I believe it was a very unexpected event to our Ministers, and made more sensation than even the destruction of

---

* This treaty of peace was signed at Basle, on the 22nd of July, 1795. See "Annual Register," vol. xxxvii., State-papers, p. 297; or Martens, "Recueil des Traités," vol. vi. p. 542.

the Emigrant army at Quiberon; I understand they
are still undismayed, and think of going on with the
war, as much as they did, and with as good hopes as
when they put that foolish paragraph in the King's
speech at the prorogation, in which they made him
foretell the restoration of monarchy in France.* However, my brother, who was here yesterday, says that
he thinks Lord Moira's expedition to France is at
last given up, though I am told that ministerial people
in general hold a different language. To be sure the
idea of going on with it is madness; but then what is
the whole of the war? and if the attack upon France
is abandoned, where can they flatter even themselves
with the hope of making any impression? I always
like to hear from you what your accounts are from
France, because, though ours are fresher, yours come
untainted with the English prejudices, which in one way
or other warp the minds of all those who either come
over from France, or write from thence to England.
Poor Sombreuil, who is taken and whose fate I think
very doubtful at best, is a man universally well spoken

---

* The following is the paragraph in the King's speech on closing the
session, June 27th, to which Mr. Fox alludes; but it perhaps hardly bears
the construction which he puts upon it :—" It is impossible to contemplate
the internal situation of the enemy with whom we are contending, without
indulging an hope, that the present circumstances of France may, in their
effects, hasten the return of such a state of order and regular government
as may be capable of maintaining the accustomed relations of amity and
peace with other powers. The issue, however, of these extraordinary
transactions is out of the reach of human foresight." It seems very absurd,
however, to state that a government which maintained the relations of
amity and peace with Prussia, and the United States, was not capable of
maintaining these relations with other powers.

of even by those who are most prepossessed against
the Emigrants.   I am sorry for him.*

"Pray if you have an opportunity tell MM. Manfredini and Neri Corsi that I am very happy to find
they are pleased with what I said about Tuscany.
Nothing ever disgusted me more, than the way in
which the Grand Duke and the Republic of Genoa
were treated by us in the hour of our insolence, and
I should not wonder if the opinion which you mention
as being given to the King of Spain, that his great
object ought to be, the lowering of the British power,
were the general opinion given by all wise Ministers
to all the Princes and States of Europe.   I think there
is something more truly diabolical in the part we are
acting now, than in the conduct of any nation in
history.   Peace is the wish of the French, of Italy,
Spain, Germany, and all the world, and Great Britain
is alone the cause of preventing its accomplishment,
and this not for any point of honour or even interest,
but merely, lest there should be an example in the
modern world of a great and powerful Republic."

SAME TO SAME.

"St. Ann's Hill, September 10th, 1795.

"You say nothing about your coming home, nor
will I, only this, that if you have thoughts of coming
this autumn, it is my opinion that Parliament will

---

* The Comte de Sombreuil, who had been taken prisoner at Quiberon,
was removed to Vannes, and there shot, with a large number of other
royalists.

meet early in November, as I understand there is great scarcity of money in the Treasury. Everybody says that the country is nearly unanimous for peace, but they do nothing in consequence of their opinion, and the Ministers are I believe as warlike as ever. An expedition is, after all, gone to France under General Doyle, consisting of 4000 British, besides Emigrants, &c.; it is supposed they are destined to Noirmoutier.* I think nothing can show the complete infatuation of our Government so much as this desperate expedition, which I believe as well as hope has not the smallest chance of success. I expect daily to hear of peace with Naples and Sardinia, and with several princes of the Empire, but with the Empire itself, I think the negotiation will proceed slowly. You will have already perceived by this letter that I have not much to say, but I write not (thank God) because I have a tooth-ache, but because I set out to-morrow for Norfolk where I seldom have time to write. By the way, when I was at Turin in summer, they told me that if I walked in the evening in a certain part of the town (I believe under the ramparts) I should have the tooth-ache. I disbelieved as you may suppose, I did walk there, and sure enough I had the tooth-ache, but I do not believe in their nonsense for all that. It would be whimsical enough if you had done just the same thing.

---

* A body of 4000 British troops, under General Doyle, joined Admiral Warren, the commander of the Quiberon squadron, in September. They sailed to Noirmoutier; but, finding it strongly defended, they landed at the Isle d'Yeu, a small island fifteen miles off; and having occupied it for three months, they returned to England.

" It is supposed the French will certainly accept, or rather, that by this time, they have accepted the Constitution; * but I am not one of those who think that merely by having a Constitution upon paper they are much the nearer to a real settlement. I am glad to hear that the Bishop of Autun has leave to return to France, and it looks as if Montesquiou would have leave too, and probably a great many more. The worst is, that they will find it quite impracticable to do what is right, I mean, to restore confiscations ; such is the inextricable mischief which a nation will always be involved in which attempts to make the punishment of crimes a resource of finance to the State. Adieu."

" September 11th.

" I believe I told you in my last that Clairfayt was superseded at the desire of our Court.† What you say confirms what I had heard, that the Spanish peace was an unexpected blow here. I do not believe we shall go to war with Spain, but many people do, and that the end of all this contest for regular government, &c., will be our fighting for the natural rights of man in South America. Nothing is too foolish, too unprincipled, or too rash, for our Government, it is true, but yet I cannot believe that they will enter into a new war.

" Yours affectionately."

* The Constitution alluded to was adopted by the Convention on the 23nd of August. It consisted of a Council of Ancients, and a Council of Five Hundred: with the addition of the five directors, it was carried into operation.

† Clairfait, however, commanded one of the Austrian armies on the Rhine during this autumn.

SAME TO SAME.

"SOUTH STREET, *November 15th,* 1795.

" MY DEAR HENRY,

" It is a long time since I wrote to you, but till a few days ago I had not one letter from you since the 11th of September last. I have now three, one by a courier, and two by the post. I think as you do, that probably some of my letters have miscarried; but I hope you received that in which I desired you to return my thanks to M. Manfredini for the information he had enabled you to communicate, and to express my esteem for his character. The public papers will have informed you of what passed on the opening of the Session; and, although Pitt's declaration * was by some thought equivocal, I rather thought, and still think, he meant to try negotiation; and we all thought that it was right to give him a little time to try his sincerity, before we urged him more upon the subject. I expected, therefore, a very quiet Session, at least in the early part of it, when, very unexpectedly to me, Ministers, upon the pretext of the insults to the King on the first day of the Session, brought in two Bills, one in the House of Lords, the other in the House of Commons,† whose

---

* Mr. Fox appears to allude to Mr. Pitt's speech on the first night of the session, October 29th, 1795.

† A Bill for better Securing the King's Person and Government, introduced into the House of Lords by Lord Grenville; and a Bill for the Prevention of Seditious Meetings, introduced into the House of Commons by Mr. Pitt.

direct tendency it is to prohibit all public discussion, whether in writing or in speaking, of political subjects. I really do not think I exaggerate in so stating them; but I will send copies of them to you by the first opportunity. In one of them there is transportation to Botany Bay, for what may be termed seditious writing or speaking; in the other, power is given to a magistrate to disperse any public meeting (whether assembled for the purpose of petitioning or any other) whenever, from *special circumstances, in his judgment,* such meeting appears to *him* dangerous.

" You will easily suppose that, in both Houses, we have opposed as strenuously as we were able (though with very small numbers) these Bills, upon their first introduction; but we have not thought this enough, and we are endeavouring at public meetings, and petitions against them in many parts of the country; how successful we shall be I know not; perhaps I am not very sanguine, but I feel myself quite sure it is right to try; and I hope you will agree with me that, upon such an occasion, it is an act of duty to brave all the calumny that will be thrown upon us on account of the countenance which we shall be represented as giving to the Corresponding Society and others, who are supposed to wish the overthrow of the Monarchy. There appears to me to be no choice at present but between an absolute surrender of the liberties of the people and a vigorous exertion, attended, I admit, with considerable hazard, at a time like the present. My view of things is, I own, very gloomy; and I am convinced that in a very few years

this government will become completely absolute, or
that confusion will arise of a nature almost as much
to be deprecated as despotism itself.   That the
Ministers mean to bring on the first of these evils
appears to me so clear that I cannot help considering
any man who denies it as a fool, or a hypocrite ; and
I cannot disguise from myself that there are but too
many who wish for the second.

> 'Between two seas, on one *small* neck of land,
> Wearied, confounded, and amazed we stand.'

" But among all the dangers of which we have the
option, I have no doubt but the right part of a man
who means well to the country is to endeavour to
rouse the people, before it becomes too late, to act by
any other means than those of force, and by giving
them, or rather trying to give them, leaders who mean
well, to direct their efforts to such remedies to the
present evils, as are least likely to create confusion.
The Duke of Bedford feels just as I do on the subject,
and takes up the business in a style that makes me
honour him more than I can express.*   We are to
have a meeting in Westminster Hall to-morrow, where
he is to move a petition ; I hope, and believe, we shall
avoid riot, though I know the Ministry mean to make
a stir to create one, by sending among us persons
who, under pretence of opposing our measures, will
endeavour to excite one.   I shall not finish this letter

---

* The Duke of Bedford presided at a meeting of the Whig Club,
to oppose the two Government Bills, held on the 11th of November.
Concerning the public meetings, at this crisis, see "Annual Register."
vol. xxxviii. p. 40.

till the day after to-morrow, when I will give you an account of what has passed. This is a great crisis. Do not be angry with me for saying, Why is not Henry here? Can he deceive himself to such a degree as not to know that he ought not to be a *spectator* of the struggles that are likely to ensue?"

"*November* 17*th*, 1795.

"I have just time to tell you that our meeting yesterday succeeded beyond my hopes, incredibly numerous, yet very peaceable. The House of Commons is very bad indeed, and really seems to like these violent measures, which I consider as a sympton that the country, or at least the higher classes, are of the same opinion. However it is clear that *here* we have the popularity, and I suspect we shall have it universally among the lower classes. I need not tell you how much I dislike this state of things; but I cannot submit quite passively to Mr. Hume's Euthanasia, which is coming on very fast.

"Yours most affectionately."

"Mrs. A. desires her love to you, we shall go to St. Ann's on Saturday to celebrate your birthday."

SAME TO SAME.

"*December* 24*th*, 1795.

"MY DEAR HENRY,

"I write to you now not because I have anything to say, but because it is a long time since I wrote last, and the Lady of the Hill says it is a shame

to be so long without writing to young one.* I
had such a glut of business both in the House of
Commons, and out of it, while I was in town that I
am more than usually glad to be here, in a little
idleness, and hardly like even to write to you about
politics. However, I must just tell you that I think
the country behaved better than I expected, upon the
subject of the bills, and that except in Yorkshire, (a
most material exception I admit), we have the people
with us every where, in some parts of course more and
in others less decidedly. I take it we are strongest in
and about the Metropolis. We made very bad divisions in the House of Commons, but nevertheless, I
think we are much more of an opposition than we have
been of late years. Thurlow came out at last, and
though I do not think this a circumstance likely to have
so much effect as some suppose, still, it is something.
You will easily conceive that the *existing circumstances*
(Pitt's favorite phrase), have made Lansdowne more
cordial with us all than formerly, and I should hope
the Duke of Leeds, Lord Moira, and other outlying
parts of opposition, will soon see the necessity of
acting more in concert, and if the public cry continues
to be with us, I have no doubt but they will. Pitt
certainly meant to parry our attacks, by the message
from the King relative to peace,† but how far that

---

* Lord Holland was generally called young one, or rather young 'un,
by his uncle.

† On December 8th, 1795, Mr. Pitt brought down a message from the
Crown, informing the House of Commons of the King's disposition to
enter into a negotiation for peace with the Government of France. He
moved an address expressive of the readiness of the House to concur in

will answer his purpose I doubt much ; I think not
at all, unless he really gets peace, and as to the question
whether he will get it or not, I think it so doubtful,
that I have altered my opinion upon it several times.
A week ago I thought it almost certain, not from any
particular information, but from general reasoning,
grounded upon a belief, that both sides wish peace
heartily enough to make them get over small difficulties.   However the later accounts from Paris lead
me to think that the French are less earnest in their
wishes than I had supposed, nor do I find any reason
to think that our ministers have made up their minds
to make the first overtures, in that decided manner,
which in my judgment would be most likely to ensure
them success.   Pray tell me all you think and hear
upon the subject.   All your information has hitherto
turned out to be very correct, and your speculations
as right as can be expected, in these times of improbable events.   I should like particularly to know
what you hear of the inclination of Austria to peace
since her victories.* It is true, those victories have now
received a check, but her situation is still far better
than it was when you wrote last to me.   However,
how she can go on in point of finance, I cannot conceive, for I hear it is quite impossible to send her any

such a measure. Mr. Sheridan thereupon moved an amendment to the
address, signifying the concern of the House that any form of government
in that country should induce the King to be averse to peace ; and to
request that, setting aside all considerations of that nature, he would
direct his Ministers to treat with the enemy on safe and honourable terms
    * Mr. Fox alludes to the successes of the Austrians on the Rhine in
the latter part of 1795.

more money from hence.   Now here is quite enough
I think of politics.

"Lord Ossory tells me you are determined to be at
home by Midsummer.   I need not tell you, my dear
Henry, how very happy I shall be when that happens :
if you could contrive to be here before parliament
rises, I own I should be still more so, but I will not
teaze you, though indeed, indeed, these are times in
which the country has some claim upon persons in your
situation.   Nothing but activity and exertion on the
part of those who love liberty can prevent Mr. Hume's
Euthanasia from taking place.

"Adieu, my dearest Nephew."

SAME TO SAME.

"February 18th, 1796.

"MY DEAR HENRY,

"Till I received a letter from you a few days
ago, without date, I had been longer without hearing
from you than ever before since you have been in
Italy.   Pray write often.   You are quite right in
thinking that the circumstances of the times will of
themselves bring Lansdowne and me together, much
better than any explanations or messages or communications, &c.   We are indeed now upon a very good
footing, and quite sufficiently so to enable us to act
cordially together, if any occasion offers to make our
doing so useful.   I do not know what to write to you
about our politics here, the whole country seems dead,
and yet they certainly showed some spirit while the
Bills were pending; and I cannot help flattering

myself that the great coldness at present is owing to people being in expectation and doubt with respect to what Pitt means to do in regard to peace. What he does mean, I am sure I do not pretend to guess; but I am convinced that this ministry cannot make any peace without incredible sacrifices. The minds of the two Governments are so hostile to each other, and their mutual diffidence so rooted, that it must be next to a miracle, if they can agree till absolute necessity forces them. Add to this, that Pitt, I really believe, is weak enough to think that the French cannot go on much longer, and they, on the other hand, have but too good grounds for thinking that we cannot. In short there has been no period of the war in which I had less guess of what was like to happen, than the present. I should like to hear your speculations. I own I thought Sheridan's amendment quite right, but many people were of your opinion at the time.* However, I think it was very material to mark our disapprobation of putting our peaceable disposition on the ground of the state of the French Government, for two reasons; first, because in so doing, we appear to adhere to that principle of the war, which gave justly to the French nation the greatest offence ; and also, because we rest our inclinations to peace upon a circumstance in its nature so liable to be changed, for who could tell then, or even now who can foresee how long this Directorial Government is to last ?

* Sheridan's amendment to the address on peace with France is intended. See note, p. 127.

" I was yesterday in an unexpected majority upon the Slave Trade, 93 to 67 for bringing in the Bill, but I fear we shall do no good, for though Pitt spoke very well, I cannot think him in earnest, as Dundas took so eager a part on the other side.* What a rogue Pitt is ! it is quite unpleasant to think that a man with such parts should be so totally devoid, as he seems to me, of all right feelings.

" I never observed before in reading the ' Odyssey,' that Homer does not mention Polypheme's being one-eyed, and it is only to be inferred from his being blind when his eye is out ; and yet he does describe his size, &c., when he first sees him.　Can you account for this ? †

" Yours, most affectionately."

" South Street, February 19th.

" Burke's pamphlet is advertized under the title of

---

* Mr. Wilberforce moved for leave to bring in a bill for the Abolition of the Slave Trade on the 18th of February, 1796.

† Homer describes the Cyclopes as a race of savage giants, who lived separately, each in his own cave, with his wives and children, who did not till the ground, or navigate the sea (" Odyssey," ix. 106-35).　Nothing is said here of their being a one-eyed race.　In the description of the blinding of Polyphemus, it is implied that he has only one eye; and, indeed, if he had had two eyes, the stratagem of Ulysses would have been ineffectual (Ib. v. 380-98, 453-516 ; compare i. 79).　For the same reason, Polyphemus is represented as living alone in his cave, without wives or children ; for .heir presence would have rendered the escape of Ulysses and his companions impossible.　It is easy to explain why Homer should have represented Polyphemus as one-eyed; but there seems to be no cogent reason why he should not have mentioned this circumstance upon the first introduction of the giant, v. 234.　Hesiod, " Theogon." 143, says expressly that the Cyclopes were distinguished by their having a single eye in the middle of their forehead.　The same defect, or monstrosity, is pointed out by Euripides in his " Cyclops," v. 21, and by Virgil, " Æn." iii. 636.

K 2

Thoughts on the prospect of a regicide peace; if the book keeps up to the temper of the title, it will be worth reading."*

SAME TO SAME.

"*September* 16*th,* 1796.

" You will think perhaps, my dear Henry, that the reason of my not having hitherto answered your letter, is because I could not ; however, that is not the case, for the truth is that you have not at all persuaded me ; but as things seem likely now to go, the propriety of our two ways of thinking will not come into question ; for if Parliament meets (as I think it will) before the result of the Paris negociation if any such exists, (what a number of ifs !) is known, it will certainly not be prudent for us, in such a state of suspense, to come to any strong question respecting the Ministry.   But I will fairly own there is no degree of clamour that I would not meet rather than be a party to so monstrous a delusion, as that of the possibility of the present Ministers, and the present system, extricating the country from its difficulties.   I will go further and say, if they could, it is not desirable they should, and the error of those who think otherwise arises from the most general cause of all errors, both in morals and politics, a too partial regard to the present difficulty or advantage, without due consideration of the bad consequences of a mischievous *general* rule and of evil example.   Read Paley upon

* This work was entitled " Three Letters addressed to a Member of the present Parliament, on the Proposals for Peace with the Regicide Directory of France," and was published in 1796.

the subject, for upon all subjects I think he is masterly.* Now I would ask, if the present Ministers can enjoy not only impunity, but power, after all their misconduct, is not the mischief like to ensue from the example, far greater than any good that can result from *their* making peace? If it is once understood, that Ministers may safely make any war the most unjust or most unpolitic, provided they can get out of it by a peace *quelconque*, and that we are to acquiesce in their making such a peace (nay, to thank them for it), as can be justified only upon the consideration of the situation in which *they* have brought us, if this lesson (I say) is taught and subscribed to by opposition itself, what reason have we to hope that upon every passion of a King, upon every party advantage that a minister may fancy to himself from a war, we shall not be again involved in similar misfortunes to the present? Peace or war is comparatively of no consequence to the great question of whether the people (or if you like it better, the public,) shall attend to their affairs as they ought, and shall or shall not discriminate between those who betray and those who serve them. The famous passage of Demosthenes is as remarkable for sterling sense as for eloquence, Τέθνηκε Φίλιππος; τί δ' ὑμῖν διαφέρει; καὶ γὰρ ἂν οὗτός τι πάθῃ, ταχέως ὑμεῖς ἕτερον Φίλιππον ποιήσετε, ἄν περ οὕτω προσέχητε τοῖς πράγμασι τὸν νοῦν.† Read *War* instead of *Philip*, and the whole of the sentence is perfectly

---

* See Paley's " Moral and Political Philosophy," b. ii. c. 7.

† Philipp. i. §. 14. "Is Philip dead? but what difference does it make? for even if he were to die, you would soon raise up another Philip, by your mode of conducting the affairs of the state."

applicable to the present times, as also what precedes it relative to the curiosity of the Athenians about the life or death of Philip. Now considering that I have been shooting in this hot day from ten to six, and am as you may suppose reasonably tired, I think I have written you a pretty long letter, especially as the principal subject of the difference between us, as far as it relates to practical conduct, is for the moment suspended. Only one word more about popularity; unless the people are prepared to be completely hostile to Pitt, I have no desire for popularity with such a people, and I do not say this from passion; but because such popularity could neither be useful to the public nor gratifying to myself.

" Yours ever.

" I have just begun ' Heliodorus ' and like him very much ; I have not quite finished the story of Cnemon. Pray tell me if you know when Heliodorus wrote.* If you write (and pray do write), direct to me at Castle Acre, near Swaffham."

SAME TO SAME.

"St. Ann's Hill, Wednesday, 1796.

" My dear Young One,
    " I cannot help writing to you a line to tell you that I read your paper yesterday, and am quite

---

* An account of the romance of Heliodorus, entitled " Æthiopica," and of all that is known respecting his life, is given in Dr. Smith's " Dictionary of Ancient Mythology and Biography." Heliodorus lived at the end of the fourth century of our era. The story of " Cnemon " ends in the fifth book.

delighted with it ; I think it very well done, and not
at all, as you said, deficient in arrangement ; but
what delights me so much is to find that your
opinions are so exactly the same as mine ; I do not think
there is a word to which I do not subscribe.

"However, except among ourselves and the few
politicians who are philosophers, whether there is now
any use in recurring to, or, at least, in dwelling much
upon the transactions of 1784, I much doubt. The
party which those events should have bound together
for ever are now scattered and dispersed ; and the
bulk of mankind, always judging by effects, will consider that as a bad bond of union which has been an
ineffectual one. Perhaps, therefore, instead of saying
now that the power of the House of Commons ought
to be first restored and its constitution considered
afterwards, it would be better to invert the order, and
say, Parliament should first be reformed, and then
restored to its just influence. You will observe that
I state this opinion as being mine *now*, in contra-
distinction to those times when the Whig party was
only beaten, but not dispersed, and when I certainly
was of a different opinion.

"At present I think that we ought to go further
towards agreeing with the democratic or popular
party than at any former period ; for the following
reasons :—We, as a party, I fear, can do nothing, and
the contest must be between the Court and the
Democrats. These last, without our assistance, will
be either too weak to resist the Court,—and then
comes Mr. Hume's Euthanasia, which you and I

think the worst of all events,—or, if they are strong enough, being wholly unmixed with any aristocratic leaven, and full of resentment against us for not joining them, will go probably to greater excesses, and bring on the only state of things which can make a man doubt whether the despotism of monarchy is the worst of all evils. I perceive you have rather asserted, than endeavoured to prove much by argument, the injustice and impolicy of the war, which certainly does not want much argument to prove it; but if your paper had been meant for the public, that part should have been more enlarged upon; for, in arguing with the public, you should do the reverse of what you would do with a philosopher, and dwell most upon those points upon which your readers or hearers are nearly convinced beforehand.

" Yours affectionately,

"C. J. F."

SAME TO SAME.

"*August 7th,* 1797.

" PRAY, if you have an opportunity of talking about the Secession,* say, what is the truth, that there was not agreement of opinion enough upon the subject to

---

* On Mr. Fox's secession from Parliament, see Lord Holland's "Memoirs of the Whig Party," vol. i. p. 84-90, 143. The secession appears, as indeed Mr. Fox represents it, to have been rather a voluntary dispersion of an army often beaten, than a regular agreement to retire. Secessions are not properly justifiable, as a parliamentary course; but lax attendance, accounted for by proved inability to contend with a compact majority, may be reconciled with a statesman's sense of duty, so long as his constituents are content with his absence from the House of Commons.

make it possible to take what one may call a *measure* upon the subject ; but that most of us thought, that, after the proposition for reform, we might fairly enough stay away, considering the preceding events of the Session and the behaviour of Parliament upon them."

SAME TO SAME.

" October, 1797.

" IF you will not read the ' Iliad ' regularly through, pray read the tenth book, or, at least, the first half of it.   It is a part I never heard particularly cele- brated, but I think the beginning of it more true in the description of the uneasiness in the Greek army and the solicitude of the different chiefs than anything almost in the poem.   It is one of those things that one cannot give an idea of by any particular quo- tation, but which is excellent, beyond measure, in placing the scene exactly before one's eyes ; and the characters, too, are remarkably well distinguished and preserved.   I think Homer always happy in his accounts of Menelaus ; remarkably so, you know, in the ' Odyssey ; ' but I think he is so always, and in this place, too, particularly.*   You see I have never done with Homer ; and, indeed, if there was nothing else, except Virgil and Ariosto, one should never want reading."

* See the excellent account of the character of Menelaus in Colonel Mure's " History of the Language and Literature of Ancient Greece," vol. i. p. 324-8.

SAME TO SAME.

" October or November, 1797.

" I AM glad to hear Lansdowne, at last, approves of our secession ; whether it will ever produce any effect I know not ; but I own I think it has a better chance of doing so than attendance ; mind, I mean *my* attendance, for I think the more any new ones show themselves the better ; and I shall be very sorry if Moira makes his motion when you cannot attend it. Indeed, I think the Duke of Bedford and everybody ought to attend his motion, as it is reasonable to suppose that you will have from him a more authentic account of Ireland than we have yet had."*

SAME TO SAME.

" November 19th, 1797.

" I OWN I remain very averse to the thoughts of more than one day in the House of Commons for *me*, but I confine my opinion exactly to my expression, and do not see why those who have any inclination, or who fancy there is any good opportunity, should not attend ; I am sure it would do no harm, and if it excited any sensation it would do good."

---

* A motion was made by Lord Moira, on the state of Ireland, in the House of Lords, on Nov. 22nd, 1797. Further debates on the same subject took place on the 26th of March and 15th of June, 1798, in the latter of which the Duke of Bedford and Lord Holland expressed their opinions.

SAME TO SAME.

" December 14th, 1797.

" DEAR YOUNG ONE,

" It has occurred to me that if this business (*i.e.*, the Assessed Taxes Bill) goes on, it will be necessary not only to vote and speak against it in the House of Lords, but to protest also ; and, as you do not dislike writing so much as I do, I think you had better try your hand at a Protest ; which need not be confined to the Tax, but may enter into the general state of things.

" I wish you would think of the Protest, for even if it is not read it will be of service to yourself in speaking." *

SAME TO SAME.

"St. Ann's Hill,
" *Thursday, December 21st,* 1797.

" DEAR YOUNG ONE,

" I hope you will set about the Protest, and I think as you do, that the impropriety of granting extraordinary supplies to men who have caused the mischief should be made the principal argument against it, though the particular measure ought also to be exposed. I have not yet heard of much stirring upon the business in distant places. It is a pity

---

* Lord Holland acted upon this advice, and entered a protest against the bill upon the journals. See his " Memoirs of the Whig Party," vol. i. p. 99. The protest is printed in Ann. Reg., vol. 40. State Papers, p. 220.

there is not, for if all the country would speak as Westminster, &c., it must produce one of two good effects : either we should beat Pitt, or a proof utterly undeniable would be furnished that the sense of the people, even if unanimous, is not strong enough in the House of Commons to outweigh the influences of a Minister.

" Pray set about the Protest, and pray neither in that nor in what you say consider what is supposed to be popular. I am convinced in these times (and that is the only good belonging to them) that the boldest and sincerest language is likewise the most prudent; if, indeed, there be any room for prudence in a situation so near absolute despair. I think there can be no occasion for my going up till the third reading, which will hardly be till this day se'nnight.

" Yours affectionately,

"C. J. F."

SAME TO SAME.

" St. Ann's Hill,
" *Monday, January 8th,* 1798.

" I think there should certainly be opposition to the Bill in the House of Lords, and particularly that the Duke of Bedford should be there, as they are attacking him about the surcharge; and besides, I own I long for an opportunity for you to do something. Nothing will I believe do good, but nothing is so likely to do some little as a new and young champion for reform.

" What I hear corroborates what you say, that the opposition to the Bill is slackening.

" Yours affectionately,

"C. J. F."

SAME TO SAME.

" January 12th, 1798.

" MY DEAR YOUNG ONE,

"I hear from several quarters an excellent account of your speech, and I do not like it the worse for your having been embarrassed.* I believe you know my opinion on that subject. I cannot address you as Dryden does Congreve, and say,—

'Whom I foresee to better fortunes born;'

for though I did not come myself into a period very favourable to eloquence exerted on the side of liberty, I fear you are fallen upon one far worse. 'In te intuens, Brute, doleo, cujus in adolescentiam per medias laudes quasi quadrigis vehentem transversa incurrit misera fortuna Reipublicæ. Ex te duplex nos afficit sollicitudo, quod et ipse republicâ careas, et illa te.' "

SAME TO SAME.

" January 16th, 1798.

" I DO assure you, my dear young one, that I do not flatter you at all, if by flattering is meant saying

---

* Lord Holland's first speech in Parliament was on the bill for the increased assessment of taxes, on the 5th of January, 1798. He likewise spoke a second time in the course of the debate. See Lord Holland's " Memoirs of the Whig Party," vol. i. p. 98.

more than one thinks, but if praise is to be called
flattery, then I beg that you will tell Lady H. that I
know enough of the family constitution to know that
it is remarkably good and wholesome for us all, and
that too, in good doses. I think your speech, whether
well or ill given, reads very well indeed, but it was
not the goodness of the speech only that I alluded to,
it was the stoutness of fighting so well, all alone
against them all, and I really was delighted full as
much as I said, or more. By what you say, I find
you had not even the expectation of the Duke of
Bedford's support to look to; I think the plan
he followed was for a determined seceder the best,
but for you, as you have begun, fight on, and do
not imagine Lord Grenville or any one can hinder
you from speaking twice. By the way, there was
nothing in the debate pleased me more than his
professing an intention of doing this. The effect of
his doing so must have been very good for you with
the audience, and particularly bad for him in the case
of one to whom he in a manner reproached the being
without support. When this was tried formerly
against the Duke of Richmond, he resisted it successfully by moving the House to go into a committee.
Whether it be that any single member has a right
to put the House into a committee, or whether in
making such motion he said all he meant to say in
his second speech I do not know, but I rather think
the first."

SAME TO SAME.

"*February,* 1798.

"I HAVE just finished Horne Tooke and like it
very much indeed; my opinion of his abilities is much
raised, for I did not use to hold him high in any
other respect, except wit, and some humour." *

SAME TO SAME.

"St. Ann's Hill,
"*Friday, March 2nd,* 1798.

"IF you have not yet got G. Wakefield's Lucretius,†
pray give orders for it directly. He seems, poor man,
so depressed with its ill success in point of sale that

* Mr. Fox probably alludes to his "Diversions of Purley," the first
edition of which was published in 1796.

† Published at London in 1796, in three vols. 4to.; a rare book, as a
large part of the impression was destroyed by fire at the printer's.
Wakefield prefixed to his edition of Lucretius the following dedication:
"Viro seculi sui illustrissimo, et vere honorabili, CAROLO JACOBO FOX,
elegantioribus ingenii dotibus eminentissimo; eloquentiæ venâ copiosæ,
facilis, inaffectatæ, vividæ, sublimis, profluenti; virtutibus iis omnibus
quæ virum politicum exornent, consummatissimo; sed ob teneros affectus
animi humanissimamque benevolentiam in primis venerabili; hoc volumen
nobilissimi poetæ carminum, e non ignobili, uti sperat, editione, et
fortasse cum Foxii ipsius nomine in ævum serius perennaturâ, vovens
omnia faustissima, dat, dicat, dedicat, GILBERTUS WAKEFIELD." To this
are subjoined some verses, beginning—

"Te salvere jubet simplex, si rustica, Musa,
Angligenum, Foxi, gloria, robur, amor."

The above dedication gave rise to a correspondence between Mr. Fox
and Gilbert Wakefield, almost exclusively on subjects of classical literature,
which was continued at intervals for several years. This correspondence
was published, after the death of both parties, by Mr. Wakefield's repre-

it would be an act of good nature, and I am convinced that, in the state he is in, every order that is given for a copy is an event to him.   If, besides buying it, you can do anything to promote its sale, pray do. It is certainly a work of great industry and learning, and however you may agree with him or not in his criticisms, it is at any rate very useful to learning to have such discussions going forward.   If you see Guilford* remember me to him, and by the way make *him* buy the Lucretius.   The small paper is five guineas only, the large, twenty guineas—a proper conclusion of a puff; but really I am very earnest in this.

" Yours affectionately,

" C. J. F."

SAME TO SAME.

" *March*, 1798.

" With regard to secession (that is, *declared* secession) I confess I do not like it as a measure, but I believe the Duke of Bedford does.   I should dislike to a degree I cannot express to attend again myself; indeed, if there is a point upon which I cannot bring myself to give way it is this, but I am so far from

---

sentatives.   See the " Correspondence of Gilbert Wakefield and Mr. Fox, in the years 1796-1801, chiefly on subjects of Classical Literature." London, 1813; one vol. 8vo   The contrast in these letters between the tasteless and dogmatic pedantry of Wakefield, and the superior judgment of Mr. Fox, though combined with a less extensive erudition, must strike every reader.   Wakefield's edition of Lucretius was reprinted at Glasgow, in 1813, in four vols. 8vo.

* George Augustus, third Earl of Guilford.

wishing others to do the same, that I even wish for
occasions where you and others may have opportunities of attending, and should be rather glad than
sorry if Lansdowne were to make motions such as
you allude to."

SAME TO SAME.

" April 20th, 1798.

" Do you know that Prior* has taken in part what
he says of the dead horse from Ariosto? I believe it
is the thirtieth canto, but the book is not in this
room; it is where Orlando offers his dead mare for
a living one.† I like Polybius exceedingly; by the
way, what a complete telegraph his was ! ‡ I have been
reading Orpheus's 'Argonautics,' and think there are
some very pretty passages in them. Is it known by
whom they are written, or when? I think I have
heard about Solon's time.§ I have been reading, too,

---

* "So Harlequin extolled his horse,
   Fit for the war, or road, or course;
   His mouth was soft, his eye was good,
   His foot as sure as ever trod ;
   One fault he had, a fault indeed ;
   And what was that? The horse was dead."—"Alma," c. iii.

Prior seems to have borrowed the idea from some Italian writer, who had
probably derived it from Ariosto.

† The passage is at the beginning of the 30th canto of the " Orlando
Furioso."

‡ See Polyb. x. 43-7 ; a very interesting passage.

§ It was the general belief of the early scholars that the "Orphic
Argonautics" was a poem of high antiquity; but it is now universally
considered to be of late date. Bernhardy, "Grundriss der Griechischen
Litteratur," vol. ii. p. 268, places its composition between the second and
fourth centuries after Christ.

the Ἀσπις attributed to Hesiod, which is really a very
fine poem, if you do not mind gross plagiarism from
Homer.   I do not imagine there is any guess when or
by whom it was written.   I observe that if we are to
judge of antiquity by the observance of the digamma,
and the not shortening of vowels before mutes and
liquids, we might think it as old as the Iliad itself."*

                         SAME TO SAME.

                                        "*October* 21*st*, 1798.

   " THE Duke of Bedford, who is here, confirms what
you say of Grey's intention to attend occasionally, and
I shall not be at all sorry to find myself the sole
seceder, but a seceder I will be till I see a very
different state of things from the present, and indeed
if they were to alter more materially than can be
expected, it would be with more reluctance than I can
describe, or than is perhaps reasonable, that I should
return to politics.   I see little or no love of true
liberty in the country, or perhaps in the world, and
I wish to have done with it as far as public affairs are
concerned, but my conduct is no rule for that of others ;
nay, I think that if I were myself younger I should
not like to give up the point without having shown to
the world my abhorrence of all that is going forward.
This abhorrence I have sufficiently shown, as I think,
for my own reputation, and, having done so, I think

---

   * " The Shield of Hercules " is a remnant of an ancient Hesiodean poem,
and approaches in antiquity to the " Iliad " and " Odyssey." See Mure's
"History of the Language and Literature of Ancient Greece," vol. ii. p. 421.

I may without reproach consult my own ease and happiness."

SAME TO SAME.

"November 23rd, 1798.

" How can you, who read Juvenal, talk of Demosthenes being difficult? difficult or not, you must read him, and read him with the view (which you probably did not before) of considering how far his manner of putting things can be introduced with success into Parliamentary debate. To be sure, his speeches are better adapted, in the present state of things, to the other side of the question, and if Pitt had any learning, or if those of his friends who have had any genius, they might make great use of him, both as to matter and manner, but the latter is good for either side.

I am sure your going to the House of Lords can do no harm, and I even think it may do some little good. I almost wish the Duke of Bedford would attend too, though his case is different from yours, and certainly I cannot advise him upon the subject, being so determined upon staying away myself."

SAME TO SAME.

"December 10th, 1798.

" DRYDEN wants a certain degree of easy playfulness that belongs to Ariosto, Parnell is too grave, and Prior does not seem to me to have the knack (perhaps only because he did not try it) of mixing familiar and serious, though he does very well in each respectively.

"The former, however, is his forte, at least I think 'Alma' better than either 'Solomon,' or 'Henry and Emma.'"

"*December* 14*th*, 1798.

"I CANNOT help thinking that Dryden has not the exact sort of playfulness, or levity, or familiarity of manner, or easy grace which I mean, and which it is very difficult rightly to define. Prior has more of it than Dryden, La Fontaine more than Prior, and Ariosto and Ovid as much as possible, which in them is the more remarkable, as I do not think it often belongs to any great genius. The 'Cock and the Fox' is the poem of Dryden where he approaches nearest to the style I mean, but as the subject there is all of the *comic* kind there is not room for a display of that style in all its merits, part of which, I think, consists in mixing occasionally a certain degree of playfulness in even the most tragic and sublime subjects, and that too without diminishing but rather increasing the interest. Besides, though in some of Dryden's fables there is a conceit and wit, I do not recollect anything of the familiar and easy kind very successful. The 'Cock and the Fox' is rather of a kind allied to the mock heroic, especially Chanticleer's speeches, which is very different from what I mean, and of which there is not a single trait in 'Orlando Furioso.' I do not know whether I explain myself thoroughly, but if we were to read Ariosto together, I could show you by example what I mean ; and indeed Spenser has some of it, but to those who are full of Ariosto, his imitation in this respect appears too close to have quite the right effect."

" *January 5th,* 1799.

" THE income bill must I suppose be dreadfully oppressive upon persons from £200 to 600 a year,* but I have long suspected that persons of this class have long become quite ciphers in respect to political power, and indeed they are most of them too dependent, either on account of what they actually have, or of what they expect for themselves and children, to dare to stir against the government and the higher ranks. I know it is in nature that when a man has taken an opinion, he takes everything to be a confirmation of it, but I cannot help feeling every day more and more, that in this country, at least, an aristocratic party is absolutely necessary to the preservation of liberty, and especially to give any consequence to the inferior classes ; but this I fear is all over.

" I am reading Aristotle's 'Poetics,' and find a great deal very obscure, and some parts (if one dared say it) rather confused. Heinsius says this is owing to his having so nice an ear for *rhyme,* and this ' maximus virorum quum aures consuleret suas, maluit obscure loqui, quam illis non satisfacere.' † Do not you think

---

* A tax upon income was proposed by Mr. Pitt, in the House of Commons, on the 3rd of December, 1798.

† No criticism can be more unfounded than to say, generally, that Aristotle sacrificed the meaning of his sentences to their harmony. Where he treats of subjects which admit of being understood, his obscurity is principally owing to his extreme conciseness.

then that he was rather *too* great a man for an author?
and that is a poor consolation to us readers when we
cannot make him out, that he was delighting his ears
with the harmony of his periods."

SAME TO SAME.

" January 19th, 1799.

"I own I think, according to the plan with which you
have set out, that you ought to attend the Union,*
nor do I feel much any of your objections, I mean to
attendance, for in all those to the Union I agree
with you entirely.   If it were only for the state of
representation in their House of Commons,† I should
object to it, but when you add the state of the country
it is the most monstrous proposition that ever was
made.   What has given rise to the report of my being
for it I cannot guess, as exclusive of temporary objections I never had the least liking to the measure,
though I confess I have less attended to the arguments
pro and *con* than perhaps I otherwise should have
done, from a full conviction that it was completely
impossible.   You know, I dare say, that my general
principle in politics is very much against the *one* and
indivisible, and if I were to allow myself a leaning to
any extreme it would be to that of Federalism.‡   Pray

* The subject of the Union with Ireland was brought before both the
English Houses of Parliament, by messages from the Crown, on the 22nd
of January, 1799.   Mr. Fox advises Lord Holland to attend the House of
Lords during the debates on this subject.   His letter was, however,
written a few days before the subject was formally recommended to
Parliament.

† The Irish House of Commons.

‡ Mr. Fox applies to Ireland the language of the French revolution;

therefore, whenever you hear my opinion mentioned, declare for me my decided disapprobation, not that I would have my wish to have this known a reason for your attendance, however, if otherwise you wish to stay away. I do not think Lansdowne * being for it, much of a reason against your opposing it, and in one view perhaps it ought to operate the other way, lest from his declared opinion and my supposed one, you should be thought to approve the thing, and yet to be too sulky to own it. As for the unpopularity of the grounds of your opposition, that is all chance, as the Public does not seem yet in this country to have attended to the question."

SAME TO SAME.

"*January 21st*, 1799.

" I am now reading Lucretius regularly ; what a grand poet he is, where he is a poet ! I shall not so easily leave him for letter writing, as I did Aristotle's ' Poetics ;' so you must not expect me to be quite so good a correspondent as I have been lately, though I like so much hearing from you that I shall not be a very bad one."

SAME TO SAME.

"*February 7th*, 1799.

" I will read ' Griselda ;' I do not remember it in Boccace, but it will be nearly a single instance, if any

according to which, the federalist system was opposed to the unity and indivisibility of the republic.

* Lord Lansdowne declared his opinion in favour of the Union with Ireland, in the House of Lords, on the 19th of March, 1799.

of his stories are mended by the imitator.* 'Minutolo,' which is one of La Fontaine's best tales, is very inferior to Boccace, † and Dryden, with all his grand and and beautiful versification in ' Sigismonda,' hardly comes up to the original."‡

" February 8th, 1799.

"If the Irish would stick to one another, they might play a game that would have more chance of doing good, than any that has been in question for a long time. They might win the battle that we lost in 1784, § and which after all is the pivot upon which every thing turns. They ought to be very careful to confine themselves however to Irish ministers, and great officers in Ireland, and they would be in no danger (unless I am very much deceived indeed) of being deserted by the people, as we were."

SAME TO SAME.
" February, 1799.

" It is certain I never read the story in Boccace, and upon looking over the contents of the Tenth Day, I

---

* "Patient Griselda," a tale from the Italian of Boccaccio, was published by Miss Sotheby, in 1799, 4to. Lord Holland appears to have recommended this book to Mr. Fox. The tale is borrowed from the novel of the "Marchese di Saluzzo," in Boccaccio, Giorn. x. nov. 10.

† "Contes," i. 2 ; from Boccaccio, Giorn. iii. nov. 6.

‡ Dryden's fable of "Sigismonda and Guiscardo," is imitated from Boccaccio, Giorn. iv. nov. 1.

§ Mr. Fox here alludes to the dismissal of the Coalition Ministry by the King, in December, 1783, and to the defeat of his party at the elections, which ensued upon Mr. Pitt's dissolution, in March, 1784. His meaning is, that the choice of the principal offices in Ireland might be made to depend on the votes of an independent House of Commons, and not upon the influence of the Crown.

am convinced I never read any of it. How this happened I do not know, but I will read the ' Marchese di Saluzzo ' directly, and tell you whether I like it as well as the ' Clerk's Tale,' which I have just read, and admire to the last degree. I suppose Chaucer did not read Italian, by his taking the story from Petrarch's translation,* and I believe, ' Palamon and Arcite,' which is the only thing (besides this) that he has taken from Boccace, was written in Latin, but this I do not know."

SAME TO SAME.

" *February* 18*th,* 1799.

" MY DEAR YOUNG ONE,

"I have just been writing a letter of such unreasonable length to Buonaiuti that I shall not have time to answer all your letter as I wish to do. First, as to the House of Lords, I am very glad you mean to speak, and think the points upon which you mean to attack Lord Grenville are all very good. The King's coronation oath should never be forgot, as I think the mention of it was one of the most disgusting pieces of impudence and folly that we have seen. As to the competency of Parliament, I will endeavour (but not to-day) to set down upon paper for you something upon it, of which you may make use or not, as you think convenient; and so I would, too, about the

---

* The passage from the " Clerk's Tale," which contains the reference to Petrarch, is cited and illustrated by Ginguené, " Histoire Littéraire d'Italie," c. 16, tom. iii. p. 109, ed. 1824. The history of the fable of " Griselda " is traced by Ginguené, ib. p. 112.

resolution of 1782 if I knew the contents of the papers referred to by Pitt in the debate between him and Uncle Dick.* Whatever may be in them may be completely answered, or rather put out of the case as connected with the present measure ; but it would be easier to answer them knowing what they are, than hypothetically supposing them to be so or so, though even in that way it might be done ; for, supposing the extreme case, that the Ministers and Lord Lieutenant of that day had actually given their opinion of the necessity of a union of Legislatures, yet nothing having been proposed upon that subject for so long a period, what was actually ratified in 1782 and 1783 must be considered as a final settlement.

"As to the use of the word ' *that*' in Spenser, I like it very much ; but it is very peculiar, and not like the prosaic use of it to which I adverted. It was not so much the general use of ' *that*' as a word of reference which I object to, as the peculiar use of it in this case, where it does not refer to an individual person or thing, but to a genus, or species, or description, and where it rather means *that sort*, or *that kind*, or some such prosaic abstracted mode of

---

* In the debate on the proposed union with Ireland, in the House of Commons, on the 11th of February, 1799, General Fitzpatrick affirmed that such a measure would involve a breach of national faith, as being a departure from the final settlement of 1782. Mr. Pitt then asked General Fitzpatrick, whether instructions had not been given to the Duke of Portland, as Lord-Lieutenant of Ireland, which contemplated ulterior arrangements. The Duke of Portland had been Lord-Lieutenant of Ireland under the Rockingham administration, in 1782, and General Fitzpatrick was Chief Secretary. The Duke of Portland was now Secretary of State for the Home Department.

conception, than *that visible, audible,* or *tangible
thing* or person. All this sounds very minute; but
so it is. The effect, as in this instance, strikes one;
yet, when one comes to compare and analyse, the
causes of the effect appear often so minute and nice
as to be scarcely intelligible. My general notion is,
that poetical language should deal as much as possible
in words conveying simple ideas, and as little as
possible in such as convey complex or abstract ideas;
it should deal in words that could be explained (for
instance) to a person who had no previous knowledge
of the nature of language, either by a reference to his
senses or by signs of one sort or other. Spenser's
' *that* ' could be explained by pointing; to understand
your ' *that,*' you must first understand the relation of
individuals to species; for you mean *of that species of
ore,* or materials similar *to that ore,* of which his limbs
were composed. In this, just as in metre, the effect is
felt by many, and the cause is known by few, perhaps
by none; but I cannot help trying to find it out, and
to erect a theory; which, however, must always be
tried by practice and effect, and must, like some parts
of natural philosophy, depend upon experiments."

" *February 19th,* 1799.

" I LEFT off yesterday in a very tiresome and
perhaps not quite intelligible dissertation upon poetic
language; but by attempting to explain myself
further I should become more tiresome, without
perhaps being more clear; only one observation
further, and I have done; and that is, that my theory

about words simple rather than complex, and appealing
to the senses rather than to the understanding, if it is
true, helps to explain why they are better poets generally in the *earlier* than in the more *refined* periods
of each language, and why many good poets are fond
of adopting the style of the age preceding that in
which they write."

SAME TO SAME.

"*February* 23rd, 1799.

" A union is not only a revolution, but a revolution
of a more complete kind than any other. In other
revolutions, the person of a King is changed sometimes, the family on the throne is expelled to make
room for another, sometimes the power of the country
is transferred from a King to a council, or *vice versá;*
but then the power remains in the representative of
the nation, however well or ill constituted such
representative may be. King William, with his parliament, was as much the representative of the English
nation as James with his, and the Directory with the
two councils is as much the representative of France,
as Louis was. But by union Scotland ceased to be
a nation, and consequently to have a representative ;
so it may be said did England, but this is a fallacy,
for whatever might be the *words* in which the treaty
was concluded, the substantial effect of it was that
Scotland was annexed to England, just as Cheshire
and Wales had formerly been, and the only difference
is, that England in compliment to her changed her

name, which she had not done in the former cases.
Revolution is, therefore, perhaps too weak a term for a
union ; it is rather annihilation. Now is Parliament
competent to annihilate itself, and the constitution
which it was instituted to preserve and protect?
There are two senses in which the phrase *competence
of Parliament* may be taken. Some mean no more
by it than this ; viz., Parliament is competent to such
an act, because when passed, all regularly constituted
tribunals and courts of justice will, and must, in their
judicial capacity, declare such act valid, and that
obedience is due to it. In this sense the Irish parliament is certainly competent to make a union ; the
British parliament was competent to tax America.
The Irish parliament would be competent to make a
union with France, and either parliament to transfer,
as it might please their whim, all the property of the
subject from one to another, or to enjoin a general
massacre. Others, when they speak of the competence
of Parliament, mean, that Parliament has a *right*
(morally as well as technically speaking) to pass such
an act if it thinks it will be beneficial to the country,
and that obedience to it is a moral duty. In this
sense I certainly deny the competency of Parliament
to destroy that constitution, which they were appointed
to uphold. It is idle to say that because it may alter,
it may destroy, for alterations are always adopted
upon the plea (whether true or false no matter) of
tending to preservation and not to destruction. Now
the Union, whatever beneficial consequences the
Parliament may foresee from it, is not an alteration,

but a destruction and annihilation of the Irish Constitution. Union therefore, like revolution, cannot be justifiable, but by the unequivocal consent of the people, and inasmuch as it is a much more violent operation than any revolution, that consent ought to be more clear and decided. Then, says Mr. Grant, must the people meet on Salisbury Plain ?* I reply, that for these violent (and therefore very rarely wise or just) operations there is not, nor perhaps is it fit there should be, any regular course or process established; but that to make such measures just or deserving (morally speaking) of obedience, the sense of the people must be not technically, and by legal fiction, but *bonâ fide* and substantially taken. It will not do to say as some one (Dr. Marriot I believe) said of the Americans, that they were represented by the members for Kent, because North America was part of the Manor of East Greenwich. Upon these principles, both in the year 1688, and in the case of the Scotch Union, the promoters of the two revolutions thought it absolutely necessary to have the consent of the people, by such a representative as was thought likely to express their opinion. In 1688, a Convention was thought preferable to a regularly chosen House of Commons,

---

* The allusion is to a speech of Mr. W. Grant (afterwards Sir William Grant, and Master of the Rolls), in the House of Commons on the 7th of February. He considered the Union as " a treaty between two independent Parliaments, who had a power to do whatever the Constitution had not forbidden. The competency of the Parliaments was not more a question than the competency of their electors, to whom, in fairness, the question must first be referred. From the electors it must go to the people at large, who must be assembled in convention on Salisbury Plain and the Curragh of Kildare."

and upon the proceedings of that Convention (which more resembled an assembly of Notables than anything else), are founded all the measures of that period, and among others His Majesty's title to the Crown. In the case of the Scotch Union, it was thought that the best means of collecting the sense of the people was from a parliament,* called and chosen *for the specific purpose* of considering a union, and this parliament so called, was thought a more eligible channel for collecting the sense of the people on that occasion, than that which had been resorted to in 1688. Apply these facts and reasoning to the present case. Is the parliament of Ireland (like the Convention and Scotch parliament), called and assembled for the specific purpose of declaring the sense of the people on the proposed revolution? and having been called for the purpose of preserving the constitution, can they be thought *competent* (except in the one sense I have stated above), to enact the destruction of it, just as they would exercise any ordinary function of Legislature? In one sense, therefore, Parliament is competent to *everything;* nay, to sell openly their country for individual benefits; for I should like to know what court of law would allow me to go into evidence to prove that the King or the members of either House had received money from France for the passing of a particular act. Yet, ought not such acts so procured to be resisted? But then they say, these are extreme cases, and in such instances the government is sup-

* I believe I am right in this fact; but, as it is a material one, it would be best to look at the history. C. J. F.

posed to be dissolved, and no ordinary rules can be
adhered to. Be it so, but is the proposition of
annihilating the constitution of our country ; nay, the
country itself, as an independent entire State ; is this
an ordinary question to be canvassed according to the
principles of ordinary legislation ? I therefore say,
that in the more liberal and popular sense of the word
competent, Parliament is incompetent to destroy what
it was erected to preserve. In the case of individuals,
if my agent abuses the powers which I gave him
against me, his employer, I have my remedy at law,
because for such individual cases, the law can, and
does provide. Between a nation and its parliament
(or other government, for the species of government
makes no difference), there is no power to decide.
Now I admit, that his principles are extravagant and
absurd, who contends that in every instance where I
can as an individual obtain redress against my agent ;
viz., wherever there is abuse, I am entitled as a subject
to resist the Government ; but surely, the other
extreme is equally or rather more absurd, which
supposes, that in the case of subject and Government,
I must take the poison the Government offers me,
because I gave it discretionary powers with respect to
the sort of medicine it was to procure for me. If
ever resistance can be justifiable it must be in the
case of Union without consent, or in other words
apprehended annihilation, and where resistance is
justifiable, Parliament is not competent except in the
very confined sense to which I have so often alluded,
e questo basti."

SAME TO SAME.

"February 26th, 1799.

" MY DEAR YOUNG ONE,

" I believe I was not quite understood by you in regard to competency, owing to my not making quite proper illustrations. I do not think competency depends upon *beneficial* or *hurtful,* because I do not think in certain cases that Parliament is the judge of beneficial or hurtful. Supposing the Stamp Act were beneficial to America, Parliament was not competent in any sense of the word to enact it. Supposing a Union would be beneficial to Ireland, Parliament again is not competent to enact it, because it is not within its commission to destroy the constitution which it is instituted to support, even though it should place a better in its stead, and here comes in with propriety what Locke says, that Parliament is to make laws and not legislatures. I cannot think, for instance, that Parliament is competent to declare Great Britain an absolute monarchy, or a republic, though it should be of opinion that the change would be for the better. For such revolutions there must be a known opinion of the people, and though such opinion be difficult to collect legally, yet for practical purposes it may be collected in a practical way, as I contend that it was, or at least that it was pretended to be, in 1688 and 1706. It is said, that this reasoning goes to say, that Parliament which is instituted to *improve* cannot be competent to *impair* the Constitution ; the answer is, that whether a projected alteration be an *improvement* or an *injury,* is a question upon which Parliament is commissioned to judge, but annihilation (which Union must be allowed to be) is not within their commission. That it is annihilation, I of course suppose proved, before I deny the competence. I agree with your present opinion of the 'Essay on Criticism,' much more than with your former one, but I am not fond, I own, of such subjects for poetry. At Pope's time of life when he wrote it, it was a prodigy, though very inferior to those productions of his which were not long posterior to it, 'Eloisa,' 'Rape of the Lock,' &c. His early works are his best by far in my judgment, as well as yours. A detractor (as I have been very falsely accused of being) might say that having little genius he soon got *au bout de son Latin*, but there are other reasons. The chief of which appears to me to be that latterly (except in the case of Homer, and that is an exception also to our remark), he chose subjects not only less adapted to poetry in general, but to his particular genius also, for with all his ostentation upon these matters, such as *from words to things*, &c., I think he is as miserable a moralist and as superficial and faulty a reasoner as ever existed, and that all the merit of his satires consists in his poetry and his wit, of both which he had a good share. Add to this, that most of his early works, and among them his best, are translations and imitations, such as 'Eloisa,' the 'Messiah,' 'January and May,' 'Sappho to Phaon' (which by the way is delightful), &c. The 'Rape of the Lock,' beautiful as it is, consists very much of parodies which are certainly not of the highest order of the productions of genius,

and all these seem to have been the species of poetry
most adapted to his talents.   In most of these early
productions he is in a kind of playful pace, and not,
as we say of a horse, *quite out* and in *right earnest*.
In his latter poems he often is, and I do not think he
succeeds so well in that pace, as in the other.   In
' Eloisa,' to be sure, he is out enough, but then in the
parts of it where he is most successfully so, the
original is so beautiful that with his talents for translation, he could not fail of success.   I am well aware,
that strong exceptions to my theory in regard to him
may be brought from some passages of the higher
style in his later works, such as the lines following,—' What arm'd for virtue, &c. ;' but these are
rare.*   I never   read   a line of   Oldham's ;   your

* Imitations of Horace.   Sat. 1, line 105.

> What? arm'd for Virtue when I point the pen,
> Brand the bold front of shameless guilty men,
> Dash the proud gamester in his gilded car,
> Bare the mean heart that lurks beneath a star ;
> Can there be wanting to defend her cause,
> Lights of the church, or guardians of the laws ?
>
> .   .   .   .
>
> Yes, while I live, no rich or noble knave
> Shall walk the world, in credit, to his grave.
> To Virtue only, and her friends a friend,
> The world beside may murmur or commend.
> Know, all the distant din that world can keep,
> Rolls o'er my grotto, and but soothes my sleep.
> There, my retreat the best companions grace,
> Chiefs out of war, and statesmen out of place ;
> There St. John mingles with my friendly bowl
> The feast of reason and the flow of soul ;
> And He, whose lightning pierced th' Iberian lines ;
> Now forms my quincunx, and now ranks my vines ;
> Or tames the genius of the stubborn plain,
> Almost as quickly as he conquer'd Spain.

M 2

character of him accords pretty well with what
Dryden says of him ; but Pope soon after was a complete refutation of what Dryden says about those
parts of poetry which are never to be acquired but by
time.   And indeed, if smoothness, as Dryden says,
be the acquisition of age, it may be one reason why
Pope, who was never deficient in this respect, did not
improve so much as others."

SAME TO SAME.

" March, 1799.

" I HAVE read the ' Clerk's Tale ' again, and aloud
to Mrs. A., who, as well as myself, admires it very
much ; and what I did not expect, that I should allow
it is a very great improvement upon Boccace ;
whether the improvement is his own or in any degree
taken from Petrarch's translation I cannot tell, as I
never saw the latter.   I think in this tale of Chaucer's
there is more of the manner of Ariosto than in anything I ever read in Spenser, where he most
endeavours to imitate him.   I think I never saw a
resemblance of manner so strong in two poets, who
were certainly strangers to each other's works, and
who did not imitate any common model ; for, though
the story is taken from Boccace the manner is not
in the least so."

" March 20th, 1799.

" I DO not know whether I told you that I read
' The Cock and the Fox' in Chaucer, and was
amazed to see how little Dryden has added.   What
a genius Chaucer was ! "

SAME TO SAME.

"June 1st or 2nd, 1799.

" I HAVE just read Grose's speech in delivering the sentence upon poor G. Wakefield, and think it the most abominable and indecent production I ever read, though its being so incredibly nonsensical is in some degree a corrective. And what a sentence too ! *
Well, it is a good thing not to think of politics in these times. You know it was said, and believed, that Wakefield was considered as a poor enthusiast, and the sentence would be mild. I never believed this, nor can I hardly believe what I hear about Thanet's sentence, though it is told me by those who think they know it." †

---

* Gilbert Wakefield, having published an answer to a pamphlet on the French war by Watson, Bishop of Llandaff, was tried, in February, 1799, for a seditious libel, and was found guilty. He was afterwards, May 30, sentenced to be imprisoned two years in the gaol of Dorchester, and to give securities for his good behaviour for five years, himself in 500*l.*, and two securities in 250*l.* each. See Adolphus, vol. vii. p. 228. Watson, in the " Anecdotes of his Life," says : " I took some pains to prevent this prosecution, thinking the liberty of the press to be the palladium of the Constitution ; but I did not succeed in my endeavours, nor did the Ministry acquire any credit for their over-watchfulness." See " Anecdotes of the Life of Watson," vol. ii. p. 54, ed. 8vo. Mr. Fox wrote to Wakefield, in the King's Bench Prison, to condole with him on account of the severity of his sentence, June 9th, 1799. See " Correspondence of Wakefield and Fox," p. 69.

† Concerning the sentence on Lord Thanet, see Lord Holland's " Memoirs of the Whig Party," vol. i. p. 126; Adolphus, ib., vol. vii. p. 48. Lord Thanet was sentenced to a year's imprisonment, and a fine of a 1000*l.* In a letter to Gilbert Wakefield, June 12th, 1799, Mr. Fox says : " The sentence upon Lord Thanet and Ferguson is, all things considered, most abominable ; but the speech accompanying it is, if possible, worse." See " Correspondence of Wakefield and Fox," p. 73. The trial of Wakefield, and also that of Lord Thanet are in Howell's " State Trials," vol. xxvii.

SAME TO SAME.

"August 16th, 1799.

"I think in parts of Lucian there is a great deal of eloquence, as well as wit. I liked Metastasio's 'Isacco' so much that I was induced to read 'Giuseppe' and 'Abelle,' but they are not near so good, though very well too."

SAME TO SAME.

"November 6th, 1799.

"I have read 'Medea' again, and like it as well as before; I am clear it is the best of all the Greek Tragedies upon the whole, though the chorusses are not so poetical as in some others."

SAME TO SAME.

"November, 1799.

"I think, both about the Duke of York's conduct and the folly of the Expedition, exactly as you do. The Convention was the best measure, and his letters were very foolish indeed.* As to the Expedition one may fairly assert, that, having 40,000 men to employ, there was no other possible way of employing them in which so small a force of the Enemy was necessary

---

* The expedition to the Helder sailed in August, 1799, under Sir Ralph Abercrombie; and the Duke of York followed with another detachment, and took the command of the army in September. The expedition was unsuccessful, and, by a convention made in October, the English agreed to evacuate Holland before the end of November.

to defeat them as in the precise way in which they were employed; but I fear all this signifies nothing; that there is discontent I do not doubt, but that such discontent is likely to operate to any good purpose in the present state of things I am not sanguine enough to hope, for reasons which it is not necessary to detail. I like some of Wakefield's defences * very much, notwithstanding the absurdities scattered here and there. There is both eloquence and argument in them to a great degree."

"*November* 23rd, 1799.

"If anything good comes (and I am not quite without hopes) from the late events, it must be confessed that it will come from a very bad beginning. I think the manner of the thing quite odious.

"I quite approve of their repealing the detestable Hostage Law; † but I give them no credit, because that was a Jacobin enormity. Let them repeal the laws against Meetings and the Liberty of the Press, and I will say something for them."

SAME TO SAME.
"*December*, 1799.

"I shall send 'Persiles' and 'Galatea' by to-morrow's coach to be left at your lodge. I remember

---

* The defence read by Wakefield on his trial appears to be here alluded to. See note to p. 166, and Adolphus, vol. vii. p. 229.

† The first measure of the provisional consuls, after the 18th of Brumaire, was to repeal the *Loi des Otages*; which made the relations of the Vendeans and Chouans responsible for the acts done in the revolted provinces, and subjected them to imprisonment or transportation.

when I read them I thought that in ' Galatea ' some
of the poetry was imitated from those parts of
Ariosto (not certainly his best) where he introduces
the praises of living persons ; but I have, in general,
forgot both the romances, only so far I remember,
that I liked the first half of ' Persiles ' much better
than the rest, and that there is somewhere in it an
idea of the modern *Parachute*.   I believe, too, that
there is in it (to the shame of Genius) a most flaming
panegyric upon the expulsion of the Moors.   I never
read (on account of the smallness of the print) more
than three books of Heliodorus, * but it struck me
that Cervantes had formed himself a good deal upon
his model.   I mean, of course, in the serious parts of
his romances.   In Don Quixote it appears to me
(contrary to what upon general principles one should
expect) that he loses more by translation in the
grave, than in the humorous parts.   Or perhaps it is
owing to my imperfect knowledge of Spanish that he
appears to gain less in the original in the comic than
in the serious, and in this way of putting it, it is less
wonderful ; but so it is, that I never feel greater
contempt for translators than in reading the serious
and eloquent parts of Don Quixote.   I shall be
very glad to see your ' Life of Cervantes,' but still
more those of the others.   That of Cardanus it is
your own fault if you do not make very entertaining ;
and as to materials, you will want little more than his
own works, which, if you have not, you may get, I
suppose, at any bookseller's.   I wish you would lend me

* The romance of Heliodorus consists of ten books.

Shaw's Apollonius Rhodius, unless you can get one for me directly, of the last octavo edition, which I had rather buy than borrow.* I should, besides, like to buy Brunck's edition of him; † but that, I understand, you may be some time in finding, and I want to read him immediately; but tell Jeffery to get it for me, as also Potter's Lycophron. ‡

"I am very glad indeed to hear you think of coming here, when we may talk over at leisure all the subjects of your letter. I agree entirely with you upon the sort of attendance I should give *if any*, but am almost wholly resolved to give *none*. If not, I should, you say, give up politics altogether, for no better opportunity is like to occur. There is no wisdom in making resolutions when they are not called for, but *if* no better opportunity than the present occurs, I have no difficulty in making the resolution of giving them up altogether. You talk of unpopularity and divisions. Can the Ministers be more unpopular than when we seceded? I really think there were not twenty men in the House of Commons who did not think they ought to go out at that time. And as to divisions among them, I must know more both of the nature of the divisions supposed, and of the grounds for believing their existence, before I can reason upon them. The Dutch expedition§ is, I believe, universally reprobated, but what then? You see, even in the

---

* The octavo edition of Shaw's Apollonius Rhodius was published at Oxford, in 1799.				† Published in 1780.

‡ Published at Oxford in 1697, and a second edition in 1702. Jeffery was a London bookseller, much connected with Lord Holland.

§ The expedition to the Helder.

common council, nothing can be done against it. Is
that, will you say, of any consequence ? of far more in
the present state of things I think, than the figure we
might make (for that is all I suppose expected by the
most sanguine) in any debate in Parliament. In short
the country is wholly without spirit, nay, I am not
sure that they are not without the power, if they had
the spirit, of resisting the Ministry, and I feel myself
more averse from attendance than ever. I have no
good opinion of the Consuls,* but shall have even a
worse than I now have, if they do nothing either to
save Napper Tandy, or to punish Hamburg.† It
seems as if all feeling for individuals was gone out
of the world, without, however, being replaced by any
great love for the Public. Hooke's Roman History,
which I am reading to Mrs. A., has led me lately to
neglect my Greek and read nothing but Cicero, whom
I admire (I do not mean his *conduct* upon all occasions)
more than ever ; one cannot read him too much."

---

* By the revolution of the 18th Brumaire, or 10th of November, 1799,
Sièyes, Ducos, and Napoleon Bonaparte were made provisional consuls.

† Napper Tandy, and other Irishmen implicated in the rebellion of 1798,
who had fled to France, were excepted from the Act of Amnesty passed by
the Irish Parliament in 1798, and were attainted. Napper Tandy joined in a
French expedition to the north of Ireland in 1798 ; returned to the continent, and took refuge in Hamburgh ; where he was demanded by the
British Government as a fugitive criminal, and given up in 1799. See
Adolphus, vol. vii. p. 76.236. It is to this event that Mr. Fox alludes.
Bonaparte afterwards remonstrated with the Government of Hamburgh
for giving up persons under the protection of France, and inflicted a heavy
fine upon the town. See Adolphus, ib. p. 242. Napper Tandy was
brought upon his attainder before the King's Bench in Ireland, in 1800,
to have execution awarded upon him. A plea was put in, and issue was
joined by the Crown ; and, upon a trial, the jury found for the prisoner.
He was discharged, and retired to the continent, where he died. See
Howell's "State Trials," vol. xxvii. p. 1191.

SAME TO SAME.

" December 31st, 1799.

" I HAVE read your dissertation upon Stonehenge, and like it very well. I wanted no convincing, so it is no compliment to say that you have satisfied me. Indeed everybody likes what makes for their own theory, and mine being almost universal scepticism, I am partial to your side of the question. Indeed we sceptics should be aware that we are almost (I will not say quite) as partial and even positive in our doubts as any other theorists in favour of an hypothesis. I have not finished the first book of Apollonius; some of it is very fine, some very prosaic, a dreadful fault with me ; and there seems to be a general want of that spirit and enthusiasm which I rank so high among the beauties of poetry ; but I cannot yet judge, perhaps, quite fairly. Pray read the eighteen or twenty lines from v. 540 or thereabouts* onwards: they are grand as well as beautiful, and should I think exempt him from the charge of equality and mediocrity given him by Quintilian and Longinus."†

* The verses pointed out by Mr. Fox describe the departure of the ship Argo from the Pagasæan Gulf.

† "Apollonius in ordinem à grammaticis datum non venit, quia Aristarchus atque Aristophanes, poetarum judices, neminem sui temporis in numerum redegerunt : non tamen contemnendum edidit opus æquali quâdam mediocritate."—Quintilian, x. 1, § 54. Ἔπειτοι γε καὶ ἄπτωτος ὁ Ἀπολλώνιος ὁ τῶν Ἀργοναυτικῶν ποιητής, ἆρ' οὖν Ἀπολλώνιος ἂν μᾶλλον ἢ Ὅμηρος ἐθέλοις γενέσθαι;—Longinus ' de Sublim.,' c. 33.

SAME TO SAME.

" January 4th, 1800.

" I AM very glad you are reading Euripides, but I had rather you had begun almost any other play than the Hippolytus, and I meant, if I had not forgot it, particularly to have recommended the Heraclidæ to you.   There are as fine things in Hippolytus as in any of his plays, but then they are almost all of them most judiciously taken by Racine and some of them even improved, so that they would not be new to you, and there is a great deal of very indifferent in it, and the plot I think vile.   I mean making Phædra kill herself and leave the lie behind her.   It is an excess of wickedness which in my conception does not suit her character.   In short, of all Euripides' plays, I think it the one the most below its reputation.   I prefer to it not only Medea, Alcestis, and the Heraclidæ, but I think both the Iphigenia and Hercules Furens, and perhaps too the Troades and Hecuba.   The Cyclops, in a style of its own, is very well worth reading.   It is so Shakesperic.   The worst of all, I think, is Andromache.   Helen you would like, if it is only for the difference of the story from the common one.   As to difficulty do not mind that, and read on till you find him easy, which is much more certain than what you bid me do, write on till I find it easy."

SAME TO SAME.

" January, 1800.

" I do not disapprove of Racine's introduction of
Aricie; on the contrary, I think it is an excellent way,
and indeed the only way of making the story tolerable,
as it makes Phædra consent to the accusation through
jealousy. Besides, Hippolytus' declaration of love to
Aricie is beautiful in itself, and Phædra's speech when
she hears of it still more so, and great beauties are
with me a complete justification of the introduction
of an episode. Only read Phædra's speech when
first she hears of his love for Aricie. Nothing can
exceed it. I have read but little of Apollonius since
I wrote last, my opinion continues the same. He is a
good poet certainly, but, like Tasso, some way he does
not get hold of me right. However, there are passages
both in Tasso and him, that are great exceptions to
this. Pray read in the first book (of Apollonius)
Telamon's and Jason's quarrel and reconciliation,
particularly from v. 1329 to 1340. It is capital, and
not I think taken from any former poet. I have not
yet perceived that Virgil has taken much from him,
but am not yet half way in the second book. If
Jason's adventure at Lemnos is the prototype of
Æneas at Carthage, and Dido is taken from Hypsipyle,
it is indeed a silk purse out of a sow's ear. I am
afraid you will not have liked the Heraclidæ as I do,
for I never heard it much praised, and perhaps the
thinking so highly, is a fancy quite of my own.

It is quite brimful of that sort of spirit the want of which I complain of in our Apollonius and Tasso. Are not you delighted where he says to Macaria

Ὦ τέκνον, οὐκ ἔστ' ἄλλοθεν τὸ σὸν κάρα,
Ἀλλ' ἐξ ἐκείνου, &c.*

"My letters tell me what I can scarce credit, that the Ministers have given a flat refusal to the Great Consul's proposition to treat.† Surely they must be quite mad. I have no doubt but the country will bear it, but if it does you must allow that it is a complete proof, that they will bear anything."

SAME TO SAME.

"*January*, 1800.

"I AM very glad you like the Heraclidæ so well. Your objections to it are very well founded. It is indeed very irregular, and so are most of Euripides' plays. Sophocles' are less so, but I agree with you that the Unities, and still less Aristotle's Beginning, Middle, and End, are much less observed in the Greek plays, than from the observations of modern critics (especially the French) one should imagine.‡ I did

---

* V. 539.

† A letter from Bonaparte, First Consul, to the King of Great Britain, was transmitted by M. de Talleyrand to Lord Grenville, on the 25th of December, 1799. A short correspondence ensued between the two Ministers, which contained a refusal on the part of the English Government to negotiate.—See "Annual Register," vol. 42 ; State Papers, p. 203.

‡ This subject is fully illustrated by A. W. Schlegel, in his Lectures on Dramatic Literature.—Lect. ix. and x. See also Manzoni's admirable remarks on the Unities in his Works.

not mention Helen as good, but thought you might
like it on account of its making the story so different
from the common one.　I never read it but once, and
believe it is one of his worst.　I will answer for your
liking Alcestis and there is one scene in the Troades,
which I am sure will entertain you at least very much,
though perhaps it is not very dramatical, nor in the
circumstance very natural; I mean the dispute or
rather debate between Hecuba and Helen.　Did
not Alcmena and Eurystheus put you a little in mind
of Queen Margaret and York in Henry the VIth?　I
am very glad you grow to find Greek so easy, and I
think if you get deep into Euripides you will grow to
like as I do his very faults.　I dare say the passages
which you and Mr. Marsh cannot make out, will be
equally unintelligible to me, but yet I should like to
try, and therefore pray point them out to me.　I know
there is a Barnes' Euripides at Woolbeding, so you
need only mention the page or verse.　I suppose
Evander's relating his having had Hercules for his
guest and sending his son with Eneas is taken from
Lycus, in Apollonius, * but it is so superior that
Apollonius looks quite like the imitation.　I admire
Virgil more than ever, for his power of giving origi-
nality to his most exact imitations.

I approve of Bonaparte's letter very much indeed,
and what an answer! Surely they must think as
meanly of the people of this country as I do.　Restore
Monarchy or show us that you can behave peaceably for

* Compare the account of Lycus, in the Second Book of Apollonius,
with the account of Evander in the Eighth Book of the Æneid.

some time before we can treat, and this experience of peaceable demeanour is desired during the war."

"January 17th, 1800.

" I have determined, against inclination, common sense and philosophy, to attend upon the question of Bonaparte's letter, &c., and shall be much obliged to you, if you will enquire about the time and manner in which it will probably come on."*

SAME TO SAME.

"January 21st, 1800.

" PRAY, my dear young one, let me know if there is like to be any alteration about the day; if there is not, I will be with you Sunday, and if seeing people is necessary that may be contrived Sunday evening or Monday morning. I have not at all reconciled myself to the resolution I have been over-persuaded to take, and when one does a thing not only against one's inclination, but one's judgment too, it must be expected that it will be ill done, but that cannot be helped. . . .

---

* " Mr. Fox was strongly urged to attend the debate on the rejection of this overture. As he was told from many quarters that great doubts of the propriety of the step, and even some disposition to call for peace existed in the public, he could not refuse the urgent entreaties of his friends. He quitted the country, however, with great reluctance, stipulated for remaining at Holland House only two nights, and when he heard that the debate was postponed, in consequence of Mr. Pitt's indisposition, sat silent and overcome, as if the intelligence of some great calamity had reached his ears. I saw tears steal down his cheeks, so vexed was he at being detained from his garden, his books, and his cheerful life in the country." —Lord Holland's " Memoirs of the Whig Party," vol. i.

I do not much see what Bonaparte is to get in any view by his second message. A controversy upon the origin of the war (though in my opinion the French cause is clearly the better) can be of no great service to him. I am very sorry for the defeat of the Anti-unionists,* but it was no more than I expected, I have not written to one person to attend, nor do I much care about attendance, though I confess that the better the attendance is, the less absurd in some small degree will my return appear. As to amendment or simple opposition, I do not care one farthing which, and still less if it is to be amendment, who moves it; I will do whatever is thought right and best."

SAME TO SAME.

"March 14th, 1800.

" I have been reading Lycophron, and have been very much pleased, partly with him and partly with the innumerable stories which his Scholiast Tzetzes gives for the purpose of explaining him."

SAME TO SAME.

"March 20th, 1800.

" I have just been reading the Phœnissæ on account of Porson's new edition, and find that it deserves a higher rank among Euripides' plays than I had given it in my mind. The scene with Jocasta and the two brothers is famous. Of all poets

---

* A motion, condemnatory of the union with Great Britain, was negatived in the Irish House of Commons, by 138 to 96 votes, on the 15th of January, 1800.

Euripides appears to me without exception the most useful for a public speaker."

SAME TO SAME.

"*August* 19*th,* 1800.

" I DO not wonder you like the Odyssey better than ever; it is the most charming reading of all. I have read near half of it over again lately. I do not know whether I do not like the book with Nausicaa the best of all, but it is all delightful, and there is such variety which I am afraid the Iliad cannot boast of. I am now reading the *Conquista di Granata* of Graziani.* It seems full of story, and the poetry sometimes good, oftener middling.

" I have read the first volume of Laing's History of Scotland. He is a bad writer, but it is a good book with a great deal of good sense in parts of it."

SAME TO SAME.

"*September* 28*th,* 1800.

" I AM very glad you have been reading the Odyssey regularly, and am sure it has well paid you for the trouble. The books you mention, Φ and X are certainly the finest, but whether the most pleasing, and particularly whether the best specimens of the characteristic beauty of the Odyssey as distinguished from that of the Iliad, I rather doubt. I have read

---

* Girolamo Graziani, an Italian poet, born in 1604, and died in 1675. His " Conquista di Granata," in twenty-six cantos, is stated to be founded upon the " Guerras de Granada" of Mendoza, who died in 1575.

the Υ and the three following books since I received your letter yesterday morning, and do not wonder at your admiring them as you do. I had a perfect recollection of the *second sight* passage,* which is a very singular one. I believe it would be very difficult to match it in any poet, whether real or pretended, of the second-sighted country. As to prosody I once set down all the peculiarities of it in the Odyssey upon paper, but I think there was only one line (and I do not know what that is) that I could not reconcile to the common rules; in the four books I read yesterday I observed nothing much out of the way ; ἔμπᾰιὄς is used as a dactyle,† but diphthongs in such positions are often made short, as τοιος εῶν, ὅιὄς οὖτις Αχαιων—‡ἔπἔιῇ πολυ φερτερον εστι,§ and many other instances; στἔᾰτὄς, as a dissyllable, may seem strange,‖ but why should not the εα *there* be contracted like the εα in τευχεα, τείχεα, &c., which in Homer are always written at length, but in more modern authors τεύχη, τείχη, &c. The same observation applies to ἐκφόρεον for ἐξεφόρουν.¶ Tell me your difficulties, and I think I can, in most cases, resolve them. I do not wonder Marsh** does not know so much about it, for he was not, I believe, at Eton, and though it

---

* See "Odyssey," b. xx., v. 350—71 ; and compare Mure's "History of the Language and Literature of Ancient Greece," vol. i., p. 425.

† In the following verse of the "Odyssey," xx., 379 :—

ἔμπαιον οὐδὲ βίης, ἀλλ' αὔτως ἄχθος ἀρούρης.

‡ "Iliad," xviii., 105.   § "Iliad," i., 169, &c.

‖ In "Odyssey," b. xxi., v. 178, 183.

¶ In "Odyssey," b. xxii., v. 451.

** Rev. Mr. Marsh, a great friend of Lord Holland ; afterwards Canon of Salisbury.

sounds impertinent to say so, I think none but those who have been there ever have a correct notion of Greek, or even Latin metre. What you say about v. 120 in the Λ is not quite correct ; what Tiresias there says about the oar Ulysses is to carry, &c. is not mentioned as a circumstance necessary to his return (as you erroneously state it), but as a circumstance which is to take place after his return, and after his conquest of the suitors in a voyage which he (Tiresias) enjoins him to make, and accordingly Ulysses after-wards mentions it to Penelope as *what is to happen,*[*] but you had not got to the passage when you wrote. The Odyssey ends with the massacre of the suitors, and the mutual recognition between Ulysses and Penelope, and consequently could not relate the sub-sequent events of Ulysses' life. Perhaps Homer meant to make another poem of them, and I heartily wish he had. You are to observe that among the many suspected parts of the Odyssey all that part of Ψ which is subsequent to v. 299 and the whole of Ω are the most generally supposed to be spurious.[†] In regard to the Λ too, I cannot help agreeing with those who think the account of Tantalus, Sisyphus, &c., fine as they are, interpolations, and that this interpolation is the only ground for representing Ulysses as having seen the infernal *regions*. He brought up the ψυχαὶ νεκύων to him, he did not go down to them, and there is an indistinctness upon the

---

[*] Compare xi., 121, with xxiii., 268.

[†] A separate treatise has been written on this question by Spohn, "Commentatio de Extremâ Odysseæ parte inde a rhapsodiæ Ψ, versu ccxcvii. ævo recentiore ortâ quam Homerico."—Lips. 1816.

common supposition wholly unlike Homer. On the other hand if you go from v. 566 to v. 600 all is pretty clear, but I think it still clearer by going at once from v. 563 to v. 627 ; then it runs naturally :—

βῆ δὲ μετ᾽ ἄλλας
ψυχὰς εἰς ἔρεβος νεκύων κατατεθνηώτων,
αὐτὰρ ἐγὼν αὐτου μένον ἔμπεδον.*

And by this means you get rid of Hercules' deification, &c., which Homer seems to have known nothing of, or indeed of any *Man* becoming a God. It is true by this erasure we lose some beautiful verses, but I cannot help thinking it right. The passage, v. 69, &c., in the M is apparently spurious, as it is the single one in which the Argo and Jason are mentioned ;† but indeed the whole account of the Πλαγκταὶ, beginning at v. 59, seems very doubtful, as Ulysses never mentions them afterwards. Perhaps it would be right to go from v. 38 to 73, though even then there is some obscurity, as it is not quite easy to consider the keeping nearer to the one or the other of the rocks, as the two ὁδοὶ that Circè mentions, though I rather think, that is the meaning.‡ There are certainly more passages in the Odyssey than in the Iliad,

---

* The passage indicated by Mr. Fox had been rejected by Aristarchus. See Porson's note on Eurip. Orest. 5. The subject of this alleged interpolation is discussed at length by Nitzsch in his notes on the "Odyssey," vol. iii. p. 304—399.—(Hanover, 1840).

† The passage xii., 69—72, is likewise considered by Nitzsch, vol. iii., p. 376, to be an interpolation. Pelias, the King of Iolcus, is mentioned as the son of Tyro, xi., 254.

‡ Ernesti thinks that the two alternative courses which Circe, v. 57-8, points out to Ulysses are the Planctæ, or Scylla and Charybdis.

which are justly suspected; but that is no reason for doubting their having been written by the same poet, of which I cannot help thinking the internal evidence most convincing.* You are to understand, that when I speak of spurious passages, I do not mean that such passages are modern interpolations; so far from it that I think there is reason to believe the interpolations (if such they were), as ancient as any other Greek poetry we have, and many of them are very beautiful. Even in the Ω, v. 36, &c., ὄλβιε Πηλέος υἰὲ, is beautiful, but how much has Virgil improved it by his application. O! felix una ante alias Priameia virgo ? &c.† Well, here is Homer criticism enough; but it is a subject upon which I never tire.

" You have hardly seen the new edition of Burns. Currie's life of him is the most affected thing I ever read, and in some parts (particularly where he speaks of his drunkenness, an odd subject to be pompous upon) pompous to a degree of ridicule. Some of Burns' things are admirable, particularly ' Tam o'Shanter,' which is very Bermeddinish.‡ The ' Cotter's Saturday Night,' is very good too. It seems

* Mr. Fox here expresses his opinion that the "Iliad" and "Odyssey" were written by the same poet; and not each by a separate poet, as has been supposed both by ancient and modern critics. See Mure, ib. vol. ii., c. 16.

† This speech of the shade of Agamemnon occurs in the last book of the "Odyssey," which Mr. Fox treats as a later addition. See above, p. 182. The passage of Virgil with which he compares it is in Æneid iii., 321, where Andromache, reminded of her marriage with Pyrrhus, envies the lot of Polyxena, who had been immolated on the tomb of Achilles.

‡ Lord Holland had begun a Moorish poem called "Bermeddin," but how "Tam o'Shanter" should put Mr. Fox in mind of it I do not well understand.

strange, but I think it is so, that the Scotch should excel in pastoral. Except the ' Tancia '* and ' Cecco da Varlungo ;' I think some of the Scotch songs, and some of Burns' works the best pastorals in any modern language."

SAME TO SAME.

"*October*, 1800.

" I CANNOT help thinking, that Bonaparte will not be so rancorous as you apprehend, and that he will find it for the interest both of his glory and of his power to continue in the system of moderation. I think he had a clear right to ask an armistice ; nay, even a preliminary outline of peace if he thought fit, before he admitted us into the negotiation of Luneville; but, if he asks an armistice as a *sine quá non*, before he will enter into a separate treaty, I think he is in the wrong. The History has gone on very slowly, but it will mend its pace much in the winter. As to keeping pace however, with Bonaparte, I do not aspire to it, and if the war continues he may conquer half the world before I have dethroned King James. I wrote you a long letter to Cassel, which I suppose you have not got, it was of no consequence, and related I believe chiefly to Homer.

" I hear it is said, that not only in France, but here,

---

* The " Tancia " is a rustic comedy, in five acts, and in *ottava rima*, by Michel-Angelo Buonarroti, the younger (nephew of the great painter and sculptor), written in the language of the Tuscan peasants. It was first published in 1612. The " Lamento di Cecco da Varlungo " is a rustic poem, composed in the same dialect, by Baldovini, a poet of the 17th century, who died in 1716.

people are universally tired of the war; you know
my belief is, that they were so long ago, but whether
enough so, as to induce them to show themselves is
quite another question. I hear your Uncle Ossory
and Egremont * named as being remarkably eager
for peace. If Ministers pretend they *now* wish for
peace, what can they say for having refused Bonaparte's
offer in the winter? and what is become the dangers
to be apprehended from the success of the Lisle
negotiation, upon which Pitt particularly laid so much
stress? but there is no end of scrapes they got themselves into, as to reason and argument, if that were
of any signification."

SAME TO SAME.

"*January*, 24*th*, 1801.

"Concert is indeed a desirable thing, and I can
never agree to your proposition, that without me it is
impossible. You mention neither the Duke of
Bedford nor Grey in your letter, who, if any plan of
concert be to be formed, appear to me by far the
most important personages. If there is any idea of
meeting at any great man's house, the Duke of
Bedford's is the most proper, but I see no great
objection to Norfolk House. According to my notions,
however, no such meeting is like to be of service in
the first instance; but it might be a very proper
measure to follow some previous success gained in
either House of Parliament, or without doors. By

* George O'Brien third Earl of Egremont, born 1751, died 1837.

success in Parliament, you know I do not mean carrying a question, but gaining any great and palpable advantage, in point either of numbers or of popularity. The old party is too much routed and dispersed to be rallied again, but upon something like a favourable appearance, which I think the present times very likely however to furnish. What has been done at Leeds in this view, is of great consequence, and if it is followed perhaps, would furnish the best ground for a meeting to concert a motion upon the principle of the petitions. As to the Northern business, I have forgot a good deal what passed twenty years ago, but I remember I was a friend then to the Russian system, and *that* to a degree that in the Rockingham Administration I was upon one question alone or had only Lord John Cavendish with me, but what that question was is quite out of my head. What the precise subject of dispute now is I do not even know, for if the treaty upon the signing of which our embargo is founded, has been in the newspapers, it has escaped me.* It is altogether a sort of question in which there is good reason to suppose, that the weakest are sure to be in the right. I quite agree with you, that whatever may be the justice of the

---

* An embargo was laid by Russia upon English vessels on the 7th of November, 1800; and a confederacy against England, upon the principles of the armed neutrality of 1780, was signed by Russia, Sweden, Denmark, and Prussia, in December. In consequence an embargo was laid by Great Britain on the ships of these nations in January, 1801. See "Annual Register," vol. xliii., p. 103. The official correspondence on the subject is printed ib., State-papers, p. 233—47. The treaty referred to by Mr. Fox is in "Annual Register," vol xlii., State-papers, p. 261. See Alison's "History of Europe," vol. iv., c. 33.

claim, its coming now, and in such a manner into discussion, is and must be owing to the misconduct of this country. The refusing Bonaparte's offers, first in January and then in October,* are faults in my judgment, without a parallel in History. The first was far the better opportunity no doubt, but the last is the one, the rejection of which is the most unaccountable, because there could be *then*, no sanguine notions in respect to the success of Austria, and what had passed with Denmark, marked out the approaching dangers from the North."

SAME TO SAME.

"St. Ann's Hill, *Sunday, February 8th,* 1801.

"A noble Pole (I'm proud to call him friend),
Tells me of things I cannot comprehend."

Addington, Chancellor of the Exchequer, as against Pitt !† If I do believe it, it must be *quia incomprehensibile*. I think the line you propose is exactly the right one; but I cannot help admiring the ease with which you talk of the new administration, as if any such thing existed. And Lord Spencer supports Ministry in everything, except Catholic Emancipation! I suppose you mean *resistance* to

---

* The first refusal was in the answer to the letter of the First Consul, already mentioned; the second, in the negotiation with M. Otto, in September and October, 1800. The correspondence relating to the latter negotiation is in "Annual Register," 1800, State-papers, p. 209.

† The resignation of Mr. Pitt, on account of the Catholic Question, was announced early in February, 1801. He was succeeded by Mr. Addington (who was then Speaker), as First Lord of the Treasury and Chancellor of the Exchequer.

Catholic Emancipation; but what, and whom is he to support? In short, I understand nothing of what is going forward. The line of conduct to be taken seems quite clear, as Lansdowne would say, simplicity and consistency. Removal and censure of Pitt and his associates, Religious Liberty to its utmost extent, Reform in Parliament, Liberty of the Press, in which I include pardon in all instances, and indemnity in others, to Libellers, &c.; not only peace, but a good understanding if it can be had, with Bonaparte, and everything that is mild and conciliating to Denmark, Sweden, &c.

"I think my going to town *now* without any call upon me to attend any particular motion in the House of Commons would be absurd, and liable to ridiculous constructions. I have not heard from Grey, or the Duke of Bedford, but I take for granted they will approve of the language which you propose to hold. I cannot help suspecting that when the resignations appear so numerous, the King and his mad advisers will give way, and we shall be blessed with the old administration.

" Yours affectionately,

"C. J. F."

SAME TO SAME.

"St. Ann's Hill, *Sunday February 8th,* 1801.

" Dear Young One,

"If Pitt be out, whatever may be the grounds he goes out upon, and however 'speedy and certain his reinstatement may be, it must be productive of some good ; since whatever the result may be, such divisions among them as those must have been which have produced such an event must weaken them. Besides no inconsiderable part of Pitt's strength consists in his long and *uninterrupted* enjoyment of power. Some of my letters mention the fact as certain, but yet as Parr would say, ἐπέχω. If the Speaker is employed as is said, to make a new arrangement, it must be indeed a notorious juggle, and it seems to me not unlikely that it will proceed thus. The Speaker will converse with some men of consequence, possibly Grey or others, and will report that he cannot find it practicable to make a Ministry upon the principle of rejecting the Catholic claims, &c., and then Pitt will be restored and the King will submit. This is the event that will do the *least* good, but still there will remain the consequences of a *shake*, and religious liberty will have gained a great point. If the King does make another Ministry and can keep it, first of all they will be very weak, which in itself is good, and besides they will feel the absolute necessity of making peace, and it is possible the inclination of France may induce Bonaparte to make it with them, and peace however obtained is in every point of view a real good. But if a new Ministry is tried and fails there is a better chance than any which has appeared of late years of overturning the whole system. Such are my speculations, but though since I began my letter a person has called who has had letters from town confirming the news, still ἐπέχω. His letters say that Dundas (which was of course) and Grenville (which seems very extra-

ordinary) go out with Pitt.* If this is so it would
confirm the notion that it is all a juggle to cheat the
King and that *He* will be the person to yield.

" Yours affectionately,

"C. J. FOX."

SAME TO SAME.

" ST. ANN'S HILL, *Sunday, April* 19*th*, 1801.

" NEVER did a letter arrive in a worse time, my
dear young one, than yours this morning; a sweet
westerly wind, a beautiful sun, all the thorns and
elms just budding, and the nightingales just beginning
to sing, though the blackbirds and thrushes would
have been quite sufficient without the return of those
seceders to have refuted any arguments in your letter.
Seriously speaking I cannot conceive what you mean
by everybody agreeing that something may be *now*
done ; I beg at least not to be included among the
holders of that opinion, for as it appears to me there
never was a moment when all exertion on our part
was more certain to be useless if not worse. Pray
therefore put a stop to any trouble or expense (as soon
as possible) that you or any one else have been at or
are incurring about a house. My present notion is
that, except for Tooke's business† (which I could not

---

* Lord Grenville resigned his office of Secretary of State for the Foreign
Department, and Mr. Dundas his office of Secretary of State for the War
Department, at the same time that Mr. Pitt resigned.

† The Reverend John Horne Tooke was returned to serve in Parliament
in the Session of 1801, for the borough of Old Sarum, upon the nomi-
nation of Lord Camelford. His right to sit was contested, on the ground
of his being in priest's orders; and measures were taken for excluding

desert without shabbiness) and the May Whig club, I shall go to town no more this year. My feeling is this, that notwithstanding nightingales, flowers, literature, history, &c., all which however I conceive to be good and substantial reasons for staying here, I would nevertheless go to town if I saw any chance of my going being serviceable to the public or (which in my view of things is exactly the same thing) to the party; which I love both as a party and on account of many of the principal individuals who compose it. I feel myself quite sure that this is not now the case, and that if I were to go the best I could hope for would be that I should do no mischief; and with such a hope only, you will allow that I cannot be expected to make any great sacrifice of my own comforts and enjoyments. I am curious to hear more about Russia.* If Alexander has really (which however, I do not believe) done all that is said, I think he must exceed even his magnanimous Sire in true Royal magnanimity, that is disregard of all principles of honesty and good faith. The Danes have made, I think, a famous resistance, but I suppose they must give up.† We shall be happy to see you when you can come. Remember what I have often told you, and now think more than ever. It must be from movements out of

him, which were opposed by Mr. Fox. A Bill was ultimately passed, disqualifying persons in holy orders from sitting in the House of Commons. See Adolphus, vol. vii., p. 486; Lord Holland's "Memoirs of the Whig Party," vol. i., p. 178.

* The death of the Emperor Paul took place on the 22nd of March 1801. He was succeeded by his son Alexander.

† The battle of Copenhagen, under Sir Hyde Parker and Lord Nelson was on the 2nd of April.

doors and not in Parliament that opposition can ever gain any strength, I mean of course *as* opposition. What the King's death or illness might produce is another question.

"Yours most affectionately,

"C. J. FOX."

SAME TO SAME.

"*June*, 1801.

"My journey to Wales, if it were to take place at all, would be entirely with a view to more leisure than I can have here in summer for the History, which, alas! goes on very slowly; but I will mend my pace, I am resolved. I have been a good deal diverted from it this last fortnight by a rage I have taken for looking over all Dryden's works, both prose and poetry. I fell into it, upon honour, with real diligent views in regard to history, but soon forgot the object, and read him with views entirely critical. I mean, some day or other, (but not till I have done at least one, if not two volumes of History,) to publish an edition of Dryden; therefore, if anything that could be useful to such a purpose should come across you, pray keep it in mind for me, though for the present I am full as well, or better without it. I mean particularly anything relative to Dryden's history, or any scarce edition of any of his works.

"The Indemnity Bill does, indeed, exceed all; but, as you say, I have long ceased to wonder. As it is worded it seems to me that, even if the Ministers themselves were to discover any abuse of authority by their under instruments they could not punish it." *

SAME TO SAME.

"St. Ann's Hill, Thursday, July 23rd, 1801.

"My dear Young One,

"I will answer your questions as well as I can. The Λόγος Αἰγύπτιος is, I suppose, the work of Aristides the sophist, who lived in the time of M. Aurelius, and travelled a great deal in Egypt. His works were printed at Oxford, 1723.† I do not know where you can find an account of all the Arabian authors, but it is not unlikely that sufficient information upon that subject may be in d'Herbelot's 'Oriental Dictionary.' I have no doubt but there are both English and French translations of 'Aboulfeda,' who is constantly quoted by Gibbon and others; but I know there is a Latin translation of him, which was published, together with the original, in London, 1650. Nota at a time when, according to modern courtly writers, no good literature was cultivated in England.‡ The

---

* This was a Bill introduced by the Attorney-General in the House of Commons, May 27, 1801, "for indemnifying such persons as since the 1st day of February, 1793, have acted in the apprehending, imprisoning, or detaining in custody, in Great Britain, of persons suspected of high treason or treasonable practices." The Bill was opposed, and divisions were taken upon it in both Houses.

† Ed. Jebb, Oxford, 1722, two vols. 4to.

‡ A list of the translations of the history of Abulfeda is given in the "Biographie Universelle," in v. A Latin translation of that portion of his Geography which relates to the countries beyond the Oxus, was published by Greaves, at London, 1650, 4to. This is the work referred to by Mr. Fox; it consists only of 64 pages. Mr. Fox's remark does not apply

generally received opinion is that Moses left Egypt about 1500 years before Christ. The date (and of late, as you know, the existence) of the Trojan war is more disputed. I believe the commonest opinion is that it was about 1100 years before Christ,* and consequently 400 years after Moses; but some maintain it to have been in the time of Rehoboam, Solomon's son, which would make it near 200 years later. As to Homer, Herodotus says positively that he lived 400 years after the Trojan war; † but the more common opinion has been that he lived and wrote within a century after it; nay, some suppose that he sung his verses to the sons and grandsons of his heroes. One of the most modern guesses (for it appears to me to be nothing more) is that Homer, or at least his family, were among the numerous emigrants from Greece to Asia, on the return of the Heraclidæ to Peloponnesus, which is supposed to have happened about 50 years after the destruction of Troy,‡ and that the poem was written in Asia Minor, in compliment to the chiefs of those emigrants, and intended to show that they were the true authors of the Grecian glory on the one hand, and that their

in this case, for Greaves was an adherent of the royalist cause, and had been patronised by Laud, and the publication of his translation of the entire Geography of Abulfeda was prevented by the civil war.

* The date of Eratosthenes for the taking of Troy is 1184 B.C.

† Herodotus nowhere says expressly that Homer lived 400 years after the Trojan war; but he states, ii. 53, that Homer lived above 400 years before his own time; and ii. 145, that the Trojan war was about 800 years before his own time. If these two statements are put together, it follows that Homer lived about 400 years after the Trojan war.

‡ Thucydides, i. 12, places the return of the Heraclidæ to the Peloponnesus in the eightieth year after the capture of Troy.

superior valour might make them easily masters of
the country to which they had emigrated, on the
other.* This appears to me a specious hypothesis,
and that it was that made me remark, not, as you once
misunderstood me, that he never mentions Hercules,
but that he never exalts him; that in one instance,
in the ' Odyssey,' he ascribes to him a horrid and
treacherous outrage,† and never speaks of him with
much respect. It is observable that several passages
where he is mentioned are very suspicious from internal
evidence relating to digammas, &c. Herodotus says
that he was 400 years younger than Homer,‡ and
consequently, according to *his* calculation, that 800
years had elapsed between the Trojan war and his
writing; but we know that he wrote 450 years before
Christ, and therefore, according to him, the Trojan
war would be 1250 years before Christ, and so only
250 years subsequent to Moses. If the era of Moses
is as I have stated it, and I believe it is very generally
understood so, between Moses and Herodotus there
are only 1050 years; and consequently, if the
Pyramids were built 1200 years before Herodotus, as
your author says, they must have been built near
200 years anterior, instead of 200 years subsequent
to Moses; but I suspect he follows some different
system of chronology from that generally received,
and plenty of systems there are built upon very
slender foundations. That Homer should not have

---

* This, and other theories relating to Homer, are stated and discussed
by Colonel Mure, in his work already quoted, vol. ii. c. 18.

† See "Odyssey," xxi. 24-30.   ‡ Ante, p. 195, n.

noticed the Pyramids, if they existed in his time, is very wonderful, as he speaks so much about Egypt; that there should be no mention of them in Hesiod is not extraordinary, for, his only work extant being a Georgic,* they would not come in his way. Among Joseph's adventures they would very naturally have found a place. After all, I cannot conceive what difficulty you can have about these Pyramids in 'Bermeddin;' Abdelrahman may get out any way; and if you wish to say anything about them and their history, you may choose any account of them you please, and Herodotus's seems made exactly for such a poem as 'Bermeddin.' I do not want to read White, or any author, to learn that the famous library at Alexandria was destroyed long before Mahomet was born; that is to say, when Julius Cæsar was at Alexandria (not it is to be supposed intentionally) by fire. But it is possible, that though the library of the Ptolemies was gone, the city of Alexandria might have collected a considerable library afterwards, and this is the more likely on account of the great renown of that which had been destroyed, which they might wish to emulate; but of this second library nothing I believe is known, but that, such as it was, it was destroyed by Amrou; nor is even that fact by any means certain.† I do not wonder you are delighted with Lucretius. I have always thought

---

* Mr. Fox here treats the " Theogony " and the " Shield of Hercules " as the works of a poet different from Hesiod, the author of the " Works and Days."

† On the Alexandrine libraries, see "Gräfenhan, Geschichte der Klassischen Philologie," vol. iii. p. 53.

Virgil alludes to him in the passage '*Felix qui potuit*,'* &c., and that he means to say Lucretius has the first place; and then, by '*Fortunatus et ille*,' &c., gives himself the second. The passage you mention is indeed an imitation, and in some respects a pretty close one, not in all parts either an improvement.†
I think the four lines, '*Nec varios inhiant*,' &c., very heavy in comparison of Lucretius. In the counterpart, '*At secura quies*,' &c., Virgil is more beautiful to be sure; but yet by being more general he is less picturesque, or (since Price has given such a fanciful meaning to that word) I suppose I must say less descriptive, which last word does not explain my idea half so well.‡ Lucretius too, as his subject required, (Virgil's did not) is, as he always is, argumentative in the midst of his poetry, and puts '*non magnis opibus*' to make out his proposition; whereas, Virgil's '*parvo assueta juventus*' is of no great use, either to the sense or the poetry. '*Inhiant*' is the only reading I ever saw; nor is there any hint of another in the three editions of Virgil which I have. One of the notes in the '*Variorum*' says it belongs to '*Salutantes*.' I had always understood it to belong to '*Agricolæ*;' and the Roman and Delphin editions favour my construction, as Annibal Caro translates it '*bramano*,' and the Delphin interprets it '*appetunt*,' which must

---

* "Georg." ii. 490.   † Compare "Georg." ii. 461, with Lucret. ii. 24.

‡ The sense which Mr. Uvedale Price affixes to this word, in his "Essay on the Picturesque," is, that quality in external nature which fits it for being the subject of a picture. Mr. Price was a friend of Mr. Fox; they travelled together in Italy when Mr. Fox was a young man. See vol. i. p. 29.

refer to the '*Agricolæ.*'* By the way, I do not approve
of Caro's or the Delphin's sense, though I do of their
construction. I conceive '*inhiant*' to mean simply
to 'stare at,' or to 'gape at.' I should be at as much
difficulty to construe '*inhians*' as you seem to find in
'*inhiant.*' I hope the grand passage in the first book
of Lucretius about the winds did not escape you.†
Virgil, if I recollect, has pillaged that too pretty
well, though I cannot immediately point out the
places. I am very glad to hear Charles is so much
mended. I have not yet seen the Russian treaty;
but suppose I shall in to-morrow's paper.‡ Bonaparte's conduct in respect to Tuscany is obvious
enough, upon the principle of keeping the Austrians
out of Italy; but if he did not act in concert with
the King of Prussia, in regard to the indemnity
to be given the Grand Duke in Germany, I shall
think his conduct difficult to be accounted for.

"Yours affectionately,

"C. J. F."

SAME TO SAME.

"*October 22nd*, 1801.

"MY DEAR YOUNG ONE,

"After a good deal of hesitation, I have determined to be at the House on the 29th, § though I
rather think it might be as well to stay for the day

---

* Heyne also interprets it by "*habere cupiunt.*"

† See Lucret. i. 272-95.

‡ A convention between Russia and England was signed in June, 1801.
See "Annual Register," vol. xliii., State-papers, p. 212.

§ The first day of the session.

when the preliminaries are to be taken regularly into consideration.* I like Thurlow's opinion better than the Duke of Richmond's; if I were induced to find fault it would be with the having preferred Trinidad or Ceylon, to Malta or Minorca; a port in the Mediterranean is something. I can easily believe all you say about Pitt's friends, but you do not mention from whom you have gathered your opinion. I dare say Pitt does right in approving the peace, because I who am not his friend would rather wish him to do otherwise; but yet I should think it must be very humiliating to him after all his blusters.

"Indeed, Young One, I cannot attend the House of Commons *con amore*. I feel somehow that that account is settled, I am perhaps vain enough to think to my advantage, and I do not like opening it again."

SAME TO SAME.

"*January 26th*, 1802.

"I AM not very sanguine about your being able to accomplish what you call my magnificent idea of building up a new opposition, but yet industry and youth can do much, and unless such a thing can be done no good can."

SAME TO SAME.

"*February* 1802.

"IT is a sad thing, My dear Young One, to come

---

* The debate in the House of Commons on the preliminary articles of the treaty with France was on the 3rd of November, 1801, on which occasion Mr. Fox spoke.

young and vigorous into an old, worn out, jaded opposition : however if you can in any degree *rajeunir* it you will do in my opinion the greatest possible service to the country. I did this in some degree with the Rockinghams, but then every circumstance was as favourable to me, as it is otherwise to you. I had heard that Albemarle was to give notice of a motion which would have included yours, and I rather wish he had, but I suppose he had not brought himself to determine upon it. I am quite undecided about attending Burdett's motion,* or any other ; my inclination (mind I mean the inclination of my opinion) is rather against all attendance, but I sometimes doubt. The not bringing on the Catholic question, is, I think, very disgraceful ; but you saw last spring how much it would have been against the grain to have started it, and I suspect it would be still more so now. The case against paying the King's debts is a very strong one, I do not know where to refer you for the particulars except it be to Burke's Bill, and to the different payments and exonerations of the Civil List, which took place before and after that Bill.† If the debates upon the increase of the Civil List in 1777 are tolerably preserved, they would afford a good deal of information. Sir Fletcher Norton's speech to the King, which the House of Commons by thanking him for it (and that too after the debate) adopted, is

---

* Sir Francis Burdett made a motion in the House of Commons for an inquiry into the conduct of the late administration of Mr. Pitt, on April 12, 1802. It was negatived by 246 to 39 votes.

† Burke's bill for an economical reform, in 1780. See Adolphus, vol. iii. p. 95.

particularly to be attended to.* If, after failing in the
opposition to the measure it could be made use of, as it
fairly may, to get the Prince of Wales' debts liquidated,
I very much wish it should be done; as some mark of
kindness from opposition to the Prince would I think
be very proper in many respects. The argument is
unanswerable. We made the Prince pay his debts
out of his income, Why? because upon the former
arrangement of his income, it was understood that he
was satisfied. Now the King's debts have been repeatedly paid, and his income once directly, and once more,
indirectly increased, and the provision was acknowledged by his ministers to be satisfactory. Surely
therefore the reasoning which prevailed against the
Prince is stronger against the King, and if in one case
we overlook it, in order to show our generosity, we are
more bound to do so in the other, where the favourable interference of Parliament has occurred in one
instance only. Mind I only recommend this attempt
for the Prince as a secondary object, for, in the first
instance, I think the payment of the King's debts, and
still more an increase of income, if proposed, should be
opposed *totis viribus;* you recollect that so far has the
Civil List been from being loaded by Extraordinary
expenses that we paid even Dr. Willis and the other
physicians out of the public money.†

---

* In 1777 a bill for paying the arrears of the Civil List was passed ; and,
on presenting it for the royal assent, the Speaker, Sir Fletcher Norton,
made a speech to the King, for which he received the thanks of the House
of Commons, and he was desired to print it (May 7). See Adolphus,
"History of George III." vol. ii. p. 424 ; see also vol. iii. p. 111.

† The debate in the Commons on the arrears in the Civil List took
place on March 29, 1802, when Mr. Fox delivered his views at length.

SAME TO SAME.*

November 21*st*, 1802.

"MY DEAR YOUNG ONE,

"After our engagement of regularity in our future correspondence it has turned out that we were hardly ever so long before without writing to one another; but besides that at Paris I really had no time, I waited in constant expectation of hearing something of your intended projects. Not a line of yours since you left Tours had reached Paris, when I left it on the 11th of this month, and though Mrs. F. had a letter from Bourdeaux, and Adair one from Toulouse, from Lady Holland, there was not in either any information of your intentions whether for Spain or Italy. I now begin on your birthday, and mean to write every fortnight or three-weeks at least. We left Paris on the 11th, and went to Charles Lameth's, where we stayed only one night; it is an excellent house, and a very pretty situation and he is arranging the place upon a largish scale *à l'Angloise*; how far he will succeed remains to be seen, the lying of the ground certainly favours his plan. We got to Calais, the 14th, crossed the 15th, in the night, a good passage, and got home on the 17th without going through London. I have certainly seldom spent time pleasanter than at Paris, but yet I never in my life felt such delight in returning home. '*Hic amor, hæc patria est;*' mind I mean the *hic* and *hæc* in a very confined sense.

---

* Mr. Fox left England for France, on the 29th of July, 1802. See Trotter's "Memoirs of Fox," p. 32.

Indeed I have little or nothing to tell you of my life at Paris, the sight of Lafayette and his family, and the perfect attachment of them all to him, and of him to them, was very charming. The only new acquaintance I made worth mentioning were Livingston, who, though deaf, is far the most agreeable American I ever conversed with, besides being a very well informed and sensible man,* and Berthier,† with whom, from shooting together, I became very intimate. I like him very much, and if I had not been too ignorant concerning the campaigns to know the proper questions to ask, I might be sufficiently informed to write a history of them. He seems to like being questioned, and answers with the greatest frankness and readiness. I ought perhaps, too, to mention Villoison the great Grecian, if it is only for his volubility which exceeds all belief; Graham the judge here, and even every Frenchman you have ever heard, are slow in comparison of him,—and what is remarkable is, that notwithstanding his speed he speaks very distinctly. It is well he knows a great deal, for at the rate he goes a moderate stock would run out in half an hour.‡ I do not reckon Lord Henry Petty§ because I have been speaking of foreigners only, but never did I see a young man I liked half so much.

---

* Edward Livingston, an American jurist and statesman, the author of the code for Louisiana. He died in 1836.

† Alexandre Berthier, Prince of Neufchâtel and Wagram, born in 1753. He died by a fall from a window at Bamberg, in 1814.

‡ J. B. D'ansse de Villoison, an eminent Greek scholar. He was born in 1750, and died in 1805.

§ Now Marquis of Lansdowne. He succeeded his elder brother in 1809.

Whatever disappointments Lansdowne may have had in public life, and of a still more sensible kind in Lord Wycombe, he must be very unreasonable if he does not consider them all compensated in Lord Henry.

We met Lord Whitworth* near Amiens, and I believe, as well as hope, that there will be peace; but by all accounts the nonsense that has been talked in this country exceeds even past times, not that I believe the wish for war is at all general, but all the newspapers writing in a cry for it has the appearance of public opinion, an appearance only I am satisfied. I shall go to town for the address on Tuesday, not with any hope of dissuading the warlike, but for the chance of being of some use in encouraging those who are said to be pacific, especially the Ministers. I am told I shall be as much abused for pacific language now, as I was ten years ago, but as I am in Parliament I must not blink such a question. With all the noise there is, it is difficult for those who most wish war to find a pretence for it; to make use of Switzerland for that purpose is not only a base hypocrisy, but one which nobody will or can believe, for not only Poland, &c., prove that such are not the causes for war with us; but it is evident to all men, that we have no means of protecting the Swiss or even assisting them in the smallest degree, in ·the present state of things. I do

---

* Charles Lord Whitworth was sent ambassador to Paris near the end of 1802, and remained there till April, 1803. Mr. Fox, returning to England, met Lord Whitworth on his road to Paris. The preliminaries of a treaty of peace between England and France had been signed at London, in October, 1801. The definitive treaty was signed at Amiens by Lord Cornwallis, in March, 1802.

not yet know what to make of this cursed plot of
Despard and his associates to seduce soldiers, &c.
I hear the Ministry mean to do what is right, and send
the persons accused to immediate trial.   I hope, and
indeed I believe, that the intention of assassination
which is imputed to these criminals is not founded.
It is one of the points in our national character, on
which we may with justice pride ourselves, that
assassination is not one of the crimes which it occurs
to Englishmen to commit in almost any circumstances.
I believe the first commitments upon this business
took place Wednesday or Thursday, and nothing
is now publicly known further than what I have
mentioned.   The numbers said to be concerned are
as usual stated very differently, but I believe, besides
Despard there are thirty, or thereabouts, apprehended.*
Pray let me know as soon as you have determined
whether or not you are likely to go to Madrid.   Don
Pedro de Ronquillo's † correspondence with his court
from 1685 to 1688, both inclusive, would be most
valuable to me, and if the copying of it would not
cost more than 100*l.*, I would willingly be at the
expense.   But if you, or anybody I could trust, were
to read it, and direct what extracts should be made,
a great proportion both of trouble and expense might
be saved.

* Colonel Despard, and thirty-two obscure persons, were arrested at a
public-house in Lambeth, on Nov. 20, 1802, charged with high treason, in
intending to kill the King on his way to the Houses of Parliament.
Despard and nine of his associates were afterwards convicted of high
treason, and hanged, February, 1803.

† Spanish Ambassador in England during the reign of James II.   See
Sir James Mackintosh, " History of the Revolution."

" I saw Mddlc. Duchénois,* again in ' *Phèdre*,' just before I left Paris, and thought her a good deal improved, though still unequal. I saw her also in '*Roxane*,' in Bajazet, which I think by far her best part. I saw La Fond once or twice, and like him better than Talma. In ' *Tancrède*,' I really think him very good, especially in the good part of ' *Tancrède*,' which is the third act and perhaps that act only."

SAME TO SAME.

"St. Ann's Hill, *Dec.* 19*th*, 1802.

" As to myself, my studies of all kinds have been much interrupted, as you will have guessed from newspapers, by politics, '*iterum mergor civilibus undis;*' but it shall be for a very short time, I swear; only while there is hope of contributing to prevent war, I feel myself in a manner bound. I mentioned in my last how I was threatened in case I spoke warmly for peace, and if those threats were not realised, it was not for want of inclination in the warriors.† ' Apologist of France,' ' agent of the first consul,' ' no dislike of the power of France,' were dealt about pretty well both in newspapers and in the House, but they would not do, for the real wish for peace is such (and indeed I had always some hope that it would be so notwith-

---

* Mlle. Duchesnois, the celebrated tragic actress, was born in 1785, and first acted at the Théâtre Français in the year 1802. See Trotter's account of this visit to the Théâtre Français, "Memoirs," p. 201.

† Mr. Fox alludes to his speech on the Address at the opening of the session, November 23rd, 1802.

standing the clamour), that I was popular both in and
out of doors to the last degree, and in the House
particularly, if I am any judge.   I do not think for
many years, certainly, not since the Russian business,
I ever had the House so much with me while I was
speaking.   To say, as those inclined to flatter me will
say, that I have done anything considerable for peace
is more than is true ; but it is true, that by speaking
a pacific language more decisively than others dared
to do, and by that language being well received, I
have been the means of showing that the real sentiments of people are strongly for peace, and it is very
important that this should be known.   By letter, of
course, I should not touch upon any more secret parts
of politics, even if I had (which I have not) anything
material to communicate to you.   Pitt is generally
believed to be friendly to Addington, and to peace ;
but yet the warriors are continually calling for him to
return ; and therefore, I think, he will find himself
obliged after Christmas to say something pretty decisive, or to make his retirement (for a time at least)
a complete secession.   Canning and his clique, as well
as the Grenvilles, keep no terms with the Ministry,
and what terms they can keep with Pitt, if he supports
Ministers handsomely, remains to be seen.   Sheridan
made a very foolish speech, if a speech full of wit can
be with propriety so called, upon the Army Estimates,*
of which all who wish him ill are as fond as I, who
wish him well, am vexed at it.   He will however, I
do not doubt, be still right in the end.   In the House

---

* On December 8th, 1802.

of Lords, you will easily conceive that Lord Grenville
(I mean in point of debate only, however), is very
powerful, and I think there never was a time when
your absence was so unlucky, for there seems to be
nothing on the peace side but the Chancellor.   So
much for politics, only I may add, that rise of stocks
and all other public circumstances look as one would
wish them for peace.   If I have my fears, it is only
from a suspicion of a want of courage in Ministers to
speak what they really think, and if they should *long*
continue to be afraid of speaking bold pacific language,
ill humours may arise, and war begin without any real
wish for it in either government.   I have begun my
work again, but have had very little time for it; for
idle moments I am chiefly reading the old favourites,
Euripides and Spenser, and admire more every day,
especially the former.   I repeat what I believe, I once
said to you before, that if a man's object is public
speaking, Euripides ought to be his constant study
scarcely less than Homer himself.   Apropos to the
latter, what do you think is meant by the *chain* in the
beginning of the eighth book of the Iliad?*   Clark
quotes Plato, for its meaning the sun, and Pope
translates the two words, σειρὴν χρυσείην :—

> ' Our golden everlasting chain,
> Whose strong embrace holds heaven, and earth, and main.'

Pope has too, I believe, a note upon it, and its
meaning.   Now my opinion is, that nothing is meant
but the literal sense of the words; not *our* golden

---

* Iliad, viii. 19, and Plato, Theætet. § 27. Compare Heyne's note, in his
edition of Homer, vol. v. p. 414.

chain, or *my* &c., or even *the* &c.; for there is no
article, but simply Jupiter stating his superior strength
says, try; take a golden chain and hang it so and so,
and pull, and I'll show you what I'll do. Pray tell
me your opinion, I am particularly anxious to defend
mine, because I think it one of Homer's peculiar
qualities, that he is able to produce the sublime to at
least as high a degree as any other poet, without ever
resorting to the mysterious, the obscure, or unintelligible; and merely by images and thoughts, which
human senses and common human understandings,
are capable of examining and comprehending. By
the way, you should tell me, as I do you, what books
you are reading, with a little criticism, if it is ever
so little.

" Yours affectionately,

"C. J. F."

SAME TO SAME.

"St. Ann's Hill, January 1st.

" I am convinced the Ministers mean peace, and
while they do so and that question continues in
agitation, they ought to be supported. The conduct
of France in the Swiss business is no doubt very
disgusting, but there is no remedy: as to more or less
decency with respect to the points which they take up,
it is what the war party are no wise solicitous about,
but yet I think, they have thought other points fitter
for their management than that of Switzerland.*

* On the conduct of Bonaparte to Switzerland at this crisis, see
Adolphus, vol. vii. p. 615., also Alison, vol. vi.

Upon the arrangement of the German Indemnities,* they lay most stress, which I dare say you think as I do of no consequence whatever. Indeed, I think Bonaparte quite in the right in that affair. I do not wonder the *Morning Post* frightened you; when I left Paris every body there was frightened, and even here such a consent of newspapers made some impression, but I have every day more and more reason to think the wish for peace is warm and general, only there is some pleasure to many people to hear the Consul well *railed* at. You know the English are what is called a high spirited people! I should indeed be glad if Lord Henry † were to make a figure, and indeed I have little doubt but he will; only my political career, which I hope will not last more than a few weeks or months at most, may be over before that happens. There have been two young speakers, Kinnaird, ‡ and Lord Cowper's brother, § by what I hear, the latter the most promising. I have seen Roscoe's pamphlet, and a poor one it is, insipid to the last degree, but well intended. I hope you will succeed in your embassy from him, and I promise myself great pleasure in reading Leo. X., ‖ I am only afraid he will not praise Ariosto

---

* On the indemnities in Germany consequent upon the treaty of Luneville, in which Hanover was interested, see Adolphus, ib. p. 616-36.

† Lord Henry Petty, now Marquis of Lansdowne.

‡ Charles, eighth Lord Kinnaird, born 1780, died 1826.

§ Edward Spencer Cowper, younger brother of the fourth and fifth Earls of Cowper.

‖ Roscoe's work on the "Life and Pontificate of Leo X," was first published at Liverpool, in 1805, 4 vols. 4to. The list of Roscoe's works in Watt's "Bibliographia Britannica" does not mention any pamphlet at this time.

enough.   We have had people here lately, and I have
neither written nor read except a little Homer, and
Euripides at chance moments.   I see Cowper translates
σειρὴν χρυσείην the chain, but leaves the question in
doubt, only quotes in a note a supposition of its being
a chain of love, quite nonsense, which he seems inclined
to approve.

" Everybody seems to think that peace is more and
more safe ; but yet what you say of ambiguous
menaces, which is applicable to both sides, bad blood,
&c., is very true, and till a language more friendly is
adopted on both sides there can be no safety ; this is
what I will work at as well as I can.   Petitions,
when men are persuaded that the Ministers are
already pacific, would not in your judgment or mine
be improper, but what is more to the purpose they
would be impracticable.

" There is a report in the papers, I hope a false
one, that Bonaparte is to be Emperor of the Gauls.*
I am not one of those who think names signify
nothing."

SAME TO SAME.

"St. Ann's Hill, *January 24th*, 1803.
" My birthday, 54.

" I write my dear young one, because my three
weeks are up, though I have no letter from you, and
nothing new to tell you from this country.   The same

---

* Napoleon assumed the title of Emperor of the French on the 18th of
May, 1804.

wishes for peace continue (I believe) on both sides of
the water, and the same perseverance in language
most calculated to bring on war, however, I say as
Pallas in Homer, A. v. 210, and surely *she* was
wise :—

> Ἀλλ' ἄγε λῆγ' ἔριδος, μηδὲ ξίφος ἕλκεο χειρί·
> Ἀλλ' ἤτοι ἔπεσιν μὲν ὀνείδισον, ὡς ἔσεταί περ.*

and I am sure we might say in answer to the Consul,
as Hector does, Υ. v. 432 :—

> σάφα οἶδα καὶ αὐτὸς
> Ἡμὲν κερτομίας ἠδ' αἴσυλα μυθήσασθαι.†

Those who are for war might quote Æneas' speech,
in the same book of the Iliad, from v. 244 to the
end ; and indeed, we peaceable men might quote them
properly enough, if it were not for the conclusion, *let
us fight.* Pitt has been in town, and it is *said*
Addington is satisfied with him ; but it is *said* too,
that he returns to Bath. This is difficult to reconcile.‡
Dundas, whom they have just made a peer, § says,

---

* " The force of keen reproaches let him feel ;
  But sheath, obedient, thy revenging steel."
  　　　　　　　　　　　　　Pope's Translation.
† " Hector, undaunted, thus : 'Such words employ
  To one that dreads thee, some unwarlike boy.
  Such we could give, defying and defied,
  Mean intercourse of obloquy and pride !'"
  　　　　　　　　　　　　　Pope's Translation.
‡ Mr. Pitt, being in London on his way from Bath to Walmer, visited
Mr. Addington at Richmond Park, early in January, 1803, and repeated
his visit shortly afterwards. No immediate result followed from these
communications. See Pellew's " Life of Lord Sidmouth," vol. ii. p. 112.
§ Right Honourable Henry Dundas, created Viscount Melville, 24th
December, 1802.

he shall stay away as he cannot support and does not
like to oppose ministers. Since parliaments, parties,
ministers and oppositions have existed, was there ever
anything like all this ? and if with all this together
with their own unaccountable conduct, the ministry
can stand (and I have no doubt but it can and will),
what is, or rather what is not, the power of the crown ?

" Knight * agrees with me, that there is no allegory
in the golden chain ; but he does not go the whole
length, that the meaning is take a chain, and he
supposes there was such a piece of furniture lying
about in Olympus. I feel on the other hand quite sure
I am right. ' You are pretty fellows, take a chain and
let us try,' is the true translation ; I do not know
whether I had looked at Cowper's ' Homer ' when I
wrote last, I have not had it long, and what little I
have read I cannot approve. We have read the first
volume of Madame de Stael's ' Delphine.' It is
heavy, but mends as you go on. I thought at one
time I should have given it up. I have been reading
(not a new favourite you will say,) the fourth Æneid,
and marking every passage I do not like in it. Pray,
if ever the fancy should take you to do the same,
make memorandums of it that I may see whether we
hit upon the same passages. I have also marked all
that I know to be taken either from ' Homer,'
' Apollonius,' or others, and when all is told it is

* Mr. Payne Knight, born in 1750, died in 1824 ; an accomplished Greek
scholar ; in 1820 he published an edition of Homer, with prolegomena
and notes. He was likewise the author of a " Monody on the Death of the
Right Honourable C. J. Fox," 8vo. London, 1806. A notice of his life
may be seen in the " Penny Cyclopædia."

incredible what a quantity of excellence, all original, remains. There are more little carelessnesses, or what we used to call *botches,* than many persons who have taken Virgil's character upon credit would imagine. Did he intend to make Æneas as odious as he appears in it? I suppose not, and yet it is incredibly well done if we could suppose the affirmative, and I do not know whether the effect is not upon the whole better than if we could either have admired or pitied him. Dido has us all to herself."

SAME TO SAME.

"CLARGES STREET, *Feb.* 23.

"I DO not agree that Spenser is as mysterious as Milton in the sense of the word as I used it; in the proper sense of the word he is perhaps full as much so; but I alluded only to that sort of sublime which is affected by images above the capacity of human senses, or abstract ideas beyond the conception of human understanding. Of the first class, are all descriptions of Chaos and the like, of the second, all that is in any way connected with infinity, eternity, omnipresence, immateriality, &c. &c. Knight, I find, thinks that Homer means a real chain, but then he does not admit that it means *any* chain; but supposes there was such a piece of furniture in Olympus, so well known in Homer's time (though now forgotten), that it was unnecessary for him further to particularize it. I see no use for this hypothesis, and though the absence of the article does not prove my interpretation it certainly favours it; the Greek article answering nine times out of ten to our English *the*. I am very glad you think of taking a note of those Spanish plays, from which you recollect Dryden to have taken. The truth is, that the Spanish theatre is clearly the parent theatre of Europe, I believe even as to tragedy, but certainly as to comedy. Corneille almost always imitates from the Spanish in his comedy, and in the ' Cid,' Voltaire has put in the notes, innumerable passages from the Spanish play. I have read some French translations of Calderon, which I liked very well; but the principal merit appeared to consist in comic situations, resulting from the intrigue of the plot. I remember I particularly liked one from which an English farce is, as I am told, borrowed, called the ' Pannel;' I never saw it ; but I am told that, by Mrs. Jordan's acting, it has a very good effect.* As to your ' Jovellanos ' † (if that is his name), the subjects he treats of are, I believe, very fit to be studied, but not by me. The truth is, I cannot endure them. By the way, this puts me in mind of the bank business (though not by a very near con-nection), and I was very happy to hear from some persons who came from the House of Lords to where I was dining yesterday, that Lord King ‡ had made

---

* Perhaps the " Padlock."

† Gaspar Melchior de Jovellanos, born in 1749, was killed in 1812 ; a Spanish writer, chiefly on political economy and legislation. See " M'Culloch's Literature of Pol. Ec.," p. 226.

‡ Peter, seventh Lord King, born 1776, died 1833. The speech here alluded to was delivered on the 22nd of February, on the second reading of a Bill for the Renewal of the Bank Restriction Act.

a most excellent speech, full of good sense and information, and his argument quite clear and well stated.
It was a subject he had much thought of, and is I
think quite right, excepting the general error of all
people on such subjects ; I mean that of supposing
their speculations more certain than they are.   I hope
and believe he will have gained great credit, and that
is the principal point.   You will of course have heard
of Despard's execution ; * it was generally thought
right ; indeed, I question whether I am not the only
man in London who would have advised a pardon,
but I would have done so.   The whole business has
produced little or no sensation.   As to other politics,
you know my complete despair of any real good ;
but the mischief of a war may perhaps be prevented,
at least I hope so.   The new Opposition have been as
dumb since Christmas as they were loquacious before,
only Lord Grenville in the House of Lords yesterday
seems to have threatened a line of opposition, something more rational than his former one, I mean upon
revenue and expenditure, &c.   In this I suppose he
will be joined by Moira, and indeed so he would by
me, if I attended to general politics.   Here am I then
come to town for nothing ; I am told however that
something will soon come relative to the evacuation of
Malta, in which case the new opposition must come
forward or never.   Pitt is ill with the gout, at
Walmer—I believe *really*, but half the world say

---

* Colonel Despard, sentenced for high treason, was executed, with six
others, on February 21, 1802. See " Annual Register," vol. xlv. p. 72, and
above, p. 204.

sham. There seems to be a sort of deadness in the House of Commons, worse than even in the worst times of the House of Lords. The Prince's business comes on to day, where however that deadness will be all to the good. He is to get a great deal, but not enough to set him quite clear, which is very foolish ; but that is the way these things are always done.*

" Yours affectionately,

" C. J. F."

SAME TO SAME.

"*March* 23rd, 1803.

" MY DEAR YOUNG ONE,

" Much more than three, I believe full four weeks have elapsed since my last, and I have had three letters from you ; but I have delayed writing latterly because I thought I should be too late for Valencia, and I had no other direction till I yesterday received yours of the third.† The view of public affairs is, indeed, altered since I wrote last. I had misgivings things were going not quite right, but I was willing to hope our Ministers were not quite such fools (and I might add another epithet too) as I now suspect them, *fuisse, esse et semper futuros* (translate that, literally, into French or English if you can). The causes of the message and all this bustle are not more known than they were when first it came. My

---

* Concerning the proposition made in this session, for the payment of the Prince's debts, see Adolphus, ib. p. 695.

† Lord Holland was, at this time, travelling in Spain.

belief is, that there was no cause. In short, I am
half mad at the thoughts of what is likely, I will still
hope not quite sure, to happen. I have very little
hope, and yet I think peace is perfectly in the power
of the present Ministry; but I cannot find that they
have proposed anything to France for the preservation
of it, or left Bonaparte any alternative but war or the
most abject humiliation. Perhaps there is more than
I know, but I sadly fear not; for, next to peace, what
I should least dislike would be a war in which Great
Britain should have justice on her side, but I despair
even of that. If there is war, I have a kind of second
sight of very unexpected jumbles in parties here;
and I will not say a probability, but a possibility of
junctions of a very important nature; if anything
of the sort can be of importance in the present
state of the Constitution. Your supposition that
Addington's strength may be owing not wholly to the
power of the Crown, but to the division of parties,
may be plausible to one at a distance, but if you
were here you would clearly see the contrary. You
ask whether if Pitt had appeared, and for war, he
would have succeeded? My answer is, not the
smallest chance *against* the Ministers; nay, if I and
all our friends had joined him, we should have made
altogether a very small minority. No, the King's
Minister, be he who he may, is in peace at least all
powerful; whether or not, in case of war, the
universal apprehension of mischief from the weakness
of these men, if such apprehension was supported by
junctions of different parties, could do anything, may

be more of a question ; but even in that case (a case, by the by, very improbable to happen), I think the Crown, in earnest, would beat all. The only chance the other way would be, if, in addition to all the rest, the Prince of Wales was to declare himself; but whether even that declaration (which, considering the present circumstances of the King's age and health, would be very very important indeed), would be decisive I have great doubts."

" March 29th.

" I HAD begun, as you will perceive by the dates, near a week ago, when I was interrupted; and Mrs. F. being taken very ill the next night with the rheumatism, and continuing so for some days, has hindered me writing since. She is now much better indeed. Though so many days have intervened there is nothing more known of importance. It is true the hopes of peace are more sanguine, but upon what ground I cannot discover. Indeed the very person who interrupted my writing last week informed me that we had made something like a proposition ; but when he came to explain it, it was so general as to amount to nothing. It was no more than this, ' We do not mean that Malta is the only possible security —if any other can be devised we will give up Malta.' It will immediately strike you that this is exactly analogous to the language in the last war. We do not insist on the restoration of monarchy ; any other adequate security will do, but what such security shall be we do not say. But though there is no

alteration, as far as we know, since the message in
the state of the question, I believe, and hope, there is
a good deal in public opinion; as everybody now
sees that Bonaparte's wish is for peace; nay, even
the most warlike say he does not yet think himself
ready.   Everybody, too, now sees there was no
violence on the part of France (which was at first
supposed to cause the message), and I believe all
indignant feelings are subsided, and the wish for
peace as general as ever.   Grey is come to town, which
is a great comfort to me.   He is quite right in everything.   Now here is politics enough for two letters
at least.   When you are at Madrid do not neglect
Don Pedro Ronquillo.   His correspondence from
1685 to 1688, both inclusive, would give me advantage of the greatest consequence over all other
historians.   I should think the whole, if permission
can be obtained for copying it, might be done for
100*l.*, and I would not grudge three times that sum.
Pray attend to this.   I have attempted to go on with
history a little in town, but have found it in vain;
when I get home I am resolved to work double and
treble tides for it.   I have read little here but bad
novels.   I like ' Delphine' both in style and sentiment; but it is heavy and totally deficient in exciting
curiosity.   Hayley's ' Life of Cowper' is quite
delightful.*   I do not mean Hayley's part of it, but
Cowper's letters, &c., and some poetry.   His character appears to have been quite different from what

---

* "Life and Posthumous Writings of William Cowper, Esq.," by W.
Hayley, 3 vols. 4to., 1803-4.

it has been generally supposed;—amiable and affectionate to the last degree, and, when he was quite well, very gay and cheerful. I am very glad you are reading so much of Lope de Vega, for I have the greatest curiosity about him. He is certainly the father of the modern stage; and it seems very whimsical that the Spaniards—who, comparatively with Italy, England, and France, are so deficient in poetry in general—should have led the way in the most popular department of it. By the way, do not omit to note the parts, either in Lope or other Spanish authors, from which Dryden has borrowed; for I have not by any means given up that scheme."

SAME TO SAME.

"St. Ann's Hill, *June 6th*, 1803.

"My dear Young One,

"I have quite forgot my last number, and the rule of three weeks; I have transgressed so long, that I do not now remember when I wrote last. My excuses to myself for putting off were, that you would not get my letters for a long time, they being directed to Madrid, and that I was in hopes, from day to day, of telling you some decisive political news. As to national politics, the news is, alas! too decisive; and how we are to escape absolute ruin, as far as finance goes, I cannot conceive. You will have heard, from newspapers and other letters, the general account of what has passed; but if you have not seen the papers laid before Parliament, you cannot conceive the extreme weakness of our cause. I do not think there was a single period since the peace when there was so little ground for war as that at which we armed. It is indeed lamentable; but the whole secret of the affair is in my old quotation, ' *Vuolsi cosi colà dove si puote Ciò che si vuole.*'* As to the probable duration or issue of the war, no man can form any well-founded conjecture, except with regard to the latter, the negative one—that we can get nothing by it. How far France may aggrandise herself by it may be more doubtful. My opinion is that she will. I foresee dreadful things if Bonaparte. takes (as is most natural to him) violent measures; and, on the other hand, if he refrains from violent measures, and could also abstain from such *desperates* as that of stopping the English, &c., I think France will gain a great deal in reputation, and will have the good, as we shall have the ill, will of all the world. Ministers gave in so handsomely to my proposition of the Russian mediation,† that many people conceive hopes from it; and so should I, if it were not for two reasons; first, that ' *non vuolsi cosi colà ;*' next, that the business requires some address, and, above all, some moderation—of neither of which I see any traces in the conduct of these people. As to party politics, there has yet happened nothing decisive—at

---

* The words of Virgil to Minos, in the fifth canto of Dante's "Inferno,' which Mr. Fox applies to the King.

† Mr. Fox moved an address to the Crown, respecting the mediation of Russia for the prevention of war with France, on the 27th of May, 1803.

least, with regard to *us*. The Grenvilles, &c., at the
suggestion, it is believed, of Pitt, chose to separate
the cause of the war from the consideration of the
conduct of Ministers, so as to leave us in a small
minority of 69.* When they came to their question
Pitt deserted them : and our friends, contrary to my
opinion, judged it best not to vote ; so that they, in
their turn, were left in a still smaller minority than
ours.† It was certainly not unfair to do by them as
they had done by us ; but, for our own character, I
think we should have done better to divide for propositions which I think true. However, I yielded
to a very general—nay, almost universal—opinion the
other way. Thus you will see the House of Commons
continues still divided into three, or rather four,
distinct parties ; for Pitt separated himself both from
Addington and the Grenvilles. From the divisions,
the result would be—that there are Pittites 58,
Grenvillites 36, Foxites 69, and all the rest Ministerial.
Things cannot long continue in this precise state ; but
for this session I think they will ; and how they will
jumble afterwards God knows. There is a great
unwillingness in our friends to have anything like a
junction with the Pitts or Grenvilles ; and whether

---

* This division was upon the address to the Crown on the renewal of
hostilities, May 24th ; when the numbers were—for the address 398, for
the amendment 67.

† In the division on Colonel Patten's motion of want of confidence in
Ministers, 3rd June, 1803, when Mr. Pitt moved that the House pass to
the orders of the day, and the numbers were—for his motion 56, against
it 333 ; after which Mr. Pitt left the house. Mr. Fox likewise declined to
vote. The numbers then were, for the motion 34, against it, 279. Mr. Fox,
in his numbers, counts the tellers.

some of them may not be *so alarmed* at the possibility
of such an evil as to act like the alarmists of old, is
what I am by no means sure of.   However, what you
will most care about, I think we stand very clear and
well in public opinion at present.   Grey went into
Northumberland the 1st of the month ; and from that
moment I consider our share in the campaign as over,
though I could not resist the curiosity I had to attend
to hear Pitt on the last question.*   Both the substance and manner (of Pitt) were as bad as his worst
enemy could wish ; and Hawkesbury answered him
extraordinarily well, shewing both a proper spirit of
resistance, and a proper feeling at being compelled to
make it against an old friend.   It was far the best
speech he ever made.   Pitt's speech on the former
day, on the address, was admired very much, and
very justly.†   I think it was the best he ever made in
that style ; and there were several circumstances that
rendered it peculiarly popular with the House.   The
contrast between the reception of that speech and of
his last was perhaps the strongest ever known.   I
dare say you have heard puffs enough of my speech
upon the address,‡ so that I need not add my mite ;
but, the truth is, that it was my best.   The House of

* Colonel Patten's motion of want of confidence in Ministers, June
3rd, 1803.

† Debate, on May 23rd, 1803.

‡ May 24th, 1803.   Mr. Abbott, in his Diary, has the following remarks
on this speech : " In the debate Mr. Fox spoke from ten to one; and
in these three hours delivered a speech of more art, eloquence, wit, and
mischief, than I ever remember to have heard from him.   His principles
were rather protested against than answered by the Attorney-General and
Mr. Windham."   See Pellew's " Life of Lord Sidmouth," vol. ii. p. 182.

Lords is scarcely worth mentioning; no tolerable speeches there but Grenville's; and if the House is analysed upon the same principle as that upon which I have done the House of Commons, there are— Pittites 18, Grenvillites 14, Foxites 10, the rest Ministerialists. As to out-of-doors opinions, they were, in London, particularly in the City, very violent and warlike upon the first publication of the papers; but I suspect they are a good deal cooled already; and from all I hear of distant counties, and see of those nearer London, I am very sanguine in my hope that the war is and will be very unpopular. I know Fitzwilliam thinks it so in Yorkshire. I do not know how to put you more *au fait* of politics of all sorts here than I have done; only I must add, what I think, however, scarcely necessary, that Grey and I are, if possible, still more *one* than ever; indeed, the good humour with which he bore staying in town so long against his will, and his kindness in shewing his agreement with me upon all occasions, have made me love him more than ever.

" We are now here for good; and beautiful and delightful it is beyond measure. The nightingales have almost done; but the singing of the other birds, the verdure, the flowers, the lights and shades of this April-like weather, make the scene from this window such that I do not envy the orange trees, &c., of your southern climates. My last letter from you is from Granada; and I do not wonder you are so delighted with it, it is true classical ground for your ' Bermeddin;' but yet, by your letter to Caroline,

I fear the *admonitus locorum* is in vain.   Dryden must have taken Almanzor, I think, from some hero of romance ; with respect to his conquering powers ; I believe Artaban, in one of Scuderi's or Calprenède's, is his model ; * but then, if I remember right, there is nothing, or at least not much, of his boastful qualities in Artaban.   Do you know that I had an opportunity of quoting Almanzor in my speech ?—yes, and the most extravagant lines in his whole part.† If they are not in the newspaper you see, try and guess.

" P.S.—Your friend King has published an excellent pamphlet upon Bank Issues, &c.,‡ but I am afraid people's minds are too much taken up with other things to attend to it just now.   His speeches in the House of Lords have been all good, and very generally acknowledged to be so.   The budget is put

---

* Artaban is a character in the "Cleopatra" of Calprenède.   See Dunlop's "History of Fiction," vol. iii. p. 247.

† Speaking of Bonaparte's conversation with Lord Whitworth, and the reproaches on account of Bonaparte's despairing language on the subject of invasion, Mr. Fox said: "It reminds me of the most extravagant passage in a great, and, with me, most favourite poet, Dryden; who, in the most extravagant perhaps of his pieces, puts into the mouth of Almanzor a sentiment which has always appeared to me to outsoar every flight allowable to the wildest fictions of the imagination. He says, in anger, to his rival :

> "Thou shalt not wish her thine; thou shalt not dare
> To be so impudent as to despair."

‡ "Thoughts on the Restriction of Payments in Specie at the Banks of England, and Ireland." London, 1803, 8vo.   Concerning this celebrated tract, see M'Culloch, "Literature of Political Economy," p. 169.

off for Tierney's re-election,* and I do not know
whether it comes on Friday or Monday. It is supposed Pitt will attend, and find fault ; and, as far as
one can judge from his speeches, stimulate the Doctor
to the most drastic medicine. I shall not attend ; but,
if anything material arises out of it, there will always
be time enough to take one's part. All that is known
is, that there is not to be an Income Tax. Malt, it is
said, is to be the principal article ; take care and
avoid the pun of Malta being the principal object,
and malt the means. I hope you will come home
immediately ; you certainly ought."

SAME TO SAME.

" October 16th, 1803.

"MY DEAR YOUNG ONE,

"Instead of fourteen days it is nearer, I suspect,
fourteen weeks since I wrote to you. There was at
one time so long an interval without hearing from
you, that I thought you were on your road through
France, and that to write would be in vain. This
produced the bad habit, and bad habits are not
always so easily broken. I have now several letters
of yours, the last written by Lady H., and dated the
12th of September, which I received this morning.
Mrs. F. has one from her, dated 20th September,
which mentions your gout being pretty violent ; but

---

* Mr. Tierney vacated his seat on acceptance of the office of Treasurer
of the Navy, 3rd June, 1803.

perhaps, as I understand from Buonaiuti that you
had some extraordinary and unusual pains, it was best
it should come to a fit.   Thank you for your news;
which, as far as it goes, is good, as our moderation
in the instances you allude to, is at least creditable,
and, as I think, politic.   I have none to send you in
return; for any discussion of what is going forward
here, by the conveyance of a foreign post, would in
every respect be improper; and as to the facts, the
newspapers will tell you more than I, who am a
careless reader of them, could do.   Invasion is
expected by many immediately, and some go so far
as to say the embarkation is to be made to-morrow,
the 17th.   Many think Ireland will be the principal
object, and draw their argument from recent occurrences and preparations, to which perhaps I am
inclined to give more weight from my opinion having
always leaned that way.   Parliament meets the 22nd
of next month; but, if the apprehensions of invasion
should be as lively as they are now, I should suppose
its sitting then would be very inconvenient.   Of
myself I have very little to say, except that, what with
company, farming, and fine weather, I have found
scarce a moment for real business (such I call history),
and hardly any even for idle reading.   What do you
think of my not having yet read the new letters of
Lady M. W. Montague,* a little dipping in Euripides

* An enlarged edition of her works and letters was published from her
genuine papers, by permission of the Earl of Bute, in 1803. London,
5 vols. 12mo. See "Edinburgh Review," vol. ii. p. 507, where there is an
account of this edition.

and in Tiraboschi,* of whom Mathias has published
an edition and sent it me, has been all my studies, if
such it can be called.   What can you mean by 1800
plays of Lope?   Consider, if he was thirty years at
it, that would make five per month.   It must be
a great satisfaction to have Frere at Madrid.†   You
do not say whether he mentions any other Portuguese
poet besides Camoens.   I shall be very happy when
you are returned, if you can spare a morning to read
with me two or three of Lope's plays, for I do not
think I shall be equal to them myself.

" I hope you will get Don Pedro's papers ; *poco a
poco* is my motto in history writing, but I think
I shall be here a great deal in the winter, and then
I feel quite sure I shall go on pretty fast.   If I had
never so safe a conveyance, I have very little to tell
you at all interesting in politics.   The result however is, as I have always said, that I expect to be a
good deal at home."

SAME TO SAME.

"St. Ann's Hill, *November 27th*, 1803.

" I am much obliged to you for Don Pedro's
letters, but possibly they had better come by some
less expensive conveyance than the post, as there is
no pretence for decreeing *urgence*.   Though they do not
relate to my period exactly, they may be very useful to

---

* Mathias published Tiraboschi's "Storia della poesia Italiana." London,
1803, 3 vols. 12mo. ; being an extract from his large work on the "History
of Italian Literature."

† Right Honourable John Hookham Frere.

me, and at all events entertaining, nay, possibly they
may make me go on further than I had intended.
As to the other period of history you mention, I
mean that immediately subsequent to the Peace of
Utrecht and the accession of the Brunswicks here,
and the intrigues in the Court of Spain, which produced a temporary connection with that of Vienna, I
am more ignorant with regard to it than of any other
times whatever, and the *neant* into which Spain has
fallen, makes it less interesting than ever. I have
little more to tell you of the opening of Parliament
than you will have learnt from the newspapers. I
suspect the Doctor is much stronger, even if Pitt
should declare his hostility in the most open manner,
than many persons imagine. The old *vuolsi cosi colà*
is more true and applied to more occasions than ever,
as you shall hear when we meet. I propose attending
on the day of the Army, and supporting the New
Opposition, if they take good ground, and they can
hardly fail doing so. We have been on a tour to
Southill and Woburn, and very pleasant it was.
The young Duchess is very gay, good-humoured, and
pleasing. The Temple, and still more some marble
antique columns, which are put up in the greenhouse
(at Woburn I mean), are magnificent and beautiful
beyond anything in England. I have seen my
brother and his family, who are at Ogilvie's house,
in Harley Street.* His appointment to an important

* Lady Amelia Jane Lenox, daughter of the second Duke of Richmond,
married, first, in 1746, James, Duke of Leinster; and, secondly, William
Ogilvie, Esq. The Duchess of Leinster was aunt to Mr. Fox. Concerning
Mr. Ogilvie, see vol. i. p. 425, of these Memorials.

district here is a decided mark that his conduct is approved. Indeed there was not the least colour for blame; but the Castle has acted with a folly, and worse too, that is incredible.* I must leave off, so God bless you.

" Yours affectionately,
"C. J. F."

SAME TO SAME.

" St. Ann's Hill, December 17th, 1803.

" With regard to politics as they affect Spain I know nothing but from you, and it looks as if in this instance (but it is certainly the only one) the Doctor had acted with some sense. If he is attacked for his moderation, as some say he will, though I do not believe it, I will defend him. One should never discourage too much industry; but I own it seems to me, that turning Lope into rhyme is unnecessary labour, unless he wrote in rhyme himself; but as you please. I shall be very impatient to see your translations, and equally so to read one or two of the originals with you, for I have a great curiosity about the Spanish dramatic writers. The passage in Calderon's ' Heraclius ' which Corneille has imitated seems to me very grand; but I cannot quite make out the construction, owing, I suspect, to its being ill printed in Voltaire's edition, where I read it. *Hijo de su valor*, I suppose is another expression for *Higo suyo;* but *che*, so spelt, is not surely a Spanish word. A

---

* The appointment of General Fox to the command of a military district in England is alluded to. By the " Castle," Dublin Castle is meant.

play written in twenty-four hours sounds strange to me, but even then it does not follow that seven plays could be written in a week, and so on. In short, as Parr would say, ἐπέχω.

"It is not the fault of the Grenvilles that the Irish question is not brought on; when one knows one's letters may be opened, one cannot write comfortably, especially about individuals, but that it is not brought on is a sad thing indeed. I repeat the G.'s are not in fault, and *they* will, if there is occasion, behave well about it. As far as keeping it alive by conversation, in and out of Parliament, I will take care of that; but that is not enough. None of us here, neither Uncle Dick, nor Mrs. F., nor I, understand what you mean by calling the French a *canting* Government. We think it has faults and vices enough, God knows, but not *that*. Perhaps it wants rather that degree of dissimulation which decency requires. As to invasion *now*, I think it impossible. In Ireland, if they can get large ships out, it is another thing; but that I hope cannot be done. I do not like the Governor of Cadiz's answer to the Lady at all, and I think those fellows who pique themselves upon severity, and what is called decision, are generally fools. However there are exceptions. When you speak of reported reforms to be made by him, do you mean in the church? Dick could not understand. He is grown a great chess-player, not a good one, for he has not yet got above me; but he is fonder of it than I ever saw any one.

"Yours affectionately,

"C. J. FOX."

SAME TO SAME.

"*January 9th*, 1804.

"THE rumours of invasion for these last ten days have been very prevalent, nor do I know that even now they have much subsided. Some affirm, others deny, that this frost will be a decisive impediment. What I think is, that every occurrence in the channel demonstrates more clearly every day the impracticability of the undertaking, barely possible it may be. What our domestic politics will be by-and-by is as doubtful as ever, one thing appears to me clear if possible beyond demonstration ; and that is that in the quarter so often referred to by me, *si puote ciò che si vuole*. There is not a power in Europe, no not even Bonaparte's that is so unlimited. When I said that some good moves might be made, you remember I said no check-mate ; and therefore good only with a view to very distant prospects. Yet even those good moves will not be made, through whose fault I will not discuss by letter. I think upon a fair hearing I can acquit myself, and yet sometimes I think I do not do all that I might; on the other hand consider how totally I am without assistance ; but no more of this.

"History goes on, but it goes on very slowly, the fact is I am a very slow writer ; but I will, I promise I will persevere. I am too scrupulous both about language and facts, though with respect to the latter it is hardly possible. It is astonishing how many facts one finds related, for which there is no authority whatever. Tradition you will say does in some cases, but it will not apply to others. Barrillon's letters are worth their weight in gold. Buonaiuti does not know what pamphlets &c. to send you; I shall advise by all means Cobbett, because though I have read but little of him, he is as I am told generally amusing, and then a weekly paper is more convenient to persons at a distance. There is a good pamphlet on the means of defence, but I should not' think it interesting at a distance. I shall direct the two pamphlets called Addington's and Pitt's to be sent, the first is very dull, and the second (I am told, for I have not read it) still duller.* The matter of them is however curious. We have been reading Plowden's ' History of Ireland,' † which is as bulky and as heavy as himself. It is chiefly a compilation from journals, state papers, parliamentary debates, &c.; but it tells me many things I did not know, and reminds me of still more which I had forgotten, which makes it a very useful book at this time. Its bulk (three massive quartos), has I believe deterred almost everybody from reading it. The first part is I think very amusing, and of course of quite a different texture from the latter parts. There is a remonstrance from the Irish Chieftains to Pope John XXII., which is admirable.‡ Lord King calls here very often and of

---

* Concerning the war of pamphlets between Mr. Addington and Mr. Pitt, at this time, see Pellew's " Life of Lord Sidmouth," vol. ii. p. 145. The first pamphlet put forth on the former side is stated to have been written by a Mr. Bentley, the answer to it to have been by Mr. T. P. Courtenay.

† " An Historical Review of the State of Ireland," by Francis Plowden, Esq. London, 1803. 3 vols. 4to.

‡ See Plowden, vol. i. p. 31.

course inquires about you; I like him better and
better every day, and from what I hear he comes on
very well in the House of Lords. Your friend Lord
Archibald, though I seldom see him but in the House
of Commons, is quite cordial with me.* Lord Henry †
I have seen but little of since last winter, but continue
to like him very much, I wish he would speak in
Parliament. By-the-by, I do not know whether you
have had Cowper the poet's life and letters, they are
delightful, but Buonainti proscribes quartos. To
Godwin's life of 'Chaucer' there is the same objection, and I suspect another also, that it is in some
parts very dull and tiresome.‡ I have not read it,
but I looked into it when I was at Woolbeding. I
observe, that he takes an opportunity of showing his
stupidity in not admiring Racine. It puts me quite
in a passion, *je veux contre eux faire un jour un gros
livre*, as Voltaire says. Even Dryden, who speaks
with proper respect of Corneille and Moliere, vilipends
Racine. If ever I publish my edition of his works,
I will give it him for it you may depend. Oh! how I
wish that I could make up my mind to think it right
to devote all the remaining part of my life to such
subjects, and such only! Indeed, I rather think I
shall, and yet if there were a chance of re-establishing
a strong Whig party (however composed) :—

> ' Non adeo has exosa manus victoria fugit,
> Ut tantâ quicquam pro spe ten†are recusem.'

[Passage cut out for an autograph.]

---

* Lord Archibald Hamilton, son of the ninth Duke of Hamilton, born
1769, died 1827.   † Lord Henry Petty.
‡ "The Life of Geoffrey Chaucer," by W. Godwin. London, 1803.
2 vols. 4to.

" Grey too is in Northumberland, and will not (come) except I press him which I do not feel myself justified in doing at present. He is perfectly right in all his ideas. Poor Holland House is said to be in a bad way; I have not seen it; but I find there is a terrible outcry against its weakness so that I fear it cannot stand. Why not as well as the Doctor you'll say, against whom there is a similar outcry? Why, if you were as obstinate as Doctor's supporters, perhaps it might, but I fear it cannot be. . . . I never heard of any other Portuguese poet but Camoens, and concluded there was no other of note; but you will bring over I hope some of those whom you say Frere so much admires. Lope de Vega is still I own the great object of my curiosity, and I must not only see your translations but read two or three of his plays with you in the original. If his extravagance is of the Drydenish style, it seems odd that the earlier dramatic poets, Fletcher, &c., who probably copied from him and other Spanish poets should have little or nothing of the sort.

" P.S. I have employed my odd five minutes' &c. lately in looking over Horace's Odes, pray tell me which you think the most perfect and beautiful of them in their different styles. I think ' Quis desiderio '* the most perfect of all; and next ' Quem tu Melpomene;'† in the lighter style, ' Ulla si juris tibi pejerati '‡ and ' Quis multâ gracilis.'§ In the grander style, ' Ille et nefasto,' ‖ ' Descende cœlo,'¶ with the exception however of the three last stanzas; the

* Carm. i. 24.   † iv. 3.   ‡ ii. 8.   § i. 5.   ‖ ii. 13.   ¶ iii. 4.

Regulus ode,* about half of ' Qualem ministrum,'†
and ' Pindarum quisquis.‡ I like what are called
the *flat endings* in many of his odes, but dislike them
extremely in others, particularly the last stanza of
' Qualem ministrum.' "

SAME TO SAME.

" WHAT can you mean by saying there is little good
of the new poetry in Cowper? what, not the triplets
to Mary?§ not the verses about his first love, in the
early part,‖ not *one* of the sonnets?¶ not the ' Ship-
wreck?' or ' Outcast?'** pray read them over again,
and repeat your former judgment if you dare. I have
not the book here, having lent it, or I could quote
I believe much more. Hayley's part of the book is
no doubt lamentable, and what I am most angry with
him for, is that he seems to have withheld much that I
should have liked to read. I think in general, however
(not in this publication), that you hold poor Hayley
too cheap. His ' History of old Maids,' and parts of
the ' Trials of Temper,' are I think very good.†† I
like Frere's translation very much, and shall be glad
to see the original.‡‡ I read a little and very little of

---

* iii. 5.   † iv. 4.   ‡ iv. 2.

§ The stanzas beginning, "The twentieth year is well nigh past," in
Southey's edition, vol. x. p. 85.   ‖ "Catharina," ib. p. 61.

¶ Ib. p. 189-92.   ** "The Castaway," ib. p. 96.

†† See the "Life of Hayley," by himself, 1823. His "Triumphs of
Temper," a poem, was published in 1781.

‡‡ Probably his translation of the poem of the " Cid," printed at the end
of Southey's "Chronicle of the Cid."

' Gifford,' and thought it vile.*   To catch the manner
of Juvenal is difficult, and without his peculiar manner
he is not himself.   Dryden catches it sometimes
admirably, only compare his conclusion of the tenth
Satire with Johnson's, and I hope you will think the
superiority as great as I do.†   The part about

---

* His translation of Juvenal, London, 1802, 4to.
† The following is Dryden's version :—

> " Yet, not to rob the priests of pious gain,
> That altars be not wholly built in vain ;
> Forgive the gods the rest, and stand confined
> To health of body, and content of mind :
> A soul that can securely death defy,
> And count it nature's privilege to die ;
> Serene and manly, hardened to sustain
> The load of life, and exercised in pain ;
> Guiltless of hate, and proof against desire ;
> That all things weighs, and nothing can admire ;
> That dares prefer the toils of Hercules
> To dalliance, banquets, and ignoble ease.
> The path to peace is virtue ; what I show
> Thyself may freely on thyself bestow ;
> Fortune was never worshipped by the wise ;
> But, set aloft by fools, usurps the skies."

Johnson's "Vanity of Human Wishes," which is an imitation, not a
translation, of Juvenal, ends with the following verses :—

> " Yet when the sense of sacred presence fires,
> And strong devotion to the skies aspires,
> Pour forth thy fervours for a healthful mind,
> Obedient passions, and a will resigned ;
> For love, which scarce collective man can fill ;
> For patience, sovereign o'er transmuted ill ;
> For faith, that panting for a happier seat,
> Counts death kind Nature's signal of retreat.
> These goods for man the laws of heaven ordain,
> These goods HE grants who grants the power to gain.
> With these celestial wisdom calms the mind,
> And makes the happiness she does not find."

Messalina, in the sixth book is very good too. If the word *sin* could fairly stand for *pleasure* it would be perfect. Now we are upon criticism, do you know that if you have made out any good rule about *personification*, it is what I want more than anything of the kind. I feel clearly that it is sometimes right, and sometimes wrong, that Johnson and his imitators are excessive in it, even to ridicule, that it is often convenient and not ungraceful, and at other times detestable; but upon what principle it should be adopted here and rejected there I have never been able to satisfy myself. I have been very sparing of it indeed in what I have written, both because I think it safer to err on that side than on the other, and because it is less used by the ancients, to whose religion in matters of taste I grow every day more and more bigoted. All I remember concerning the blank verses you mention is, that I could not guess where they were, I have now forgotten them and do not know where to find the letter they were in without more search than it is worth. As to politics, invasion is still expected, and some say that a great number of troops is actually embarked; but as Dr. Parr says— ἐπέχω. No talk of the only good event, peace. Distance of place operates like distance of time, and you can never know at Madrid the exact state of things *here*, therefore I excuse your phrases of, *such things would not go down*, the *public* this, and the *public* that; but here, if I am not mistaken you will quickly perceive that, *cio che si vuole colà*, is like the old story of *actio* (a word by the way which has

never as I think been rightly understood);* first,
second, third, and so on to the end of the chapter.
Whether this point will be tried in the question of
Ireland, and the Catholics, is still uncertain, and the
very uncertainty with respect to the trial is at once
occasioned *by*, and a complete proof *of*, the certainty
of the decision. This sounds rather *riddle-like*, but
it is correct. Opinion itself is regulated from above,
and I shall not be surprised if in a short time the
Doctor is reckoned the ablest man in the kingdom,
or if that cannot be compassed, it will be thought and
maintained that a minister without abilities is best
for the country. It is no uncommon wish here, that
the enemy may land in order to show his inability to
do us any harm; and I think a good courtier should
(and perhaps does) wish a cordial union among all
parties hostile to the Ministry, in order to prove (as
it certainly would prove) the impotence of all opposition. Who was the good Christian who wished
there was much more to believe than was proposed to
him? I dare say, there are many good courtiers who
wish the Ministers were greater fools than they are,
in order to show the purity of their devotion; and
then to hear people saying the *public* opinion is very
strong upon this point, and the other; and the *public*
opinion would have brought *Pitt* back again if he
had not lost himself by this, and that, and t'other,

---

* *Actio* properly means delivery; every thing which distinguishes a
speech from a written composition; corresponding with the Greek ὑπόκρισις.
It is commonly translated *action*; which word, in its ordinary sense, is not
equivalent to the Latin term. See the saying of Demosthenes, in "Cic
de Orat." iii. 56; Brut. 38; and compare Bacon's "Essay on Boldness."

it makes me quite sick; and then the *unpopularity* of the Grenvilles, &c., *hac ipsá Sejanum* * is not in the present times a conjecture, but a proved fact, *calcemus Cæsaris hostem* † is the universal motto. If this is suffered to go on without a marked stand being made against it or at least attempted, there is not the smallest hope; but a stand might be attempted which, unsuccessful as it would be for the present, might keep something alive against other times. To humour the present disposition and temporise, is a certain, absolutely certain confirmation of the evil; no nation ever did or even can recover from slavery by such methods. Towards what Hume calls the Euthanasia, *Le penchant est si doux qu'on y tombe sans peine. Sed revocare gradum superasque evadere ad auras, Hic labor est.* I do not know that anything can do good, but if anything can I feel quite sure that some bold measure, supported even tolerably in point of numbers in parliament, is the only chance. But in my view it is essential that the measure should by its evident character prove that it is taken for its own sake, and not for the purpose of courting popularity; much less of being agreeable *colà.* Even this poor chance we shall not have, and so let us turn our minds to other subjects. I suspect Cowper's madness was the cause and not the effect of his methodism,

---

and though his disposition appears to have been often
cheerful, it is evident that he was always subject to
occasional gloom, though not of so miserable a kind
as that with which he was tormented in his latter
days. I shall be very glad of more of Don Pedro's
letters and other manuscripts of the kind, but you
are mistaken in supposing that I intend going beyond
the Revolution. I do not determine against doing so,
alors comme alors, but I have no such thoughts at
present. Our love to lady H. and the children.

" Yours affectionately,

"C. J. FOX.

" P.S.—I have forgot to mention that Lauderdale
is now printing at Edinburgh a famous book, in
which he is to destroy poor Adam Smith entirely.*
I am afraid, from what I hear, that he is too paradoxical; but Grey, who has seen part of it, speaks
wonders of it. They say the King has the gout,
here his power ceases and there is another *colà*."

SAME TO SAME.

" *March* 19*th*, 1804.

" DEAR YOUNG ONE,
    "I am ashamed to think how long it is since I
wrote, but I have been in this vile town five weeks,
and have had no time for anything. If, as some of

---

* "An Inquiry into the Nature and Origin of Public Wealth, and into
the Means and Causes of its Increase," by the Earl of Lauderdale. Edinburgh, 1804. 1 vol. 8vo. A critique on this work appeared in the
fourth volume of the "Edinburgh Review," out of which a further controversy arose. See M'Culloch's " Literature of Political Economy," p. 15.

the political economists say, (for to oblige Lauderdale I have forced myself to look at his book upon that most nonsensical of all sciences,) things are to be deemed valuable in proportion to their scarcity, time is a most precious thing in this town; but if, as others assert, we must estimate the value of articles by their productiveness, it is here the most worthless of all commodities.   I have a letter from you in Lady H.'s hand, of the 20th, and conclude, notwithstanding the tingling of your fingers, which, while it lasts, must be troublesome, that long before this time you are quite sound.   The circumstance of the bone having been broken in another part, if it is not displaced, is, I suppose, of little or no consequence.   I like your left-handed verses to Caroline very much, indeed they are quite to my taste.   You know how unpleasant it is to write on politics when one expects one's letters to be read by others than those to whom they are directed.   Our co-operation (for that I find is the common term) with the Grenvilles has no secret in it of any kind.   I should have had no objection to a closer connection, but I found some friends so prejudiced on the subject that it was agreed, with the mutual consent of both parties, that we should make no engagement of any sort, but simply co-operate upon such measures as we were agreed upon, and have that degree of concert only which might be necessary to give efficacy to our support of, or opposition to such measures.   Thus matters stand with us.   Pitt keeps aloof, but misses few opportunities of exposing the present men, and will, I am told, be inclined more and more to divide for any measure against them, but this is all very uncertain. The King's health is, as you will see by the bulletins, *recovering*, but not well.* He saw the Duke of York on Saturday, and has not, I believe, seen any of the rest of the Royal family : of his Ministers, only the Doctor and the Chancellor.† The Ministry are very weak in numbers, as well as in everything else ; but perhaps this may be owing as much to speculations on the King's health as to anything else; for, though they are weak, we are not strong. We shall have a division to-day on the Volunteer Bill,‡ I fear a poor one ; and I shall, unless something unexpected happens, go home to-morrow. Grey went last week, and I have a letter from him to-day saying Mrs. G. is brought to bed of a son,§ and is well ; if there is anything to be done he will come after the holidays. Poor Hare ! he is gone ; but it has been a hopeless case for a long time, and the last eighteen months of his life have been so miserable that one can hardly be sorry he is released; but an intimate friendship of upwards of forty years, and not once interrupted, must make one feel. ‖

" P.S.—I can never give up my liking for the end of the Regulus ode, though I must confess I have not often found anyone agree with me."

---

* Adolphus, vol. vii. p. 765.
† The Great Seal was held by Lord Eldon.
‡ See note to the next letter.
§ The Honorable Charles Grey, second son of Earl Grey.
‖ James Hare, Esq., M.P. for Knaresborough, died at Bath, March 17th, 1804. He was educated at Eton and Oxford, and in 1774 married the only

SAME TO SAME.

" March 20th, 1804.

" WE had, as I expected, a very poor division yesterday, 56 to 173 ; * but still the numbers of Ministry are small, though in this instance they had Pitt and some of his friends, as well as Sheridan and Erskine, who in general will not vote with me for fear of being found in Pitt's company. They are intolerable, and that is the truth of it. The general contempt of the Doctor and his crew increases visibly, and it is thought he cannot last ; but if that should be the case, it will be owing to the little confidence there is in his Majesty's recovering his perfect health. Lord Alvanley is dead,† and some people fancy he will be succeeded by Erskine ; not I. If the King should be well enough to appoint a successor, it will be Perceval. Our division last night was so bad owing to the Ministers giving up to us two principal points. You see *iterum mergor civilibus undis,* and more than I had intended ; but I do not know how it is that my indignation rises every day at the

daughter of Sir Abraham Hume. A short notice of his life is in the "Annual Register," vol. xlvi. chron. p. 473. His wit was the admiration and delight of all who knew him. Hare's failing state of health, when he was at Paris in 1802, is mentioned in Trotter's "Memoirs of Fox," p. 311.

* This division was on Mr. Fox's motion for the recommittal of the Volunteer Consolidation Bill, March 19, 1804.

† Richard Pepper Arden, Esq., Solicitor-General in 1782, Attorney-General in 1784, Master of the Rolls in 1788, Chief Justice of the Common Pleas in 1801, was created Lord Alvanley, May, 1801, and died 19th March, 1804. He was succeeded by Sir James Mansfield, who held the office of Chief Justice of the Common Pleas until 1814.

existence of this rascally Ministry. It seems to be a degradation to all men of talents or characters to submit to it. Poor Holland House, do not believe I give it up, I only said the outcry against it was so great that I feared for it."

SAME TO SAME.

"*April 9th*, 1804.

" I AM going to town to-morrow, to stay I know not how many weeks. I dislike it to a degree you can hardly conceive, but I feel it is right, and resolve to do it handsomely, and therefore make it a rule not even to grumble, only to you who are so far off I may. I am not very sanguine about dispossessing the Doctor, but I had much rather the attempt should fail than that it should not have been made. If it does fail, the absolute power of the Crown will be so manifest that nobody can deny it, whereas it would otherwise be said that the Doctor holding his post was owing to the want of will on our parts to dispossess him. There are many circumstances at present which give us every advantage, so that if we fail it must be owing to an intrinsic irresistible power *colà*. I have done very little, as you may imagine, in history during these three weeks holidays; I have even had very little idle reading, just a play or two of Euripides, whom I admire more than ever. I do not know whether I mentioned how much I agree with you about ' Vitas hinnuleo,' * I think the two first stanzas the *prettiest* things in all Horace; the

* Carm. i., 23.

third is rather trite and flat.   I persevere in my
singularity in liking the end of the ' Regulus ode.'

  " Lord King was here yesterday, and seems much
delighted with the badgering of the Ministers in the
House of Lords, and regrets, of course, the want of
you to assist in it.*   I hear Hawkesbury † does not do
well in this sort of work, and that all rests on the
Chancellor, who cannot bear it well either.   With us
your friend Tierney does little for them, Maitland ‡ a
trifle better, but only a trifle, and the Ministers themselves grow every day worse.   Of our young ones, I
am afraid Kinnaird will do no great matters, poor
Lord Archibald's deafness is a heavy evil, and I
suspect Lord H. Petty is the only one among those
who have yet appeared who will make any great
figure.   The little he has done is excellent ; good
sense, and good language to perfection ; a little more
force might be desirable, but that will come, possibly,
when he speaks on greater occasions than he has yet
done.   Ossulston § made one set speech, in which
there was some good matter, but in a voice that made
it impossible for any one, except two or three of us
who were close to him, to hear him.   Of older ones,
Windham has made some excellent speeches, but too
much on one subject and in one style ; though, if he

---

  * The Volunteers Bill was read a second time in the House of Lords
on March 27.

  † Lord Hawkesbury, who was at this time Secretary of State for
Foreign Affairs, had been called up to the House of Lords at the beginning
of the Session.

  ‡ Gen. Sir Thomas Maitland, brother of the eighth Earl of Lauderdale.

  § Lord Ossulston, now Earl of Tankerville; born 1776, succeeded his
father in 1822.

had been suffered to go on about Lord Redesdale, he seemed to be getting into what I think the true manner for a public assembly. Canning has done well and ill. T. Grenville seemed last year to have made a good shoot, but I do not think he has done much this year. His speech on P. Patten's motion, last June,* was of the highest order.

"P.S.—Nightingales not come yet, and it will be well if I do not quite miss hearing them this spring. It is a sad thing indeed, but I will do it so handsomely that I hope you will hear from your other correspondents that I have quite turned my mind to politics again, and am as eager as in former days. Pray remember to inquire at what time Nightingales usually appear and sing where you are? Here, you know, it is about the 12th of this month; and do the Spanish poets count them lively or melancholy?

"I say nothing about the Paris plot, or the Duke d'Enghien,† because it is too horrible on all sides."

At the commencement of this volume we have marked the ground on which Mr. Pitt placed his defence of the war, and traced the course of Mr. Fox in assailing his position. But although the annals of Parliament contain no series of speeches more replete with wisdom, argument and wit than those in which

---

* 3rd June, 1803. P. Patten was member for Newton, in Lancashire.

† The plot of Pichegru and Georges against Bonaparte, discovered in February, 1804, and the execution of the Duc d'Enghien, in March, are here alluded to.

Mr. Fox, Mr. Grey, and Mr. Sheridan appealed to the House of Commons against the policy of the minister, their artillery produced little effect. Mr. Burke indeed gives the palm of ability to the Opposition. But his own fervid writings; the general alarm felt at the subversive doctrines and horrible massacres of the French republican government; the aid of more than half the parliamentary party which had hitherto followed Mr. Fox; and the entire confidence of the King made Mr. Pitt far stronger in war than he had been in peace; nor had his followers to blush for his inferiority in debate. With a majestic and flowing eloquence he vindicated the measures of his government; denounced the crimes, the ambition and the insincerity of the rulers of France; and with the weapons of sarcasm and lofty declamation parried the rapid and ever varying thrusts of his great rival. To his friends he expressed his admiration, that whenever he thought he had spoken better than usual Mr. Fox surpassed himself in his reply. Mr. Wilberforce, in his own person a master of the art of persuasion, confessed that for a time his mind was always overborne by the arguments of the one of these two great orators who spoke last in the debate.

The time arrived, however, when Mr. Fox was disgusted with a struggle so apparently hopeless. His habits, and with his habits his passions, had taken a new direction. He had left off gaming; he lived much in the country; he returned with increased and revived zeal to his literary studies; he had married a woman as affectionate and warm-hearted as himself, but who, by her previous conduct was unfortunately disqualified from taking her place in society as his wife. Hence, with a fund of happiness in himself, he willingly and cheerfully resigned the prizes of ambition, and, ceasing from the struggle, stood by as a spectator of the games.

Such was the secession; a measure rather dictated by the inclinations of Mr. Fox and the desponding complaints of others, than founded on motives of policy and inspired by an enlightened foresight. Yet an abstinence from the usual course of opposition is not without at least apparent justification. The minister derives great advantage from constantly renewed debates followed by victorious divisions. The country is apt to attribute to unworthy motives perseverance in arguments which Parliament has constantly overruled. The people, left to themselves, may give to reflection and to facts that weight which they never would allow to a party engaged for a long time in thwarting their most favourite projects, and predicting the failure of their most cherished hopes.

But whatever may be the value of these reasons, it is certain that from 1797 to 1801 Mr. Fox's name appears but seldom in the parliamentary debates. In the collection of his speeches there are none from 1798 to 1801.

In 1801, however, occurred an event which entirely altered the aspect of affairs both at home and abroad. Mr. Pitt, alarmed by the state of Ireland, convinced that with a separate Parliament it would neither be safe to grant, nor wise to refuse political power to the

Roman Catholics, meditated the plan of the Union. He instructed Lord Cornwallis, then Lord Lieutenant, to endeavour to effect a Legislative Union, and the admission of Roman Catholics to political privilege on equal terms with the Protestants. Lord Cornwallis wrote that he could carry the first, but not the second of these measures. Mr. Canning, who was sitting with Mr. Pitt when he received this letter, exclaimed, "Then if I were you I would have neither." * Mr. Pitt, however, reproving the rashness of a young politician, pursued his scheme. He seems to have contemplated pressing on the Union, and postponing with fair promises the consideration of the Roman Catholic claims. He appears to have obtained the assent of Lord Grenville, Lord Spencer, and Mr. Dundas, to this plan.

There was an obstacle however on which Mr. Pitt had not sufficiently reckoned, or which he hoped by his great authority, assisted by the unpopularity of his rival, to overcome.

The King entertained a fixed opinion against further concessions to the Roman Catholics. In 1795, when Lord Fitzwilliam wished to enlarge the boundaries of the Constitution, so as to embrace all the King's Irish subjects, George III., alarmed at the extent of the proposed changes, consulted Lord Kenyon, then Lord Chief Justice, on the subject of his coronation oath. He understood that oath to bind him not to assent to a repeal of the Test Act, or of the Acts inflicting disabilities on the Roman

---

* Speech of Mr. Canning in the House of Commons.

Catholics. The King's own words, as used in a letter to Mr. Pitt, are these—" A sense of religious, as well as political duty, has made me, from the moment I mounted the throne, consider the oath that the wisdom of our forefathers has enjoined the kings of this realm to take at their coronation, and enforced by the obligation of instantly following it, in the course of the ceremony with taking the sacrament, as a binding religious obligation on me to maintain the fundamental maxims on which our constitution is placed, namely, that the Church of England is the established one, and *that those who hold employments in the State must be members of it,* and consequently obliged not only to take oaths against Popery, but to receive the holy communion agreeably to the rites of the Church of England." *

With these sentiments deeply engraved on his mind, the King was not likely to listen with complacency to any suggestion that, in order to render the Union efficient, it would be advisable to embrace the Roman Catholics in some liberal plan of policy. And when Mr. Dundas, in pursuance of such a suggestion, hinted that the coronation oath bound the King in his executive, and not in his legislative capacity, he was sharply rebuked by his Majesty with the taunt, " None of your Scotch metaphysics, Mr. Dundas." Mr. Pitt had, however, gone too far to retreat. He felt it necessary to state his opinions to the King, and to intimate his willingness to withdraw from the public service, adding, however, that at the personal

* Corr. with Mr. Pitt.

request of the King he would consent to remain in office, and even for a time to oppose the Catholic claims.

The King was determined, however, that there should be no concealment of his own sentiments, and, in reply to Mr. Pitt, he declared that his concurrence in the Union was mainly founded on his trust that the union of the two Churches would for ever shut the door on any further measures with respect to the Roman Catholics.

Mr. Pitt had now no alternative. He and the best part of his cabinet resigned.

There seems no reason to suppose that Mr. Pitt was driven to this step by the difficulty of continuing the war and the shame of making peace without "indemnity for the past and security for the future." On the contrary, he seems to have been quite willing to stay in office, and to have hoped to have kept his position, either with or without the concession of the Catholic claims. He could not expect that the King would send for Mr. Fox, and he evidently did not expect that he would send for Mr. Addington. Indeed, it is said, that when that gentleman informed him that he had been offered the place of First Lord of the Treasury and had accepted it, Mr. Pitt expressed his surprise and displeasure in terms more emphatic than courteous.

The ministerial revolution, however, made a great change in the position of Mr. Fox. He neither wished nor expected office at this time; but three great advantages evidently accrued to him. First,

peace was made; which, though on less advantageous
terms than those which he had advised, gave evident
joy to the people, and great discomfiture to those
who had represented such terms as dishonourable and
ignominious. Secondly, some of his old friends,
such as Lord Fitzwilliam, Lord Spencer, and Mr.
Grenville, were set at liberty and soon were happy
to revert to him on ancient terms of confidence and
affection. The death of Mr. Burke, and the suppres-
sion of Jacobinism by Napoleon, removed two of the
greatest obstacles to such a reconciliation. Thirdly,
Mr. Pitt and his colleagues had broken with the court
upon a question on which they had the hearty sympathy of Mr. Fox. If Mr. Pitt should make a public
cause of his personal disagreement, Mr. Fox and
Mr. Pitt might unite against the personal prejudices
of the sovereign; if Mr. Pitt should still cling
to the hope of a restoration by court favour,
some of his late colleagues might be found
more bold and more honest, more true to the
principles of religious liberty, and the cause of their
country, than their late leader.

After the peace of Amiens, Mr. Fox went for a
short time to Paris. His letters do not contain any
account of that conversation with the First Consul,
which has been much repeated. Bonaparte himself,
quoting some phrase of Mr. Fox, said, "Mr. Fox,
in his bad French," &c. The facility and correctness
with which Mr. Fox spoke French were however
remarkable. A Russian gentleman who met him at
dinner at that time, told me that though he talked a

great deal during dinner, it was not till afterwards that he discovered Mr. Fox was not a Frenchman.

It was not long after Mr. Fox's return, that apprehensions of war began again to prevail. The encroachments of the First Consul in Switzerland and in Italy were indeed very glaring. But they must have been expected from the character of Bonaparte, and the nature of the peace which had been made with him. The wisest policy for England was to husband her resources in peace till Austria and the continental powers should take alarm at the spirit of aggrandisement displayed by their formidable neighbour.

It has been said that when the conduct of France towards Switzerland became known in this country, Mr. Pitt and Mr. Canning urged Mr. Addington to declare war, promising him their support.*

However this may be, in the situation of affairs at that time, Mr. Addington had but two courses to pursue, the one to declare war, and lean wholly on Mr. Pitt, the other to maintain peace, and rely on the support of Mr. Fox. But he had not sense and decision for either of these courses ; neither the vigour to declare war, nor the firmness to preserve peace. He showed neither skill in negotiation, nor when at war energy in its prosecution. The natural consequence was that as Lord Chatham and Lord Holland had acted together to displace Sir Thomas Robinson, the deputy of the Duke of Newcastle, so Mr. Fox and Mr. Pitt combined their forces

* Adolphus, vol. vii.

to overthrow Mr. Addington, the favourite of George III.

The victory then gained, and its consequences, must be reserved for the next volume.

Mr. Fox's correspondence with his most intimate political friend Mr. Grey at this period is full of interest.   Mr. Fox, as usual, is very candid and explicit.   His hopes of reviving the importance of the Whig party gradually gain strength, and he is ready to exclaim,—

> " Non adeo has exosa manus victoria fugit,
>   Nec tantâ quicquam pro spe tentare recusem."

In all his numerous and splendid contests for liberty of conscience, for political freedom, for peace, for the abolition of the Slave Trade, and for Parliamentary Reform, Mr. Fox never forgot that he was a Whig.   He devoted his life to maintain the genuine principles of that party, and he died in attempting to vindicate them.

Yet eager as Mr. Fox was as a party man, his letters to Lord Holland, which occupy the former part of this volume, are more truly characteristic of him than those which are now to follow.   To Lord Holland alone he dilated on the literary occupations, which, far more than political contests, absorbed his mind and delighted his taste.   Despondent beyond due measure on the prospects of our domestic liberty, he loved to turn away his eyes from the carnage of contending armies, and the servility of a confiding country, and to fix them on the immortal works of the great heirs of literary

fame.   Reading with ease and pleasure to himself
the poets of Greece, Rome, Italy, France, and England,
he loved to compare kindred passages, to trace the
history of a simile, and to weigh in his critical scale
the rival beauties of Homer and of Virgil, of Euripides
and of Racine.   The period comprised in this correspondence reaches only to the time when Mr. Fox
resumed with assiduity his active duties in Parliament.
His complete junction with Lord Grenville, the overthrow of the Addington ministry, and the events
which followed, including Mr. Fox's short tenure of
office, will be reserved for the next and last volume.

It was not without a pang that the great leader
left his quiet home, his flowers, and his nightingales,
to perform a last public duty.   But he made no
boast of his reluctance.   Simple and unpretending in
everything, it was only to his nephew, then living
abroad, that he confessed his reluctance to engage
again in political strife.

Without further explanation, I proceed to give Mr.
Fox's letters to Mr. Grey, Lord Lauderdale, General
Fitzpatrick, and Mr. Adair.   They will be found to
contain many expressions, which, in these days, will
be thought wanting in moderation, and even in
patriotism.   But his familiar friends knew that his
heart was full of kindness, and that he dearly loved
the country whose errors he blamed.

TO ROBERT ADAIR, ESQ.

" *November* 14*th*, 1792.

" Dear Adair,

" I think as you do, that there is a good deal of nicety required in recommending any conduct to this country with respect to France ; but difficulties are not impossibilities, and I should be very glad to converse with you upon them, especially as I think something upon the general situation of Ministers as to foreign countries is exceedingly desirable at this moment.

" I shall not be in town till the next Whig Club, but shall be very glad to see you here at any time that is convenient to you. We dine at four, and you have experienced our exactness.

" Yours ever,

" C. J. FOX.

" St. Anne's Hill, *Wednesday*."

TO SAME.

" *November* 26*th*, 1792.

" Dear Adair,

" Notwithstanding the apparent good spirits you saw me in, the truth is, that what I saw and heard in London has made a most deep and painful impression on my mind ; and I grow very doubtful about the possibility of preserving those connections which I love and esteem as much as ever, and without which I do not feel that I ever can act in political matters with any satisfaction to myself.

" My reason for writing to *you* upon this now, is that I overheard you say to Sheridan that there was much disposition in what is called the aristocratic part of the party to concede and conciliate; and though I confess this is totally contrary to my own observation, I cannot help catching at anything that gives me the least glimpse of hope. Perhaps you only said this to Sheridan in order to inspire him and others with similar dispositions to those which you described on the other side, and this I fear to be the case, for I must repeat that not one symptom of the kind has appeared to me. If any such disposition existed, I cannot help thinking that on the other side *I* ·should have weight enough to produce a correspondent disposition, if it did not exist without my interposition. I am sure that Lauderdale, Grey, and Sheridan, are all manageable men; and the rascals of the democratic party (for there are such on all sides) have not set their wits to pervert *them*, in the way that those on the aristocratic side have to pervert the Duke of Portland, Fitz-william, Windham, &c. Just as I was leaving town yesterday, I heard a report that Lord Loughborough had accepted the Great Seal, but I have reason to fear that it is not true. That event would open many eyes, and I should be full of hopes that the destruction of the Whigs was not irrevocably pre-destined. The circumstances of the times ought

rather to excite you to going on with your plan
than to deter you from it, if you have spirits
for it.

       " Yours ever,
         " C. J. FOX."

      TO SAME.

       " *November* 29*th*, 1792.

" It is good not to despair, but I do assure you
I am forced to use considerable exertion with
myself to avoid it. I still am blind as to any
disposition to what I call conciliation. The very
word *forgive*, if it were mentioned, which I hope it
never will, would put an end to all hopes of it.
But what is worse than this is that I do not see
any express renunciation of the plan of suspending
opposition for the purpose of giving strength to
Government. This with *me* is the most real cause
of separation of any that has been started, and this
I know was mentioned and not reprobated before I
came to town. It is given out to be the Duke of
Portland's intention by Pitt and his friends, and
sorry am I to say that when I hear it I have no
authority to contradict it, though that was the point
I laboured most hard for when I was in town.
This point must be cleared up. Is the Duke of
Portland ready to go on with the same sort of
opposition we have been engaged in for years past?
or is he not? I am *sure* the world thinks *not*, and I
believe Ministers have reason to think not, though I
           s 2

do not believe the Duke of Portland ever authorised
any assurances to them upon the subject. Till this
is cleared up, I must remain in the state in which I
described myself to you ; and in such a state it were
no wonder if I did make continually these large strides
which are complained of, though I am not conscious
of having made any. I do not think I said a word
respecting Parliamentary Reform which I had not
said months ago to the Duke of Portland and Lord
Fitzwilliam, and years ago to Lord Rockingham.
And upon that subject let me observe that though it
was not, as Burke says, in the original contract, yet
neither was opposition to it in that contract; and
that Grey, &c., had good reason to be surprised at so
violent a storm arising from his undertaking what
the Duke of Richmond, when he was upon the most
cordial terms with the party, what Sir George Savile,
and what so many of us had done before him ; what
was supported by the Rockingham Administration;
what was voted for by Lord John Cavendish, and
assented to by some of Lord Rockingham's best
friends (mixed, I grant, with some of his wickedest
enemies) in Yorkshire. Indeed the taking such an
alarm on such a ground, and running to Pitt upon it,
were very bad symptoms ; but what is passed cannot
be recalled. What creates the present embarrassment
with me is Windham's late rash visit to Pitt, and the
inclination of others to take similar steps. Till this is
disavowed, not by words only, but by acts, I cannot
be easy. Before I quit the subject of home politics,
I will just go over the points that have been mentioned.

About Ireland we are all agreed, but nothing respecting it can be *done* in our Parliament ; though something may and I hope will be said.   In regard to Scotland, Reform is full as necessary in the borough repre- sentation as in the counties, and is of the two that to which I am most pledged.   On this subject I shall press Sheridan and the Scotch Committee to form a plan, which, if approved and supported by the body of the party, will certainly in my judgment pro- duce a good effect.   However, if Lord L. * is consulted, as I fear he must be, I shall despair of its being a secret from Pitt.   With respect to the Penal Acts, it is true that Lord Titchfield stayed to vote for the repeal, and I hope all our friends, with very few exceptions, will support me in that point if we can agree upon others.   I own I think the Duke of Portland's opinion upon the Test Act peculiarly wrong, for a point of toleration is the last thing upon which the Church ought to be consulted, and we are the last persons who ought to consult her upon anything, for if the Church party is not the most determined enemy of the Whig, there is no trusting experience in anything.   I do not wish the Duke of Portland to do anything inconsistent, but I never heard any declara- tion of his against the repeal, and considered Lord Edward's vote as a compliance with a meeting in Nottinghamshire.   Now, as to the question of Parlia- mentary Reform, I never had even a wish that the Duke of Portland should recede from his former

---

* Lord Loughborough.   It is apparent that Lord L.'s anxiety to obtain the Great Seal had great influence on the course of the Whig Party.

opinion upon the subject. He and Lord Fitzwilliam were always against it; but what I want them to do is to adhere to their former line of conduct, as well as to their former opinion, and to oppose it without any *hostility* to the supporters of it or any friendship with those who resist it. If this is said to be a difficult line, I answer it was theirs in 82, 83, 84, and 85. Indeed, indeed, instead of my making strides forwards towards new opinions, or even leaning to them, they are adopting systems of conduct entirely *new*, and in so doing are, I am convinced, the dupes of those who have the worst intentions. I do not mention the proclamation, because that mischief is over and irreparable; but I cannot help wishing to know to what length they consider themselves bound to support the sort of measure to which it points. Is Lord Grenville's circular letter to be supported? Is every absurd prosecution Ministers institute to be supported? Am I to say that it is right to crush every paper that does not atone for its sins by gross libels, upon myself for instance? or is it possible that they are so blind as not to see that they are arming Pitt with a power to support his own libels, and to put a stop to all others? I mean that they are doing this if they succeed; for I think the probability is that they will wholly fail, and that libels of all sorts will if possible increase. I must own I think that in addition to their other means of influence a monopoly of libels in the hands of a Minister who we know would not be scrupulous in the use of it, would be rather too dangerous a power for wise men to give.

I must finish now, or I shall be too late for dinner. Foreign politics to-morrow.

> " Yours ever most sincerely,

" ST. ANNE'S HILL, *Thursday.*"

SAME TO THE HON. RICHARD FITZPATRICK.

"*January* 1*st*, 1794.

" I HEAR the ill success at Toulon, and Lord Howe's failure, make more impression than the other misfortunes of the year, and that the Ministers particularly (and I do not wonder at them) are in great consternation about Toulon. To keep it will be very difficult, and for the purposes of the war quite useless ; to carry off all the inhabitants impracticable, and to leave them to the guillotine quite horrible to think of. Indeed, even if it were practicable to remove the inhabitants, how to dispose of them would be a new embarrassment. Lord Moira's expedition created very sanguine hopes at first, and now as I am told people scarcely inquire about it; whether it is over, or to take place immediately, or put off till spring, nobody seems to know or care. As to the King's speech, I think, by attending to the different declarations, one may form a guess what will be the language of it. From what I hear, our old friends * are worse than ever upon the subject of the war ; but, till I see it, I cannot bring myself to believe that they can think any circumstances of the country sufficient to justify the judicial transactions of

---

* Lord Fitzwilliam, Mr. Grenville, Lord Spencer, &c.

this year, especially those in Scotland, which I am quite confident are as contrary to law as to substantial justice. I think the prosecution of the convention in Scotland a very absurd measure, and I am very glad they have taken it, as I think it will help to call the attention of people to Muir's and Palmer's cases, when they see that the irregularities belonging to their cases are like to be extended to so many others, unless measures are taken to prevent it. I dare say you will think me too sanguine in hoping for the concurrence of our old friends, or even for much public attention on these subjects, and perhaps I am so; but I am sure a stand must be made now, however disadvantageous the moment may be; for, if what has been done is right, there is not a pretence left for calling Scotland a free country, and a very thin one for calling England so. Some say they have, and others that they have not, issued a warrant against Lord Daer.* I hope they have, because I have such an opinion of the people's love of aristocracy, that I think they would feel it to be much worse to send a man of fashion to Botany Bay than another. You will judge by my writing this long letter that my mind is pretty full upon these subjects. I have been reading Muir's trial, in which the manner is full as disgusting as the matter, and very like that of the trials in Charles the Second's time. I have desired Adam to press Serjeant Adair to attend to these matters. If he is right, I think it will be a great

---

* Lord Daer, eldest son of the Earl of Selkirk. I know not the grounds of the report here alluded to.

point, and I cannot but think it impossible that he
should be wrong.　He being a most zealous friend to
the war, will have a great weight upon this business,
and I think more than anybody with our friends.　I
saw Thurlow, who is quite right, and I think will
come forward ; but, *il faut voir.*"

TO SAME.

"*August 24th,* 1795.

" Dear Dick,

　　" I know nothing with any certainty concerning
what you ask me about.　My belief is that they are
stout.*　Just after you left us, I had an opportunity
of hearing that they were remarkably sanguine, to a
degree of folly approaching to madness ; but that
was before the final defeat at Quiberon, and the
Spanish Peace.†　As far as I can collect, I understand that the last of these two events (contrary to
what one should have imagined) struck them with
more dismay than the former ; but still I do not
hear, from any good authority, that they are coming at
all to their senses.　My brother, who was here on
Thursday, said that he understood that Lord Moira's
expedition was given up ; but I do not think even
this certain, though it seems impossible it should be
otherwise.　Sheridan indeed says, as I heard from
Lord Robert ‡ yesterday, that he knows that after

---

* The Ministers.
† The treaty between France and Spain, signed at Basle, July 22, 1795.
‡ Lord Robert Spencer.

the account of the Spanish Peace, Pitt, Dundas, and Grenville consulted, and determined to give up the whole thing and to go out; but afterwards, upon conversing with their other colleagues, took heart, and decided to go on stoutly ; but, though Sheridan knows this, I do not believe it. There is no likelihood at all in the manner in which the story is related. I think they will go on with the war ; but it is only my speculation. I have no intelligence ; and, on the other hand, the evident eagerness for peace in France and in the French Government would certainly afford Pitt a facility in making a turn which one should think would be tempting. I used always to consider his making peace as impossible, because I conceived it to be a work of some time and of some difficulty, which, in his circumstances, he could not execute ; but, if peace can be made, as I suspect it now can, by a negociation of a few hours, and by saying ' done and done,' like a bet at Newmarket, the case is very different ; and, bating the shame, the loss of reputation, and other like considerations, about which Pitt is often very careless, I do not see why he cannot make it as well as anybody else. However, there is certainly no symptom at present of any attempt at negociation, and I am of opinion that there will be none."

" *August*, 1795.

" Since I wrote in the morning I have heard some things which confirm me very much in my opinion that they * are as stout, or, in other words, as mad as possible. I believe there is no doubt but that war is as much the order of the day as at any former period of this business."

TO SAME.

"*August 27th*, 1795.

" I HAVE no news that I can at all trust to since I wrote to you last; but I believe it is pretty certain that General Doyle is going to France to attempt some co-operation with Charette, in case Charette should be in force, which I think doubtful.† If you have looked at Louis XVIII.'s letters and pro-clamations I think they must have exceeded your expectations of folly, however high they may have been."

TO SAME.

"*Monday, November 9th*, 1795.

" WE certainly mean to make a stand against the Sedition Bills; for there are to be two, one of which is to be moved to-morrow by Dundas.‡ I think there certainly will be a division, and we talk of measures

---

* The Ministers.

† Charette was one of the royalist leaders in La Vendée. He was captured and put to death by General Hoche, in March, 1796.

‡ A bill for better securing his Majesty's person and government, brought into the House of Lords by Lord Grenville; and a bill against seditious meetings, brought into the House of Commons by Mr. Pitt. See Adolphus, vol. vi. p. 358-63.

without doors which I own I think right, but yet go
to with a sort of reluctance.

" Yours ever,

" C. J. F."

TO SAME.

"*September 2nd,* 1796.

" I UNDERSTAND Parliament certainly meets on the
27th of this month.* A Spanish war is expected,
although it is said that the Ministers are doing what
they can to avoid it. It is said, too, that they are
determined to set about making peace in earnest ; in
short, that they will leave nothing undone that the
most warm friends to peace could recommend ; but I
have still my doubts about their making, or meaning
to make, the attempt in a proper manner, and still
more about their success if they do. However, I
hear that in France (particularly in the Departments)
they are very desirous of peace. At Paris they say it
is wonderful how little people in general think or talk
of public affairs. Dissipation and speculation of every
kind are the rage there, and the prices of the articles
which are the object of their speculations (that is,
everything saleable) are the great objects of inquiry
and conversation."

TO THE EARL OF LAUDERDALE.

"*December 27th,* 1796.

" DEAR LAUDERDALE,
    " In the first place, send the Wild Goose here.

---

* The meeting of Parliament took place on the 27th of September, 1796.

I cannot go to town till Thursday; but I will be there on that day soon after one, either at home or anywhere else, and shall certainly be very much disposed to agree to anything that you and others think right. My present opinion is that the strongest measure will be the best, though I fear the Directory have bungled the matter, and shown themselves to be a little unreasonable.* Why did they say anything?

" Yours ever,
" C. J. FOX.

" St. Anne's Hill, *Tuesday.*"

TO THE HON. R. FITZPATRICK.

"South Street, *Wednesday, May,* 1797.

"I PUT off writing till I could tell you with certainty about business in the House of Commons. The Call is fixed for Monday, and if it does not take place St. John's motion upon St. Domingo will certainly come on when one should wish to have a good division.†

" The news of the Emperor's peace, though not come to the Directory immediately from Bonaparte, is, I think, certainly true,‡ as Moreau has made an armistice upon the faith of it. What a catalogue of

---

* This alludes to Lord Malmesbury's mission. He was sent to Paris in October 1796, and rudely dismissed by the Directory on the 19th December of the same year.

† Mr. St. John's motion, for an address to the Crown to withdraw our troops from St. Domingo came on in the House of Commons on the 18th of May, 1797, and was negatived by 116 to 31 votes.

‡ An agreement for peace between the empire and France was made by Bonaparte with the Austrian commissioners on May 24th, 1797.

victories you will receive by this day's post! and what a wonderful thing, after all that passed last year, that Kehl should be taken the first day of the campaign!*   Accounts from Ireland are every day worse and worse.   Even the Government people there now admit the extreme danger, and say that the greater part of the militia and yeomanry in the south have taken the oath of the United Irishmen.   I know nothing more of the Naval Mutiny business than I see in the newspapers, but it appears to me to be as serious as any other of our misfortunes.† I am going to Court with a petition : I am told they affect there not to believe in the Emperor's peace, but this appears to me ridiculous."

TO SAME.

"*August 16th*, 1797.

"Peace is expected less and less every day.   I do not know whether it has occurred to you how like the present state of parties in France is to that of Whigs and Tories in King William's and in part of Queen Anne's reign.   The Government and the Army Whigs, the Tories very strong, and accused (in many instances truly, but not in all) of being Jacobites.   The Whigs accused, very falsely, of intending to govern by military force.   The Duke of

---

* Kehl capitulated to the Archduke Charles, after a seven weeks siege, on the 9th of January, 1797, but it was recovered by Moreau in the following April.   It is this last event probably to which Mr. Fox alludes.

† The mutiny at Spithead broke out on April 12th, 1797, and was renewed in May and June in a more serious form.

Marlborough, Bonaparte, &c.* It is a sad thing
that we do not hear anything about the delivering of
La Fayette, &c."

TO THE EARL OF LAUDERDALE.

"June 2nd, 1797.

" DEAR LAUDERDALE,

" I am glad the debate in the House of Lords
went off to your mind and that of the Duke of Bedford.† I am sorry he made that sort of answer to
Moira's attack, as you call it, as by your account I
suppose he did. I think, from what passed in my
room, that however peremptory his refusal might have
been as to himself, he would not have given an answer
absolutely discouraging to the plan unless you had
since perverted him. I never heard that the scheme
had originated with Thurlow, nor do I know where it
began. The proposal is said to have been made to
Carlton House, not from it; and I believe the guilt
or merit of it belongs much more to your countryman
than to any Irishmen of whatever description. Who can
doubt this that knows that Dundas and Loughborough
were the two members of the Cabinet whom it was
stated that it would be most expedient to preserve.
My conjecture is that the plan was first proposed to
Loughborough by Fullarton, and that upon his refusal

* The Duke of Marlborough was indeed accused falsely of intending to
govern by military force. Whether the charge against Napoleon was
equally false, may be questioned.

† On the 30th of May the Duke of Bedford moved an address, asking
for the dismissal of the Ministry. What follows relates to some proposal
of Lord Moira.

Thurlow was thought of as a good instrument with
the King. I am glad the Duke of Bedford was in
the closet, and think him quite right in not mentioning what he said there. I cannot help wishing
he had not said what he did upon the futility of any
administration without me, for I cannot help apprehending that if all my friends hold this language, I
shall be suspected of hypocrisy in what I have said
upon the subject as well in private as in public ; when
the truth is that I am most completely in earnest. I
indeed, even supposing Royal prejudices out of the
way and all other objections of the kind, feel such an
extreme aversion to the situation of First Minister
that I am sure I should act very ill a part I so much
dislike. I have not diligence or activity enough for
the situation,—*je ne suis pas à la hauteur des circon-
stances ;* and I am quite seriously convinced that, if
yourself, Guildford, Bedford, and Grey could get the
Government, and would accept it, you would do
much better without me than with me, having of
course the advantage, whatever it may be, of my
name and of my support in the House of Commons.
You will observe that I have not named Sheridan,
though he certainly would and ought to make part of
such a system as I have mentioned ; but I must confess that his mode of conduct lately convinces me that
he would not add much to the strength of it. What I
allude to particularly is that incurable itch that he
seems to have of distinguishing his conduct from that
of those with whom he wishes to be supposed
united."

TO SAME.

" July 20th, 1797.

" I should suppose peace to be out of the question, as the only rational motive that I can conceive would induce the Directory to make an offer evidently unreasonable, must have been an apprehension lest anything like a reasonable one should be closed with."

TO SAME.

" October 8th, 1797.

" I am very strong indeed against attending Parliament. Grey and Guildford think as I do; but I hear there are different opinions."

TO SAME.

" November 2nd, 1797.

" I am very sorry to hear the Duke of Bedford is for my going to the House the first day, indeed I find many of his opinion; but I own my own is so very much the other way that I shall scarcely bring myself to give it up. As to malicious interpretations, they of course will be given to one's conduct, and will be more or less believed; but nothing one can say can prevent that evil. That secession is a measure liable enough to misconstruction, I admit, but that was considered I suppose before we absented ourselves last session; and if ever there is a time when absence or secession is like to have any effect upon the public it is at the beginning of a session. Absence at other times only passes for less vigour and activity.

" Yours ever,

" C. J. F."

TO SAME.

" November 26th, 1797.

" As to the meeting at Westminster, I have no objection to it if it does not appear to be in consequence of the wishes of my particular friends; and how to encourage it without such an appearance I do not know. I should dislike very much that it should look as if I set on foot a meeting on purpose to give me a pretence for attending this business in Parliament; which, besides, I wish to avoid if possible. The 'Morning Chronicle,' which is the only paper I have seen, and which indeed I have not read very attentively, does not seem to give a clear account of the scheme. What is meant by the 4,000,000*l*. from the sinking fund is not at all explained. I shall go home Tuesday or Wednesday. I do not like to hear again of the Duke of Bedford's being unwell."

TO SAME.

" January 11th, 1798.

" DEAR LAUDERDALE,

" I agree with you, that if the country stirs in distant parts there ought to be some centre of communication in London. The Whig Club is preferable to the Friends of the People; but I think something may be found out better than either. Holland proposes a Middlesex meeting and a committee formed out of it, which I think the best plan; and if things go on well (which I do not expect) there might be committees to join the Middlesex Committee from Westminster, Southwark, London, and even perhaps from Surrey, Kent, &c. In short, I have no hope of any good, because I am convinced that nothing but our carrying everything so triumphantly as to give an appearance of something like unanimity can save us, and of this I see no prospect. Whether the object held out be Reform, or dismissal, or both, I do not think material; but whatever it be, the less I appear publicly in it, not only the more pleasant it will be to me, but, as I really think, the better for the cause. Might not there be a petition for the repeal of the Tax Bill? I hear very good accounts of Holland's speaking.

" Yours ever,
" C. J. FOX.

" St. Anne's Hill, *Thursday.*"

TO SAME.

" *January 12th,* 1798.

" I understand the Middlesex business will not do, nor do I think the Yorkshire will. Perhaps it is as well that they should not till there is a more general right feeling in the country. By a letter I have from the Duke of Bedford, I find he has some inclination to subscribe; if he does, I shall think him as mad as the King. What I wish he would do is that he would make his motion for removal in the House of Lords ; but being so very determined against budging myself, I feel rather awkward in pressing him or others to stir."

TO SAME.

"*February 4th*, 1798.

" I THINK something complimentary to the Duke of Norfolk ought to be proposed, and, to give it the more weight, only proposed at the meeting on Tuesday, and adopted at the March meeting.* I hope that what I hear is true, and that the dismissal is grounded upon the toast relative to the Sovereignty of the People, for there cannot be a better or a more advantageous line of demarcation for us, to distinguish the two parties in the country ; for it is impossible to support the Revolution and the Brunswick Succession upon any other principle."

TO SAME.

"*March 6th*, 1798.

" I AM glad I did not hear of the Duke of Bedford's illness till he was out of danger ; and even now I cannot help feeling alarmed as well as concerned. There are not enough of such to make it at all tolerable to lose him."

---

* Alluding to the Whig Club, and the Duke of Norfolk's dismissal. See Letters to Lord Holland, in the former part of this Volume.

TO THE HON. R. FITZPATRICK.

"St. Anne's Hill, *Friday, March 9th,* 1798.

" I am much obliged to you for your letters. The report you have heard about O'Connor is, I hope, not true ; but it is not very unlikely, for when I saw him he appeared to me to be in a great degree an altered man from what he had been, owing, as I suppose, to his long imprisonment having shaken his health and shattered his nerves, for he seemed exceedingly nervous. What an engine of oppression this power of imprisonment is ! I shall be sorry if he is tried at Maidstone, as I think the juries of London, &c., are far the best ; and if the Ministers try him in the country it is evident that they think so too, and that they want a jury more likely to be influenced by the Court than they have found the juries of the metropolis to be. It must be owned they are as unrelenting hunters of lives as ever lived ; and I suppose they will have as much pleasure the first time they hit, after so many misses, as ever had the most eager shooter. I believe we shall go to town for a couple of days next Monday, as I am in hopes of selling my house immediately.

" I cannot give much credit to what you have heard of Pitt's retiring. No change can be for the worse ; and so far I should be glad if it were true. As to the question on such an event, what would I do ? my answer is, as it would be to most cases that can be put,—nothing.

" Yours affectionately,

" C. J. F."

TO SAME.

"I AM much obliged to you, my dear Dick, for your account of O'Connor, &c. If anything more transpires pray write. I earnestly hope your last account is true, and that they have got nothing against him. I think it next to impossible that anything should make me go to the House of Commons; I am sure nothing concerning the Land Tax * or the Plot † will make me. No, not if they pass laws to seize all the land in the kingdom, and to give Pitt the power of life and death over all of us. No good can ever be done now, but by ways in which I never will take a share, and for which I am as unfit as I am indisposed to them. You may say, and truly, that neither Cato nor Brutus, nor perhaps even Cicero, would approve of my way of thinking, nor should I myself as a general rule of acting; but there are cases, and times, and situations, that are exceptions to general rules."

TO SAME.

"ST. ANNE'S HILL, *April* 9*th,* 1798.

"I THINK you were quite in the right not to wait for the Slave Trade; it is a most ridiculous farce. It

---

* Mr. Pitt proposed, in the session of 1798, a plan for the redemption of the Land Tax.

† Mr. Fox perhaps alludes to some proceedings taken about this time against some members of the Corresponding Society. See Adolphus, vol. vi. p. 693; see also the message from the Crown, on April 20th, ib. 701.

was right, I suppose, that we should not be beat too
much, and therefore Dundas and Rose were absent
with a *corps de reserve* ready to beat us in a subsequent stage if we had been victorious in the first.*
From what I hear, the fears of invasion increase. I
suppose Foster's † speech, with the Money Bills,
did not escape your notice. How they can ask
Abercrombie to stay after that speech I cannot
conceive.

" Yours affectionately,

" C. J. F.'

TO SAME.

" *May* 11*th*, 1798.

" MY DEAR DICK,

" As I suppose there is but little chance of your
coming to-day, I lose no time in desiring you to take
no step, at present at least, about resigning the Privy
Council. Nobody did it when the Duke of Devonshire
was struck out of the list; and, besides, it would have
rather a bad than a good effect, I think, if you and
Lord Robert ‡ were the only persons to do it. I
believe the late Duke of Devonshire is the only

---

　* On the 3rd of April Mr. Wilberforce moved for leave to bring in
bill for the abolition of the Slave Trade, which was refused, by 87 to 83
votes.

　† Right Hon. John Foster, Speaker of the Irish House of Commons.
The speech alluded to by Mr. Fox is reprinted at length in Plowden's
" Historical Review," vol. ii. part i. p. 665. The resignation of General Sir
Ralph Abercrombie took place shortly afterwards. See Plowden, ib.
p. 667.

　‡ Lord Robert Spencer, third son of Charles, second Duke of Marlborough, died 1831.

instance in this reign of a Privy Councillor being turned out in England, and the more the circumstances of the two cases shall appear exactly similar the better I shall like it.* I wish I knew whether it is necessary I should go to Court; I had much rather not, but would do in this as is thought right, and should be glad to know whether the Duke of Devonshire did. Unless it be Lord Frederick,† I do not know who is likely to recollect whether he did or not, and it is hardly worth while for me to trouble him with a letter about so foolish a business.

"To be sure, what they have done is of a piece with the dismission of the Duke of Norfolk,‡ and the debate on Tierney's motion;§ and yet why they should do a thing which they must know can do me no harm, and what might possibly (if we thought it desirable) rekindle some spirit in opposition, I cannot understand."

* This is singular, as the Duke of Devonshire was turned out by Mr. Fox's father. See Lord Mahon's "History." Mr. Fox's name was struck out of the Privy Council, May 9th, 1798.

† Lord Frederick Cavendish.

‡ Concerning the exclusion of Mr. Fox from the Privy Council, and the removal of the Duke of Norfolk from the Lord-Lieutenancy of the West Riding of Yorkshire, see Adolphus, vol. vi. p. 692.

§ Mr. Tierney's motion on the 7th of November, 1797, respecting the third Secretary of State for the War Department, and declaring that Mr. Dundas had vacated his seat by the acceptance of the office. The motion was negatived by 139 to 8. A similar motion was afterwards made on December 15th, but no division was taken.

TO THE EARL OF LAUDERDALE.

"*May 31st*, 1798.

" I WILL certainly be at Bedford House at three on Tuesday. I wish I could have avoided the Whig Club, for it will be difficult to avoid saying something, and I am sure that nothing of what I think is fit to be said in public."

TO HON. R. FITZPATRICK.

"1798.

" I DO not know whether one ought to be glad or sorry at the scheme of Union with Ireland being dropped; and yet one might perhaps suppose that whatever Foster opposed must have some good in it. With regard to the continental war, I have no doubt about what I wish; first against the formation of a new confederacy, and next, against its success if formed. It is whimsical enough that the Russians and Turks should be the only, or at least the first people, who are supposed to show a proper degree of sensibility upon the subject of civilised society. I dare say they add, too, upon that of Liberty and Christianity. Does anybody know yet what Pitt's tax upon property is to be? If it is to produce what is wanted for this year, besides replacing the assessed taxes of last year, it must be a trimmer; and yet this is what we must collect from the Mansion House proceedings."

TO SAME.

"St. Anne's Hill, *Wednesday, December,* 1798.

"Price* writes to me to recommend some plays; and he mentions Knight's † opinion of them, but not yours. Is it that yours is unfavourable, and that he wishes me to read them without the prejudice which your judgment might create in me? You know I reckon you so severe a critic, especially upon the first reading of poetry, that that would not be much. As to public affairs, I think what W. Smith said in the House of Commons is perfectly true; that if people will not resist this inquisition,‡ they will resist nothing. *Ergo tout est fini.*

"Yours ever,

'C. J. F."

TO SAME.

"*January 6th,* 1799.

"I am very well pleased at Young One's going on to fight so stoutly in the House of Lords alone. It would be an excellent education for him if there were anything to look to in future; but time and chance may produce anything. I think if you do not see some good things, and especially some very moving things, in the plays Price sent me, that you are as much too severe as he is, perhaps, too partial."

* Mr. Uvedale Price, author of the "Essay on the Picturesque."
† Mr. Payne Knight.
‡ The Property and Income Tax.

TO SAME.

"January 13*th,* 1799.

"You are very severe indeed upon the poor plays; Price is perhaps as much too fond of them.* As to the Preface, I am almost glad now—though it was quite by accident—that I forgot to tell Price my opinion of that part which I have read of it; which is, that it is dull, stupid, and conceited to the last degree, and, what is worse than all, has the effect of setting one against other poetry written by the author of it, and of persuading one that he has a vile, prosaic soul. The very idea of a man reading lectures upon the passions in the shape of a tragedy and comedy upon each, is a complete damper to all feeling. In short, it is detestable; and I am sure, if I had read it before the plays, it would have made me less favourable to them. But indeed there are good things in them, and they are not at all like Fuseli's painting."

TO SAME.

"January 17*th,* 1799.

"What you say about Greek and Latin verses is, I believe, true in part; but the principal reason why they are easier (the Latin ones, at least), is the simple one, that one has learned to make them earlier, and is more used to the making of them than of English.

---

* Probably Miss Baillie's "Plays on the Passions." The first volume was first published in 1798; the second in 1802.

The only copy of English verses made all the time
I was at Eton were Price's."

TO SAME.

"March 8th, 1799.

"Poor Ireland! and, indeed, if she does not some
way save herself, poor world! But I cannot help
hoping that this excess and insolent display of despotism will not do long."

TO SAME.

"March 10th, 1799.

" I am very glad the dice have been more favourable; but while the post goes and comes, all that may
be changed; and ought a wise man, who has lived
half a century of years, to allow himself to depend
upon such events? But it is in vain to preach."

TO SAME.

"March 12th, 1799.

" ' When with wild wood leaves and weeds I ha' strew'd his grave,
And on it said a century of prayers,
Such as I can twice o'er, I'll sigh and weep.'

Cymbeline, Act IV., Scene 7.

" I should think, after this, there is an end of
what Hare contends it must mean, and that it is
evident what it does mean. I have looked in ' Johnson's Dictionary,' where I found the above referred to ;

and I think he does too much honour to this new
fancy of century relating to years, by stating a century
of years to be one of the two senses of the word
century. In my opinion, it has no such sense; and
you might just as well say it meant a hundred citizens,
or a hundred soldiers, because we say Rome was
divided into centuries without mentioning citizens,
and the Roman army into centuries without mentioning soldiers. The truth is, that it is a word
generally so used as to make it unnecessary to mark
to what it relates; but this is not more true when
applied to *years* than when applied to anything else;
and it is always an abbreviation of the more regular
phrase. To say, therefore, that a century of years is
formal or pedantic, would be another thing; but to
say that it is incorrect, is just as absurd as if you were
said to speak incorrectly when you say you have lost a
thousand pounds: because, if you were to say the
thousand without the pounds, everybody would know
that you did not mean shillings or pence, or hairs
from your head."

TO SAME.

"St. Anne's Hill, *Friday, March 15th*, 1799.

"I am very sorry the continental war is to begin
again.* How can any prince who is governed, as they
say the Emperor is, by his Ministers, contrive to get
such fools for his advisers? Pitt's conduct on the

---

* The Congress of Rastadt was dissolved on April 8th, 1799. Hostilities
had already commenced in Italy.

Union does appear highly absurd; but, as to Ireland, unless he would determine (which he is quite unequal to) to gain the United Irishmen, all he does signifies nothing. If the exterminating system is adopted, whether he has a few more or less Orange supporters is a point of less consequence than it may perhaps appear.

" Yours affectionately,

"C. J. F."

TO THE EARL OF LAUDERDALE.

"*May* 13*th*, 1799.

" I BELIEVE both you and I thought the finances would go sooner than they have done (or rather than they are like to do, for they are not gone yet); but neither of us, I believe, expected that every vestige and shadow of what used to be called liberty would be extinguished quite so soon, and with such general good humour and acquiescence."

TO SAME.

"*June* 10*th*, 1799.

"THE newspapers speak of Thanet being to be pardoned, but I hear no certain account of it yet.* Erskine and others were positive that imprisonment would make no part of the sentence, and yet you see. Which of Grose's two speeches is worst in point of

---

* The Earl of Thanet and Mr. Ferguson were tried and convicted in April, 1799, for an attempt to rescue Arthur O'Connor on his trial at Maidstone. See State Trials, vol. xxvii., p. 821.

folly and atrocity ?   I rather think that on Wakefield
the foolishest, and that on Thanet and Ferguson the
most rascally, but it is a near race."

TO THE HON. R. FITZPATRICK.

"1799.

"DEAR DICK,

"I was at Holland House last week, and saw a poem
which Young One has begun, called 'Bermeddin,'
which I like of all things.   If he would give himself
the trouble of correcting the parts that want it, and if
he goes on as well as he has begun, I really think it
will be quite a delightful thing.   It is a sort of poem
exactly to my taste ; and my partiality to that style of
poetry may perhaps make me think it better than
it is."

TO SAME.

"1799.

"As to criticism and poetry (that is, reading
poetry), there is no danger of my leaving them off ;
and my late Greek studies have made me fonder of
them than ever ; but as to versifying myself, I doubt
the fit will soon be over, though as yet I have not
been able even to keep my resolution about the
Faddles, and shall send Price by to-day's post one
more Latin and one more Italian.*   I know it is not

---

* This alludes to a quantity of idle poetry, on a very idle subject, by Mr.
Fox, General Fitzpatrick, Mr. Price, &c.

fair to argue against criticisms from the poetry of the critic : if it were, I think Addison's " Cato," with all its merit, would sufficiently prove that he did not much understand the nature of dramatic poetry ; and, indeed, in this instance, I think the argument pretty fair ; but it is certainly not in the language, or poetry, or what may be called the execution, that ' Cato ' fails ; but in the plan and scheme of it.   As to the Union, I know nothing but what I see in the papers ; but Sir J. Parnell's dismission looks as if Pitt was in earnest ;—but as you say, no more of politics, and let poetry and criticism be the order of the day; and of these, if I could get Young One to meet you here for a day or two, we might have a very pleasant dose. There is a Cambridge declamation published of William Lamb,* which, though too Johnsonic in the style, is certainly an extraordinary performance for so young a man, and has, I think, many strokes of genius in it."

TO SAME.

" *December 8th*, 1799.

" I SHALL be very curious to see the great Consul's propositions for peace.   My speculation is that they will be very unreasonable, St. John thinks the contrary.   What think you ?   I have, in a manner, begun something of modern history, but I have no liking to it, and am sure I shall not do it well, as my

* Afterwards Lord Melbourne.

mind is so much more upon poetry and the ancients,
particularly Cicero: I wish you would read his letters
to Atticus; if you have not Latin enough, in French,
and his familiar epistles too. There can be no
history so interesting, of any period, ancient or
modern."

TO THE EARL OF LAUDERDALE.

" Friday.

" I AM seriously thinking of becoming an historian,
and have indeed begun, but my progress hitherto is
so little that it is not worth mentioning, except upon
the principle of *dimidium qui cœpit.* As to what
people may expect, I know not; if much they will be
disappointed,—but I certainly do not intend to decline
the labour of any research which I am able to make,
and much less to refuse any assistance I can have in
such research. I hope, therefore, you will not be
satisfied with merely recommending to me to make
use of assistance, but will give me some hint of what
nature, and from whom I can get it. To enable you
to do this better, it is necessary first to inform you
that the death of Charles II. is the period from which
I commence my history, though in my introduction I
take a pretty full review of his reign, and consequently
should be glad to get any new light in regard to it.
Even this introductory chapter, however, is not yet
finished. Next, it is fit you should know that so far
from having as yet examined or even looked into any
manuscript papers, or other documents not generally

known, I do not even know where any such exist, and
therefore any information upon that head will be very
welcome. I find one of my greatest difficulties to be,
how to discover the authorities upon which the
historians advance their facts, for they very often do
not refer to them. Hitherto, when I am only taking
a cursory review, this is of no great importance; but
in regard to the Popish and Ryehouse Plots particularly, I find both Rapin and Hume advancing so many
facts for which I cannot guess their authorities, that
if I were to give a regular history of those transactions
I should be much puzzled. Now, when I am under
difficulties of this sort, can you either direct me to
whom I can apply for a solution of them, or if I send
queries to you, can you get me answers to them?
For instance : The first point I would inquire about
is the generally received opinion that it was Charles
II.'s intention to change his measures, if death had
not prevented him. I should like very much to know
upon what authority, either written or traditional, this
opinion is founded. I have a vague notion that the
Duchess of Portsmouth told my grandfather the Duke
of Richmond so; and Burnett (I think) says that she
told Mr. Henley so ; but I should imagine there must
be something more than such slight authority for an
opinion that has so generally prevailed. Can you
inquire? As to the sale, it may very possibly happen
as you foresee ; but if it does it shall be your fault, for
in that matter I will trust entirely to your advice ; and
in this I include the question of who is to be the
publisher. You will perceive by this letter that I really

am in earnest; but yet the doubts you mention, if they relate not to my present intention, but to the completion of the work, may be but too well founded.

" Yours ever affectionately,

"C. J. FOX."

TO CHARLES GREY, ESQ.

"St. Anne's Hill, *Wednesday Night*.*

" DEAR GREY,

" Since I sent back Lord Robert's messenger I have read the papers, and now feel quite easy about not being with you in your consultation; for our way is so clear that we must be as ingenious as Malmsbury himself to go wrong. If it had been the object of Ministers to put themselves in the wrong, I do not think that they could have done more.

" I wish you would inquire about the treaty referred to in the bottom of page 52 in Malmsbury's letter. Is it before the House of Commons? I do not know whether you recollect Pitt saying, in justification of his not having made the Emperor at the time of the loan debar himself from making a separate peace, that such a condition must have been mutual, which might be objectionable for us. The date of the treaty referred to is in some respects material, though I think it is before the House. Pitt will have some ground, according to his late favourite mode, for reproaching us for not having attacked him earlier upon it. I rather wish the Directory had not in their

---

* No year is marked for the date of this letter; it may belong to an earlier year.

last note referred to their constitution, though in their circumstances I think it was excusable. Surely no man can now believe the Ministers to have been sincere in their wishes for peace, unless they think them idiots.

" Yours ever,

"C. J. F.

TO CHARLES GREY, ESQ.

"ST. ANNE'S HILL, *Friday.*

" DEAR GREY,

" I send you the enclosed two papers, according to the Duke of Bedford's desire. I should like the one marked A the best, if it were not that it seems to point at public meetings ; a measure in my judgment quite right if one saw any encouraging circumstances for it in the country, but which at present nobody seems to think of. Perhaps I am too despondent, but my opinion is that nothing can save the country (at least its constitution) but unanimity, or something very near unanimity, against the Ministers ; and of this at present there is no hope. What future events in Ireland may produce I cannot tell. If they are to produce anything, I most heartily wish they may happen before any serious invasion of this country takes place—for I have long thought that if the French once land (in any force, I mean) during the present Ministry, our slavery is decided ; and the only question, who is to be tyrant ? In this question I should prefer George III. Those who think there is any consolation *in Æneæ magni dextrá cadis* may

prefer Bonaparte. Lord Robert told me yesterday
that you seem to be rather vexed at my appearing, the
day before, desirous to get rid of the discussion we
were in. Surely if you recollect the turn it took
and the impossibility, when Erskine was in his most
talkative vein, of anything like deliberation, you
cannot be surprised at it. Besides, I will own that
my opinion leans very much against doing or almost
saying anything on the subject of invasion before the
thing actually takes place. I do not mean that there
is any objection to saying in general terms that one
would endeavour to repel it; but I own I do not much
like any specific engagement, and still less any actual
exertion, which among other effects may have that of
enabling the Ministry to send more murderers to
Ireland. However, upon this point I am ready to do
whatever the Duke of Bedford and yourself wish. My
opinion, certainly, is for doing nothing till the invasion
comes, and then for such of us as can be useful either
by their personal service or by their influence, exerting
themselves to the utmost against the French. As to
myself, I should content myself with going to the
King or his Minister and offering myself for any
purpose in which I could be serviceable. Now this
is my opinion—however ready I may be to give way
to that of others, it cannot be expected that I should
be active in making converts to opinions to which I
am not yet converted myself. I had an opportunity
of asking Lauderdale his opinion on these things. As
to Sheridan, I dined with him at Combe's and he
seems to be fuller of absurd notions than ever man

was—but do not say I say so. I wish you would
find a day to come here ; and I do assure you that if
you think you can convince me that anything can be
done either for our personal credit or to make the
invasion less formidable, I am ready to hear with the
utmost docility, and, even without conviction, to trust
entirely to your judgment.

" Yours affectionately,

" C. J. FOX."

TO THE HON. R. FITZPATRICK.

" St. Anne's Hill, *Wednesday, February* 19*th*, 1800.

" I read Young One's speech in the *Courier* only,
but thought it very good in many parts. It is impossible to judge what he ought to do with Stanhope
unless one knew his particular measure. I own I
thought it formerly injudicious in Bedford and
Lauderdale to seem so afraid of being with him as
they did, but Holland's situation is so different that a
different conduct may be proper in his case from that
which I should have advised in theirs. I agree with
you, that Stanhope is what Drake called super
imperial in these qualities you mention ; but yet, if
his proposition is right in itself, I do not think it
ought to be opposed, or even to be without support.
You are more sanguine about the Union than I.

" Yours affectionately,

" C. J. FOX."

TO SAME.

"*March,* 1800.

" I go on very slowly, and begin now to doubt whether I shall even have finished my introductory chapter by the end of this month, as I had once promised myself to do. There will certainly be plenty of observations in most parts of the work, though probably not quite so much in proportion as in this first chapter. I do not grow yet to like my work, and have been employing myself in writing a couple of Italian songs ; one a translation (but not near close enough) of Lewis's 'Pleasure and Desire.' "

TO SAME.

"*April 3rd,* 1800.

" Grey and George Ponsonby * have been here this morning to talk over the Union, &c. Nothing can persuade me to attend ; but if there were any public in this country to be operated upon, I think it one of the strongest cases that can be laid before it. I think particularly the compensation to the Borough holders will be one of the most bitter pills that ever was swallowed ; and it must, I think, be almost equally disagreeable to both Reformers and Anti-Reformers. Jurisdictions have, it is true, been bought in by the public, but then they were Jurisdictions exercised by him who sold them. Burgage lands or freeholds might be fairly enough a matter of purchase, but to

---

* Right Hon. George Ponsonby, younger brother of Lord Ponsonby.

sell directly and avowedly the influence a man has upon others was reserved for these times. You know, no doubt, that these Boroughs are all small Corporations, in which he who is called the proprietor, and who is to receive the compensation, has no ostensible power, nor any other, except the influence he has with the corporators. Add to all this, that the English, it is said, are to pay the money, which will amount to above twelve hundred thousand pounds."

TO CHARLES GREY, ESQ.

"St. Anne's Hill, *Thursday*, 1800.

" Dear Grey,

"It made both Mrs. A. and me very happy to hear you think your little girl in so good a way. I read a better account of the debate in the *Courier* than that I had before in my own paper ; but there is no symptom in either of Sheridan's having done any mischief—on the contrary, in the *Courier* account he appears as having made an excellent speech.

"Your expressing so strong a wish for having the one day upon the neutral question has made me consider ; and it does occur to me that if you think a good discussion could be had upon that subject, it might do some good abroad, if not here, by holding out a hope to the northern powers of kind treatment from England, and thereby showing them that it is not absolutely necessary for them to throw themselves into the arms of France, to which I believe them to be by no means naturally inclined. But, then, this depends entirely upon the prospect of a good division, of which I can by no means judge. There is no account of the Doctor's speech * in the *Courier*. Fitz seemed much pleased with it, and indeed it appeared to me from some things he dropped, that the Doctor was likely to have a good deal of influence with him. For this reason as well as others, take my advice, and, notwithstanding his tediousness, cultivate Lawrence. If I am to have anything to do about the neutral business, I must have some hours with him first; but that I hope is out of the question.

"Yours ever,
"C. J. FOX."

TO SAME.

" St. Anne's Hill, *Friday,* 1800.

"Dear Grey,

"From what you say of Pitt's charge against Denmark, he must either suppose this convention to be different from that of 1780, or he must (according to my conception) strangely misunderstand the matter. The convention of 1780 expressly excepts *contraband,* and just before, I think, or nearly about the time of signing it, Denmark made an explanatory convention with Great Britain, declaring certain naval stores *contraband.* This was done by the Danish Ministry, with the direct view of preventing Denmark from being obliged by the armed neutrality (which she was about to sign) to act in a manner that would give cause to Great Britain to be offended with her. If, therefore, this armed neutrality is like the former,

---

* Dr. Lawrence.

neutral bottoms do not protect contraband, and the convention with Denmark, 1780 (as I should suppose), still subsists, by which naval stores are considered as contraband; *ergo quoad* Denmark, they are not protected.

"Lord Holland said that Bernstorf, in talking to him some years ago, made a merit of having done something agreeable to Great Britain contrary to the wishes of the Empress Catherine, and I take it for granted it was this convention of 1780 to which he alluded; and in truth it was a very conciliatory and meritorious proceeding. Do you guess from Windham's answer to Banks that there is some offer from hence for negotiation? It is so like Pitt to be making one with a view to parry the effect of Leeds, Wakefield, &c., &c., that I half suspect it; otherwise, Windham's words would naturally be interpreted the direct contrary way. I have advised Wyvill to detach as much as possible any meeting that may be to take place now, from the old one. I am glad to see by the papers that Ponsonby's election is carried.

"Yours affectionately,

"C. J. FOX."

TO THE EARL OF LAUDERDALE.

"*April* 18*th*, 1800.

"Though I have not had an answer from you to my former queries, I must send you another, upon which you can find little difficulty, where you are, of getting information. Dalrymple, in his Appendix, p. 301, says the secret treaty entered

into between Charles II. and Louis XIV. in Spring
1681, was first given to the public from the
Versailles papers by Mr. Hume. Now, in my
edition of Hume, printed in 1763, there is no
mention of this treaty; and what may seem to be a
reference to it in some sort in vol. viii., pp. 201,
202, sixth edition, rather proves to me that he had
not seen it. Perhaps he has mentioned it in some
later edition of his history. I am very eager about
the work just now,—that is to say, about the mark
that you are at when you are slackest in any
business, and it is dreadful how slowly I proceed."

TO SAME.

"*April 27th*, 1800.

"DEAR LAUDERDALE,

"I certainly thought you were rather tardy,
and could only account for it by supposing that
you were getting some very full and satisfactory
answer to my first query, which might require
some time; but I find you have not even procured
an answer to my second, which might be had, I
should think, from any man of letters in Edinburgh,
or certainly from Sir John Dalrymple. You may
say, why do not I write to him myself? First, because
I had rather give up my whole plan than enter into
a correspondence with him; and next, because, if I
should be obliged to mention him in the course of
the work (which, however, I will avoid if possible)
it will certainly not be in a flattering way to him;
and I should not like therefore to do anything that

might look like getting weapons from him to be used against himself. I can hardly think, however, that he can have had the impudence to publish papers that have no existence ; and, therefore, in my introduction, I have not scrupled to make use of his papers, though certainly not of his informers. Indeed, in the introduction it is not so important to be exact to a nicety, as it is rather in the nature of a discussion alluding to known facts than of a minute inquiry into disputed points. Even this introduction is not yet finished in the literal sense of the word, much less in its critical sense, for it will require a good deal of polishing and correcting; so that you need be in no apprehension of my hurrying myself. I shall, I believe, however, have done with this part in a few days.

" I am going to write to La Fayette in a few days, and rather think I shall make the application you suggest through him, unless you think it would be better to make it in the way you propose. By the way, almost all the emigrants of that class are returned, or returning, to France ; the Lameths, Aiguillan, &c."

TO SAME.

" *May 2nd,* 1800.

" Now for a query which has nothing to do with my part of the history, but which relates to facts concerning which I have the greatest degree of curiosity, and of which I may perhaps take notice in some note to my Introduction. Harris, in his Life

of Charles II., vol. i., p. 134, quotes a Proclamation
from Thurloe's State Papers, vol. ii., p. 248, said to
be issued by Charles II. from Paris, in which he
encourages loyal persons to assassinate Cromwell
by sword, pistol, or poison. This sounds quite
impossible to be true; but whether true or not it
seems strange, that having once got into Thurloe's
State Papers, it should not be noticed by the
historians, either for the purpose of blackening
Charles if it were genuine, or the other side if it was
a forgery.

"I have no thoughts of throwing away my Greek
books, and would give up the whole plan if I thought
it incompatible with my giving a little time to them.
I hear again famous accounts of Grey's speeches. I
am told that no historian ever dealt more largely in
that mode of writing mentioned in your letter than
Hume; and that in many instances he did not
even give himself the trouble to transcribe, but
referred the printer to the original author, with a
few marginal alterations, particularly in Scotch
affairs. I have at last finished my Introduction;
which, after all, is more like a speech than it
should be."

TO SAME.

(No date.)

"I AM much obliged to you for your letter and
catalogue of Birch's works. I thought there had
been some papers published by him that related
to James the First's time, and particularly to the trial

of Somerset, and to the communications between the
King and Bacon in that affair.   I am sure I read such
papers thirty-two years ago, and have never seen them
since.   I thought they had been published by Birch,
but in this I may have been mistaken.   I rather
think all the publication consisted of papers relating
to Bacon, and of letters between him and others.
There were several, I remember, between him and
Buckingham.   What is all this, you will say, to my
history ? Certainly nothing ; but one historical inquiry
leads to another, and I recollect that the impression
upon my mind was, that there was more reason than
is generally allowed for suspecting that Prince Henry
was poisoned by Somerset, and that the King knew
of it after the fact.   This is not, to be sure, to my
present purpose ; but I have thought of prefixing, or
subjoining, to my work, if it ever should be finished,
a disquisition upon Hume's History of the Stuarts; and
in no part of it would his partiality appear stronger
than in James I.   I am sorry you gave yourself, or
rather your amanuensis, the trouble of copying the
Proclamation, for I did not doubt the fidelity of
Harris's transcript of it.   What I want to know is,
whether anything was said about it at the time;
whether it was disavowed or justified ; what historians
notice it ; and what rational account can be given of
so very extraordinary a business not having attracted
more general attention.   Now for another query, not
foreign to my history, since it relates to a fact of
which I have already taken notice in my Introduction.
Rapin says expressly that Charles II., towards the end

of his reign, published a declaration thanking his
people for surrender of charters, &c.; and among
many other things stating, *that as the Crown was
the origin, so would it be found the best security of
the People's Rights.* Harris quotes the same words
from Sprat's account of the Conspiracy; and in that
account they are sure enough, as well as the other
matters mentioned by Rapin, to be in the Declaration.
It is true that Sprat's publication purports to be a
Declaration of Charles's; but in the Preface of James
countersigned by Sunderland, it is said that it was
ready for the press when Charles died, consequently
not issued. Now what I want to know is, whether
the Declaration mentioned by Rapin to have been
issued by Charles, and Charles's intended Declaration
published by James (commonly called Sprat's
account), are one and the same thing; or whether
Charles did in his lifetime publish some Declaration,
the words of which might not unnaturally be repeated
in that published by James. I have followed Rapin,
but I should not like to be wrong in such a fact,
though not in itself very material. I have, indeed,
laid some little stress upon some parts of the
Declaration; but whether it was published or
ready for the press would not interfere with my
observations."

TO CHARLES GREY, ESQ.

"St. Anne's Hill. 1800. *Friday.*

"Many thanks to you, my dear Grey, for your letter. It is so very unpleasant to me not to comply with the wishes of my friends, that I always feel the greatest obligation to them for not pressing me. You will have a fine opportunity for making a good speech, and I dare say you will not disappoint my expectations; but as you do attend, you should persuade yourself not to be out of heart as you describe yourself. The question between Power and Liberty perhaps never was more directly at issue than upon this occasion. I will not trouble you at present for any of the books you mention, unless there are (which I much doubt) any accounts of Parliamentary debates in James the Second's reign. These, however imperfect or scanty, I should like to have whenever you come. I have some volumes of Somers's Tracts, in which there is a letter from Sunderland to a friend in the country, dated March 23rd, 1689; so that if that be the paper you mean, I will not trouble you to bring it.

"I shall go to Lord Robert's,* I believe, for a day or two next week; so that you will not be sure of finding me at home till towards the end of it. Mrs. A.'s compliments. We hope you have nightingales at Ham, for they are singing here to-day in a grand style.

"Yours affectionately,

"C. J. FOX."

* Lord Robert Spencer's house at Woolbeding.

TO SAME.

"St. Anne's Hill, *Friday,* 1800.

" Dear Grey,

" I send you back Wyvill's letter, to whom I have written this day. I enclose you also a note I have had from him to-day, in which, by the way, he seems to lay a stress upon the letter I wrote to him last week, that the contents of it, if I remember them, do not at all justify. Do you know where Fitzwilliam is ? or have you any notion about what would be the best way of attacking him ? I think he would not have much objection to a petition for removal; but whether he would be active in promoting it I do not know. Anything in favour of Reform it is impossible to propose to him; but, on the other hand, it seems to me that Reform need not be brought forward at either a first or second meeting. That it must be a part of a change of system there can be no doubt, and Fitzwilliam must know as well as anybody else, that you and I are so pledged to it that it must be an inevitable consequence of power being in our hands. Knowing this, I think he will gradually make up his mind to it; but that he should acquiesce in it immediately, and that too from Wyvill, is beyond all hope. What is the meaning of these repeated delays of the speech and the address ? The rise in the stocks is, I suppose, owing to the Bank extending their discount; but whatever be the cause, it is a very bad effect, for, from my observations, nothing discomfits Pitt like a low state of the funds ; and when I saw them at fifty-

four and a half, I thought it as good an event
for you as twenty or thirty additional votes in
Parliament.

" Yours affectionately,

"C. J. FOX."

TO SAME.

"St. Anne's Hill.   1800.   *Sunday.*

" Dear Grey,

" It is a great disappointment to me your not
coming to-day. Nothing can be more judicious, in
my opinion, than the language you propose to hold
upon the armed neutrality business. I suspect the
question of right is against us altogether; but on the
point of searching ships under convoy I am quite sure it
is. I suppose you have read "*Schlegel, sur la visite,*" &c.,
in which there is a great deal of good, though
not so well put as it might be. As to the value of
the claim, I must agree with you; and that the
madness of party has brought it to an issue now is
self evident. I do not remember exactly what was
signed by the Neutral Powers in 1780; but I am
quite sure no blame was imputed to Lord North for
not resenting it. The first act of the Rockingham
Ministry, before I had had the seals twenty-four
hours, was to make an offer to Holland upon the
principles of the Armed Neutrality : and this more
with a view to satisfy the Empress, than with much
hope of procuring peace with the United Provinces ;
and this measure was one of the few upon which that
Cabinet was unanimous. I am very much obliged to

you for discouraging all ideas of Westminster meetings at present. They would indeed be embarrassing
to me, and the result would probably be my going out
of Parliament. If Yorkshire and other places can be
stirred up successfully, Westminster might follow with
propriety; but I am sure its taking the lead could
do no good. I take for granted the Common Council
is immoveable, or that would be an important point;
next to Yorkshire, I think, the most so of any. If
the stocks continue to fall so rapidly, I think Pitt will
be more alarmed at that than at any other symptom.
If the country were not both corrupted and subdued,
you could not fail in your opposition at such a time as
this: which the more one considers it, the more it
appears the most desperate that ever existed; and in
a still greater proportion, if possible, to Ministry. But,
however, it is no use to croak or to discourage you.
As to myself, the call upon me must be very strong,
and very unequivocal, before I think I can do any
good by returning; and unless I think I can do good,
why should I do so very strong a violence to my own
inclination?

              " Yours affectionately,
                        " C. J. FOX."

" I send you back the song, which both Mrs.
A. and I like very much. Pybus's part of it
is particularly good. Do not mind Lawrence's
unpopularity, who will be of infinite service to you on
the question of Neutrality, if you should be obliged

to go deeper into it than is prudent to do at first. I am sure you will do everything you can to smoothe Sheridan's difficulties. The best way is not to appear to attend to them too much; and in the main point of the incapable conduct of Ministers he is sure to be right. By the way, the incapacity of Ministers, rather than peace with Denmark, or with France, &c., ought to be the point principally hushed out of doors,—and, to a certain degree too, within."

TO SAME.

"St. Anne's Hill. 1800. *Sunday.*

" Dear Grey,

" I am much obliged to you for your letter, and am very happy Fitzwilliam is coming so right; though I much wish he would be so about Yorkshire too, as that is of most consequence in itself, as well as the point in which his assistance will be the most efficacious. I think he is wrong, in fact, about what Wyvill did formerly at the Yorkshire meeting; but it would be of no use now to go into an examination of that matter. He is strangely prepossessed against Wyvill, and that cannot be helped; but sure he has lived long enough in the world to see that to effect anything in politics he must be content to act and concert with many persons whom he does not like. I allow his last adventure upon this principle with Pitt is not encouraging for this sort of coalitions; but Wyvill's power is not such as to make the danger at all the same. I will write to

him.   It is impossible to guess the cause of the delay
of the King's speech.   His absence from the Queen's
party appears to me, as well as to the courtiers, the
most extraordinary part of the whole.   If he was
upon business (which is next to impossible) with
whom?—that might easily be known.   Of the causes
guessed at, the difference relative to the Catholics
appears to me the most likely.   Some of them understand that they had a positive promise from Lord
Cornwallis, not only of his, but of the whole Government support; but then the mode of proceeding
was to be by a petition to be presented by Lord
Cornwallis when he should arrive, and therefore it
would not (unavoidably at least) come to so early a
decision.   If the King and part of the Cabinet are
against the measure, whatever may be the case in the
House of Commons, it will be thrown out in the
House of Lords by an immense majority.

    " I cannot much admire your answer to Jack
Townshend, who certainly meant you nothing but
kindness, but happens to differ from you in opinion
with respect to any good that can be done.   There
must have been, I think, from your account, something at least in it.   Besides, my dear Grey, he who
wishes to act effectually in politics must be content
to use conciliatory means to men, and frequently to
take the service done to the public by attendance
as favours done to himself; especially when, as in
this instance, the intention is as friendly as the
profession.   I know there is scarce anybody for
whom Jack has such an esteem and value as for

yourself. Pray excuse this preaching; but if there is anything in which I have experience, it is in these matters. I like the amendment very well. I am sorry to see stocks keep up.

" Yours affectionately,

" C. J. FOX.

" P.S.—Take care not to pledge yourself about the Brown-bread Act, for I think it not impossible but it may create such dissatisfaction as to make the repeal necessary."

TO SAME.

" ST. ANNE'S HILL. 1800. *Friday.*

" DEAR GREY,

" I am much obliged to you for sending me back my letter. I will write to Conolly. In defence of my opinion about the nightingales, I find Chaucer,— who of all poets seems to have been the fondest of the singing of birds,—calls it a *merry note*, and though Theocritus mentions nightingales six or seven times, he never mentions their note as plaintive or melancholy ; it is true he does not call it anywhere merry, as Chaucer does, but, by mentioning it with the song of the blackbird, and as answering it, he seems to imply that it was a cheerful note. Sophocles is against us ; but even he only says *lamenting Itys*, and the comparison of her to Electra is rather as to perseverance day and night than as to sorrow. At all events, a tragic poet is not half so good authority in this question as Theocritus and Chaucer.

" I cannot light upon the passage in the Odyssey, where Penelope's restlessness is compared to the nightingale; but I am sure that it is only as to restlessness or watchfulness that he makes the comparison. If you will read the last twelve books of the Odyssey, you will certainly find it, and I am sure that you will be paid for your hunt whether you find it or not. The passage in Chaucer is in the 'Flower and the Leaf,' p. 99. The one I particularly allude to in Theocritus is in his Epigrams, I think in the fourth. Dryden has transferred the word *merry* to the goldfinch in his ' Flower and the Leaf,' in deference, may be, to the vulgar error; but pray read his description of the nightingale here, it is quite delightful. I am afraid I like these researches as much better than those that relate to Shaftesbury, Sunderland, &c., as I do those better than attending the House of Commons.

" Yours affectionately,
"C. J. FOX."

TO SAME.

" WOOLBEDING. 1800. *Friday.*

" DEAR GREY,

" I am very glad to hear from all quarters that I was in the right in expecting (and you of course in the wrong in thinking otherwise) that you would make an extraordinary good speech.* I had not time to look at the newspapers the morning I left home, and so have not read the account of it, but I

---

* In April, 1800, Mr. Grey made a motion on the subject of the representation, as connected with the Irish Union.

hear everybody is agreed about it. I am sure, my dear Grey, you must see that the argument of its doing no harm is applicable to my attendance whenever there is a business of any importance upon which any of my friends would be glad to have me present. I cannot with fairness be supposed more indifferent to the question of the Union than to all the other questions of politics that have been, or are in agitation, from all which it has been my plan to absent myself. It is true that, in deference to the opinion of others, I did upon Buonaparte's offer act contrary to this plan. This I did not like, and shall like it still less if it is to be brought as an argument why I cannot stay away on other measures without the imputation of indifference to the subject in question. Another exception will furnish an argument for attendance upon some other question, and thus the whole plan of my secession completely destroyed. I shall be pestered, I know, about the wool business, and perhaps by my own constituents upon the new Income Bill, if Pitt perseveres in the objectionable parts of it; and I shall have no excuse in these and many other cases, unless I can state myself to have acted uniformly upon my scheme of retirement. Always remember that the original ground of retiring was not (that) the questions likely to be agitated were unimportant, but that our attendance in Parliament upon them was useless, and because useless, in some measure hurtful, as tending to drive the country into an opinion that the House of Commons was still a place in which it was worth while to try the effect of argument and reason.

" To show you my zeal upon the question I will *endeavour* to write to Sir Richard Quin; I say *endeavour*, for I really feel it, and so will you, to be a very arduous attempt. I do not believe I should know him by sight, and (though he married my cousin, whom I never happened to see since her marriage,) I never exchanged a word with him except once, or at most twice, that I casually met him at Miles's. However, I will try and send you the letter, which, if you think it can be of use, you may send.

" I am just setting out for home. Your salmon is excellent.

" Yours affectionately,

"C. J. FOX."

TO SAME.

"1800.

" DEAR GREY,

" Pray let me know how your little girl does, and whether you are yet satisfied what her complaint is, as I understood from Fitzwilliam yesterday that you were very doubtful about it, and a good deal alarmed.

" I have just read the debate, in which you seem to have done very well, though I suspect the whole of the debate is very imperfectly given. I congratulate you upon what appears to me a great division, and that in the House of Lords still more so. I suppose it is *their* object to confound *enemies' property* with *naval stores*, which is a question of contraband, not of property. Now, with regard to contraband, the old armed Neutrality admitted they could not carry it on. Then as to the question whether certain naval stores are *contraband*, it is of no consequence in a dispute between us and Sweden or Denmark, because, by our respective treaties with them, it is a point settled, with Sweden that they are not contraband, with Denmark that they are. This may be material to be explained with regard to the importance of the point.

" I could not get Fitz to say anything right about Yorkshire, but I still hope he will *do* right.

" Unless your little girl is better, do not bother yourself with taking notice of all this, which I should not have written but in the hopes that you and Mrs. Grey are quite easy about her.

" Yours affectionately,

"C. J. FOX."

TO SAME.

"St. Anne's Hill. *Thursday.* 1800.

" DEAR GREY,

" Immediately after I had your letter this morning, I read a debate in the ' Morning Chronicle,' and should suspect that your speech and Sheridan's are tolerably taken, and Wyndham's and Dundas's very ill.* The distinction (certainly a just one) of negociating separately from making a separate peace, is not stated, which it ought to have been ; nor is there any appearance of either Sheridan

---

* Probably on Mr. Sheridan's motion, Dec. 1, 1800.

or you having asked, if the Emperor is not now at
Luneville negociating separately, what is he doing?
which I think a very pinching question to those who
assert that he is in their sense faithful to us. More-
over, if he negociates separately and *bonâ fide*, it
must be for a separate peace, as he knows there is no
negociation pending: whereas, if we were to negociate separately, knowing of his pending negociation
at Luneville, we might make our negociation keep
in some measure pace with his, and regulate our
demands or concessions on the probability there
might be of France coming to reasonable terms
with him.

" As to the northern business, I think as you do,
that if it is Bonaparte's doing, it is serious indeed,
otherwise it may be nothing. With respect to the
question itself of the rights of neutral ships, I should
have been more pleased if Sheridan had not made
one of his Pizarro flourishes upon it (which, by the
way, if correctly given in the newspapers, is as bad
in point of taste as of discretion); and I am sure it is
not necessary to caution you against volunteering
a very decided opinion upon such a subject. I am
sure justice is altogether against the British claim,
and I have great reluctance to believe Justice and
Policy to be of different sides in great national concerns. It is a subject that may be well worth your
studying. I am very glad to hear you go on so well
together. Indeed, as to Sheridan, I told you it would
be so. His levities are sometimes disgusting; but
they must be borne with, and he is sure to come

right.   I am sorry for what you say of the inclination
to a maximum ; the folly, after the experience there
has been in different ages and countries, is incredible.
If economy is the object, I am afraid the fundamental
vice of the poor system is a dreadful obstacle ; for
how can you expect those fed by others to be econo-
mising ?   If the poor could maintain themselves, they
would economise fast enough, and might be easily
enticed from a favourite food to a less popular one,
by the cheapness, whether natural or factitious, of that
which it is wished to recommend.   Do not call here
Saturday or Sunday morning, as I shall be from
home, but I return to dinner Sunday, and shall then
be constantly at home.

" Yours affectionately,

" C. J. FOX."

TO SAME.

"St. Anne's Hill.   *Dec.* 1, 1800.

" Dear Grey,

" I hope you did not give quite so unqualified
an approbation to the corn report as the newspapers
state.   There is a part of it that I dislike exceedingly ;
I mean the scheme of parish allowances being, instead
of wheat or money, in substitutes.   The poor complain they are starving, and look (very foolishly, I
admit) to Parliament for redress ; and then the measure
proposed is to give them cheaper, or, as they term it,
worse food.   If anything can exasperate them to mischief, surely this may.   If you were to make the
allowance in money, and facilitate their buying rice

or other substitutes, you would really teach them economy; and when they find that by buying rice, &c., &c., instead of wheat, they can put a penny in their pockets, they will of course do it, that is,—if it is really as good for them as is supposed. And this voluntary economy is a thousand times more effectual for the public, as well as better for the poor, than a compulsive adoption of a new sort of food. Whitbread, you know, told us they bought rice of him more and more every week; that is because they find it answers, and that they are either richer or better by those means. In the other way I own I think it abominable.*

By the way, it is singular that the committee directly imputes the importation having been less than it might have been, to the late season at which the bounties were granted, and thereby throws the greatest blame on the Government for not having made Parliament meet sooner last autumn. This blame was, I remember, last year directly imputed to them, whether by Tierney or Lord Holland I do not recollect; and the answer was, the earlier adoption of bounties could have been of no service. I send you the enclosed to show you that I am not wholly void of all thoughts about politics. I do not perceive any new names, except perhaps Jolliffe's, in the division on Tierney's motion. I see you are all agreed that the naval armistice was impracticable, and I believe

---

* In spite of his dislike to Political Economy as a science, Mr. Fox's common sense generally led him to right opinions on subjects connected with it.

you may be right ; but then it is still more clear that
Bonaparte could not negociate conjointly with the two
powers, there being an armistice in one case and not
in the other. What then was the alternative ? Either
that there should be armistice with neither power—
which Bonaparte did not think fit to state, from
motives of generosity, as it would have carried the
appearance of a menace—or that the two treaties
should be separate. If neither of these plans are
fit to be adopted, there must be war for ever. I
rather think, taking Bonaparte's speech, and comparing
it with Paul's embargo, that there is something serious
brewing in the north ; but then Paul is such a
madman.

" Yours ever affectionately,
"C. J. FOX.

" Pitt says the Emperor has never for a moment
thought of a separate peace.

" Otto says positively that the Emperor was about
to negociate separately. Well, but Otto I suppose is
a lying Frenchman.

" What then are Cobentzel's full powers which he
has opened ?

" Will it be said that though the powers are full,
the instructions limit the use of such powers to a
negociation in which Great Britain is to be a party ?

" I say that such limitation would in any case be a
scandalous juggle, but more particularly where the
armistice is asked for and pressed for by the party
who so limits the power of its ambassador.

"But if our Ministers think otherwise, and that this is fair conduct on the part of Austria, why not imitate it?

"Why not accept Bonaparte's offer of a separate negociation? give full powers to Tom Grenville, and then instruct him not to conclude without Austria?

"The proceeding would be less exceptionable in them than in Austria, because they ask no armistice, or other boon for the purpose of negociation.

"How then is all this to be explained? Will Pitt say that the miserable state of the Emperor's affairs have driven him to a trick which we are not in so humiliated a state as to be obliged to adopt? When it is necessary, I suppose we shall."

On the 5th of February, 1801, Mr. Pitt resigned, and the King sent for Mr. Addington to form a new administration.

TO THE HON. R. FITZPATRICK.

"February 3rd, 1801.

"DEAR DICK,

"The reports of Pitt's being out come from such concurrent authorities, that, with all the disposition in the world to incredulity, I hardly know how to disbelieve them. If they are true, a state of things may happen in which the question of whether I ought to attend Parliament at all; and, if I do attend, what conduct to hold, may force itself upon me rather suddenly; and if it should, I shall want your advice very

much.   When you receive this, you will receive, probably to-morrow, letters and newspapers which will
ascertain the truth of the report.   If you find it is
true, I hope you will come as soon as you can.   At
all events, probably you did not mean to stay much
longer.   I think if the Catholic question comes on I
must attend; but that is not likely, I suppose, to be
immediately.   The story is, that Fitzgibbon and the
Bishops have pushed the King to resist Pitt in this
instance.   This sounds too absurd; but I am quite in
the dark.   The Speaker, all agree, is to arrange the
new Ministry, which is totally incomprehensible ;
and some say, Grenville goes too; others, quite the
reverse.   The Speaker's being employed looks as if
there was some strange juggle, but what is the nature
of it cannot be easily guessed.

" Yours affectionately,

"C. J. FOX.

" P.S—St. John is just come, who says, that,
besides Pitt, all the rest of the Ministers are out,
except the Duke of Portland, the Chancellor, and
Lord Westmoreland.   If this is true it is a new view
of the subject.   *Je n' y comprends goutte.*"

TO SAME.

" *February 10th*, 1801.

" Dear Dick,
    "I hear to-day Canning, Charles Long, and
others, have resigned; and Young One writes word
that Pitt's friends are furious against Addington ; on

the other hand, it is said that Lord Chatham continues. If you can make anything out of all this it is much more than I can. Grey gave notice of a motion for Monday, but I have not yet heard from him; probably after his notice yesterday he was too late, and I may see, or hear from him, to-morrow morning. I wish you were here best; but if not, in London. At present I do not know what his motion is to be, consequently cannot judge whether it may be necessary for me to attend. Nothing but my feeling it to be very much so will make me go. Lord Clare, they say, is Secretary of State; what an absurd fellow he must be! but does not it strike you that Addington appears to be still more so? I think there must be some *dessous des cartes*.

" Yours affectionately,

"C. J. F.

" P.S.—Carlisle and the Marquis of Buckingham are said to join with Pitt, and Lord Gower and Lord Granville Leveson have resigned."

TO CHARLES GREY, ESQ.*

"St. Anne's Hill, *Wednesday*, 1801.

"Dear Grey,

" I am much obliged to you for your letter, which has convinced me at least that it is not altogether the juggle that it appeared; but still there are very incomprehensible circumstances, among which Lord Chatham

* Afterwards Lord Granville.

staying in is a very material one.   However, time will
clear all up.   At all events, my opinion is that what
has passed must do good, whatever may be the upshot
for the present.   The beauty of a Government truly
royal appears in its highest lustre; and if Lord Clare
can and will state in public what you hear he does in
private, the perfidious system of the late Government
will appear in the most glaring colours.   The mischief
of clandestine and unconstitutional bargains for
support, rather than an open and public way of
declaring the intentions, whatever they may be, of
Government and Parliament, will surely be so evident
as to make all reasonable people see that *our* system
of politics is better in every respect than that which
has been pursued—and, by the way, will furnish a most
powerful argument for Parliament acting once more
for itself, and going into the state of the nation; which
I think is by far the best motion that can be made.
As to the time of making it, you upon the spot can
certainly judge better than I; but I own I think it
ought not to be made till the new Ministry are seated,
but whether waiting for them may not bring you so
near the call of the House as to oblige you to wait for
that too, is to be considered.*   I think to wait for
the Ministers, in my view of the subject, is absolutely
necessary; for the way I should reason is this, one of
my great charges against Pitt, and one of my motives
to secession, was that he had the power, and used it,
of preventing the House of Commons from examining

* Mr. Grey's motion on the state of the nation was made on the 25th
of March, 1801.—Parliamentary History.

into the state of the country, and offering the King
salutary advice founded upon that state. Of these
new Ministers I know little, but I will put them and
the House to the test, whether they will pursue the
same system of shifting inquiry, and whether the
House will support them in that system by giving
them the same degree of unconstitutional confidence
which they did to their predecessors. I confess, I
should not think it quite judicious to state that the
country is thrown into any greater degree of danger
than it was in before by the change ; on the contrary,
I would be willing to indulge a hope that the new
men may be better, as they cannot certainly be worse
for the country than the old. The grounds upon
which the old ones go out are a plain proof of the
pernicious system they followed ; and though we agree
with them about Catholic Emancipation, &c., the
manner in which they managed even that business is
highly exceptionable, and, as I think, may fairly be
contended, the only manner by which they could have
failed in obtaining it. If they had endeavoured it in
an open and fair manner, and not in the way of a
bargain, to be conceded from their co-adjutors in the
union, what passed in Fitzwilliam's time and afterwards, proves that they would have succeeded with
ease, but all this is more detail than is necessary at
present ; otherwise, one might ask why there should
be a recommendation from the Throne of the subject
at all, and why Parliament should have the appearance
of doing every act of grace at the suggestion of the
Crown, rather than from its own sense of justice and

policy. As to myself, I cannot go to town while the new Ministry is arranging, for I am sure my going at such a time would be subject to imputations and sneers, which, though I mind them as little as most people, ought to be avoided if possible. When they are settled, if you should put off your motion for the state of the nation till then, and if your opinion is that my attendance would be right for the public and for myself, I will attend; but pray do not say this yet to anybody. I wish very much to see you, and will go over to Ham for that purpose when I know you will be there, and come back to dinner. But as the Duke of Bedford, whom I wish much to see too, has not the reason for staying at home that you have, I hope he will come to me. I hear strange things of Sheridan (*i. e.* of his intention of disclaiming Reform), but I hope they are not true. Pray keep him right if you can. Addington's conduct seems so incomprehensible that I cannot help thinking yet that he must have something to say for himself that we know nothing of. I am a good deal surprised that he has not applied to you. Has he to Moira? or any other opposition man? I wish some strong expression of popular joy could take place upon Pitt's going out. Believe me, it would do more good than anything, and certainly not tend to strengthen but weaken his successors. In the Lansdowne language, I say *Simplicity and Consistency*. Pitt was a bad Minister; he is out—I am glad.

> " Yours affectionately,
>
> "C. J. FOX."

TO THE EARL OF LAUDERDALE.

"*February* 19*th*, 1801.

" Now for politics. I am very anxious to hear
your opinions upon the great point, how far all this
business is or is not, on Pitt's part, a juggle. I do not
expect that you at a distance can determine, when I,
who am so much nearer the scene of action, cannot.
Grey and the rest of our friends seem clear that it is
no juggle, but there are circumstances very difficult to
account for on this hypothesis. Lord Chatham, Mr.
Dundas, Steele, &c. Besides, it is a great gulf to
swallow, to believe that Addington himself should act
without some understanding with Pitt. On the other
hand, if there is a *dessous des cartes*, it is certain that
Lord Spencer and Canning are out of the secret. But
juggle or no juggle, what will be the consequences?
This Ministry cannot last, say our friends. So say not
I, unless the public misfortunes should be such as
would have equally forced out the others. The King's
power is, as we know, great; and when exerted in
conjunction with his ally, the Church, and therefore
in the way and upon the points which he likes best,
and into which he will enter with the greatest spirit,
will not easily be foiled; and you may be sure this
Ministry is one quite to his heart's content. But
what ought to be the conduct of Grey and his friends?
If Pitt, as is generally believed, means neither to move
the Catholic question, nor to support it if moved by
others, ought or ought not Grey or Ponsonby to bring

it on? I say yes, for if Pitt opposes it, as they say he will, it will tend more than anything both to disgrace him and to show the abject state both of the late Ministers and Parliament in the strongest light, if a measure of importance to the welfare, and as Grenville has said, to the safety of the empire is to be waived because the King is said to have prejudices against it. Consider this. Now for myself: I have consented (whether right or wrong God knows, for I think differently about it every five minutes) to attend Grey's motion for the State of the Nation, on Monday 2nd March. My ground is specious enough, that having absented myself because the influence of the late Ministers had made the proceedings of the House of Commons a farce, I return to put the House to the test, whether they will by an implicit confidence make themselves the same abject tools of the present Government as they were of the last. The State of the Nation involves of course everything, and among others the neutral question, upon which Grey says you have very decided opinions. Now I want you upon this, as well as upon the other questions, to give me sense, as the Eton phrase is. My opinion at present is, 1st, That the Law of Nations ought to be according to the principles of the armed neutrality, but that as far as we can collect from decisions, &c., it was (prior, at least, to 1780) generally understood otherwise. 2nd, That it was settled otherwise with respect to Sweden and Denmark by specific treaties between us and them. 3rd, That it is a matter of little or no importance; for Holland being entitled by the treaty of 1674 to carry hostile property, and Holland having been in the one hundred years following the principal, if not the sole carrier for foreign nations, experience shows that it is not materially hurtful to *us*.   4th, That it has upon the face of it no connection with the question of naval stores, &c., because *contraband* is particularly excepted, and because such naval stores, &c., are always the property of the neutral power while on sea, not of belligerent power.   As to the right of search which has provoked this question, I think, 1st, That to search ships sailing under convoy is both an absurd and an insulting proceeding, for if you are bound to be satisfied with the ship papers, unless there be some special ground of suspicion, surely, *à fortiori*, you should be satisfied with the sanction of the neutral Government, unless there be some special cause of suspicion; and, in point of practice, who can believe that we should grant a reciprocity, and because Spain is at war with Algiers (a war that used to be perpetual) suffer the Spaniards to search all our ships of war in the Mediterranean? 2nd. That if even we have such a right, it is one which it has not been usual to exercise, and that in our present circumstances, common sense dictated to us an opposite conduct to that we have held, and rather to waive an accustomed exercise of right than to have introduced a new one.   3rd. That there is something in what Pitt says, that the engagement on the part of Denmark *to protect by force*, &c., *the right of neutrality*, is inconsistent with the engagement of last summer not to send out more convoys.—I go to town the 1st of March; if you can answer this time enough for me to get it here on that day, which will be Sunday, that will be best; if not, direct to me at General Fitzpatrick's, Arlington Street, for I do not know where I shall be. When we are beat on the State of the Nation, I mean to attend no more; unless the Catholic question is brought on, and in that case upon that only. Do you think they could have picked out any one fellow in the House of Commons so sure to make a foolish figure in this new situation as Addington? I think not."

TO SAME.

"February, 24th, 1801.

" Dear Lauderdale,

" The King is certainly very mad, but I believe it will not be formally notified to both Houses till Friday. All sorts of absurdities are in agitation (I believe again) with those who are likely to have the power of forming arrangements; and the consequences (I believe again) will be that all those you wish well to will be out of the scrape. But all this may be otherwise, and if it should be, all of us, and most especially myself, will be helpless in the extreme without you."

TO CHARLES GREY, ESQ.

"St. Anne's Hill. 1801, Friday.

" Dear Grey,

" I send you part of Lauderdale's papers. I will send you the remainder by Sunday's post, but they are only extracts. I send also the Birmingham paper. I saw Moira just before I got out of town yesterday. His conversation was all right; but as to the great accession which he supposes the know-ledge of his having joined us to bring to your motion, I am not quite so sanguine, especially as he named no one person. However, it is pleasanter, at any rate, that he should appear openly acting with you, than to go on with a sort of secret com-munication that looks like an intrigue without being one. If his information is correct, there is no danger of a Regency; which I am heartily glad of. As to the new Ministry, I am so doubtful whether it is best they or the old one should be appointed, that I hardly know, if I had the choice, which way it would be. Fitzwilliam is very eager for bringing on the Catholic question, and seems to be persuading G. Ponsonby and others to it; but I, who see the pro-priety of bringing, or rather, indeed, the extreme impolicy of not bringing it on in a still stronger light than even *he* does, am totally against using much persuasion on the subject; and it is but fair to say that most of those whom I have heard speak upon the subject are against my opinion. Lauderdale, Fitzpatrick, Hare, and Thanet, are the only persons besides Fitzwilliam who appear at all decidedly for it. I did not therefore mention it to Moira, but I should guess he would be against it too. Mrs. A.'s cold is still bad. She sends you a violet of a size which I much doubt if you can equal at Ham; and its sweetness is in proportion to its size. I have read

Luder's Report, and am quite confirmed in my opinion in favour of Tooke. Some decisions, if there are any such, against clerks' voting at elections prior to 1664, should be produced, which in my judgment would completely decide the cause before impartial judges. Piggott thinks there are many such.

" Yours ever affectionately,

" C. J. FOX."

TO SAME.

" St. Anne's Hill, Wednesday, 1801.

" Dear Grey,

" Both Mrs. A. and I are very much obliged to you in giving us such early intelligence about Mrs. Grey, and are very happy to hear all is so well. Dick, who is gone to town to-day, was very glad to hear you have put off your motion, and I think it was clearly right. I am glad you were so pleased with Sheridan and with the appearance of the House. If I were inclined to refine, I might say that Pitt's *cut* upon my secession (which, however, in my paper does not appear) being applauded, looks as if the House, though not favourable to *him*, were still willing to support him against *me*—and that, therefore, it would be best that I should stay away. From the moment you and the Duke of Bedford left me, I began to repent the promise I made you, and passed most part of the following twenty-four hours in thinking how foolish I had been, till Dick came on the Monday; and though his opinion in favour of my going put me in much better humour with my determination, it has not quite persuaded me it was right. However I am glad it was settled any way, for I never was in a greater state of indecision in my opinion; and nothing is so unpleasant as to be thinking the same thing over and over again, and seeing it sometimes one way, sometimes another. As to *staying*, unless circumstances quite unforeseen should occur, I have nothing like irresolution. I am afraid you are over sanguine about the division : but you do not say what numbers you should reckon good. I think they will not give you the State of the Nation ; but in case they should, you should determine as soon as possible upon your first motion in the committee. Everything seems to confirm the notion that Pitt (wishes for) a motion from our side on Catholic Emancipation—and yet how he can justify himself is inconceivable. I dare say some negotiation is attempting ; but that (they) should employ Cazales, without some previous knowledge that the employing him would be agreeable to Bonaparte, is incredible.

" Yours ever,
"C. J. FOX."

TO THE HON. R. FITZPATRICK.

" March 16th, 1801.

" DEAR DICK,

" Many thanks for your letters. If the Catholic business is to come on, a petition would be by far the best mode. I cannot help thinking there is some hitch ; why did not Addington kiss hands ? Perhaps, upon a view of the vessel, he thinks it too crazy to trust to, or, at least, requires a little time to satisfy himself as to its soundness. I wish I knew about the Call and about Tooke's business, for I should neither like to make two jaunts of it nor to stay so long as from Tuesday to Tuesday. Pray continue to write. In the newspapers Sir L. Parsons's speech seems pretty good, and Lord Castlereagh's rather flat.* Surely George Ponsonby ought to have spoken. I cannot help suspecting that the King is not quite so well as he appeared upon his first returning to his recollection."

TO SAME.

"April 2nd, 1801.

"Dear Dick,

"I hear from authority I cannot doubt that the King is so ill again that something will be to be done. It is not reasonable to call you back the moment you are gone; but pray whenever you hear this intelligence confirmed, so as to make you think that business of consequence must come on in parliament, pray make no delay in coming. Mrs. A. makes me write this, because she knows how very helpless I am in difficult circumstances without advice."

TO SAME.

"April 9th, 1801.

"Dear Dick,

"It is very extraordinary, but so it is, that I have heard nothing more since I wrote last concerning

---

* On the 12th of March, 1801, Lord Castlereagh moved for leave to bring in a bill to continue the Irish martial-law acts. Mr. Sheridan moved an adjournment; and his motion was supported by Sir Lawrence Parsons. The motion for adjournment was negatived without a division.

the King's health.   Everything, however, confirms
the notion of his being ill.   The communication to
the House of Commons was not by message, as it
had been announced; and Lord Eldon is not yet
appointed.   The King not having been present at
chapel, too, at Easter time, is very remarkable.   It is
reported Lord Eldon has said that he must have a
quarter of an hour's conversation with his Majesty
before he accepts; but a favourable quarter of an
hour has not, I suppose, been found.   I will let you
know, of course, if I hear anything authentic; but
the case in which I wish you not to wait for my letter
is a possible one; I mean that you may hear from
the newspapers, or otherwise, certain accounts of his
situation being to be announced a day or two before
you can get my letter, which goes round by London.
With regard to the Baltic, the common notion is that
the enemy is so much better prepared than had been
expected that the Admiral has sent for fresh orders.
At any rate, our Ministers make, I think, a ridiculous
figure in the affair; however I do not think they will
nail themselves to the mast.   There is a boldness in
going on so, with a mad King, that I own surprises
me; but it looks as if their determination was taken to
do so."

TO SAME.

" 1801.

" Dear Dick,

" Many thanks for your letter.   I can, no more
than you, discover the grounds upon which Grey

and Young One are so sanguine. Pray continue to write. I wish I had thought of desiring you to be at their Friday's dinner to-day, for I hear strange conversations go on there, and that Tierney holds very imprudent language with regard to me. This, as you may imagine, I do not care about; but old friends ought to be put upon their guard against at all giving in to his notions. Bonaparte has been moderate and wise, and the pacific character seems to me what he at this time so much affects, that my opinion is, this Ministry, if they will give up the nonsensical neutral question, may have peace with him. The more I think of it the more I think it madness not to move the Catholic question ; I mean for those who have any wish to be ever concerned in public affairs. For me, who have no such wish, but quite the contrary, it is another thing: and if others do not think of moving it, I shall not urge them to it."

TO THE EARL OF LAUDERDALE.

"St. Anne's Hill, *April 5th*, 1801.

" Dear Lauderdale,

" I have not heard one word more concerning what I mentioned in my last. Indeed I have had fewer letters from London than usual. They speak, some of them—of the King's having had paralytic strokes; and the delay in appointing the new Chancellor, as well as the giving up of the intended mode of communication to the House of Commons by message, seems to confirm in a great degree the intelligence upon which I wrote to you. But yet the

Ministers seem to go on undauntedly. I think things cannot last so, and that either they will be compelled to state the real situation of the King to the public, or that it must be demanded from them. If so vigorous a measure as this last should be necessary, you will see plainly how much we shall want the best counsels we are masters of. I hope therefore you are coming, but I thought it necessary to let you know that my former intelligence has had no direct confirmation, as it is possible you may consider it as in some degree shaken by nothing having happened publicly in consequence. The next news from the Baltic will be curious at least, though perhaps according to my view of things, not very important.

" Yours ever."

TO SAME.

"April 9th, 1801.

" Dear Lauderdale,

" I am very sorry to hear of your ague ; there is certainly something very particular in the season, for even I had one day some feverishness, with a cold : and though I got rid of it so shortly, I had a degree of weakness for some time after it, that seemed quite unaccountable after so short an illness. I found drinking some more wine than usual set me quite right, or nearly so ; but as your case is so much worse you should take bark as well as wine, but the wine I believe to be the more efficacious of the two. I have heard nothing more from any authority since I wrote last, but all the letters from London agree in representing the King as very ill, and wholly incapable of business. It is said Lord Eldon declared he must have a quarter of an hour's conversation with him before he took the great seal, but no fit quarter of an hour has been found. I think his not having been well enough to appear at any church or chapel on Easter Sunday is a very strong circumstance; nor is it clear that any one person, except his keepers, has seen him lately. He certainly was a long time without seeing the Queen, and whether or not he sees her now regularly, is not, I believe, known. Loughborough told me himself that he did not see him when he signed the Commission for the Brown Bread Bill; and, therefore, *non constat*, that he saw any Minister when he signed the Commission for the last Bills. Their audacity in going on so is quite incredible; but it looks as if they had taken their determination for that purpose; though St. John, in a letter I have from him this morning, says there is again talk of a Regency."

TO SAME.

"*April 17th,* 1801.

" DEAR LAUDERDALE,

" I do not know how it happened, but I received your two letters of the 10th and 13th both this morning. I hope you are not set out, if travelling was at all likely to be hurtful to you, as the King certainly must be something better. You have seen in the newspapers that he had a Council, and I find too that he has seen the Prince of Wales. Your speculations about the Baltic were very wrong, and so I suspect will be the very sanguine ones which, as I am told, are entertained in London from Paul's death. The Hanover business leads to an odd question enough, concerning how far in a negotiation the interests of Great Britain and the Electorate are to be considered as united or distinct. To be sure, in this instance, Hanover has suffered on account of her being under the same Sovereign as Great Britain, but yet she is not in any way an ally of ours, and much less a part of us."

TO SAME.

"April 22nd, 1801.

" DEAR LAUDERDALE,

" I am very glad you did not stir, as you were so unwell. I dare say perseverance in bark and wine will soon set you up however. I think just as you do as to what is to be wished, and if I had written yesterday I should have said that what we wish was likely to be the case at least for some time. To-day I hear differently : and that Willis's people, after having been sent away, have been again sent for to Kew. This is so probable from all that I have heard, that I believe it ; but whether it be true or not, there is every reason to think, that if he is not again violently ill, he will sink into perfect imbecility , but this may be gradual, and upon the degree to which it is so, in a political view, much will depend. I rather suspect the public are pretty well prepared to expect such a thing happening, but this is all guess."

TO ROBERT ADAIR, ESQ.

"1801.

" As to how far the state of the King's health should be noticed to-morrow by Grey, is a point upon which those who heard Addington's speech, and are in the way of hearing recent news from Kew, must be far better able to judge than I. But indeed if I were upon the spot, it is a matter in which I would rather act than advise, as there is a risk (though I confess in my judgment no great one) of the person who mentions it incurring a considerable degree of popular odium. My opinion is that if Willis and his people are with the King he is not fit to govern, whatever his apparent state of sanity may be, and that it turns chiefly upon that point. Whoever is in fear of the rough prescriptions that such physicians may prescribe, cannot be a free agent, even supposing him to be rational. But whether this opinion of mine would be generally adopted I know not.

" Yours ever,

" C. J. FOX."

TO THE EARL OF LAUDERDALE.

" May 11th, 1801.

" Dear Lauderdale,

" I agree with you in a great measure ; but yet there is a point at which patience ought to cease, and there is some advantage in having to charge the enemy with having criminally delayed the bringing on of the

business.   However as my inclination, whatever may
be my judgment, is very strong indeed for forbearance,
I shall by no means urge any one to action.   In the
meantime Grey, and, as I hear, the Duke of Bedford,
(whom I have not lately seen) are determined to say
something.   I learnt nothing new about the King
when I was in London ; all accounts seem to agree
that he was not allowed to see the Queen, nor any
other part of his family, and that the Ministers transact
business with him by letter."

TO CHARLES GREY, ESQ.

"St. Anne's Hill, *Thursday,* 1801.

" Dear Grey,

   " If the enormity of the measure were a reason
for my attendance, I agree with you, that the Indemnity
Bill ought to bring me to town immediately.*   But
this is not the rule by which I govern myself in regard
to attendance.   If it were, I would not have staid
away from the Martial Law Bill, the repeated suspen-
sions of the Habeas Corpus, and least of all, from
that dreadful law, making loose discourse with sailors
and soldiers capital.   My only motive for attending
occurs when I have thought myself, or have been
persuaded by others, that my doing so might be of
some use.   In this instance I feel sure that it would
not.   A single speech, I do not say from *you,* but
from Jones or Robson, is sufficient to show the

---

* The Indemnity Bill was discussed in the House of Commons on the
5th of June.

tyrannical nature of the Bill; indeed nothing more is required than to notice it.   But then whether its being of so tyrannical a nature will much alarm, or even displease the public, in the present state of things, is another question.   In short, till I see that the public has some dislike (indignation I do not hope for) to absolute power, I see no use in stating in the House of Commons the principles of liberty and justice.   I see by the papers, Law said there were precedents; but I suspect it was a hazarded assertion on his part. The old contrivance in what we called *bad* times was to pass general acts of indemnity under pretence of mercy, and so by a side wind to protect the Ministers of Tyranny, but without any *pretence* (for in some of the cases the numerous exceptions made it only a *pretence*) of mercy to offenders, to indemnify the instruments of power is I believe quite new. . . . . I observe that there is no mention in the preamble of the Report of the Committee, and consequently not the smallest ground laid for supposing the arrests, &c., to have been made upon proper information, or even well-founded suspicion.

" Yours affectionately,

" C. J. FOX."

TO CHARLES GREY, ESQ.

" DEAR GREY,

" I am very much concerned indeed to hear of your father's peerage, more especially as I understand that it vexes you very much.   It is undoubtedly a provoking event; but according to my notion, the constitution of the country is declining so rapidly, that the House of Commons has in great measure ceased, and will shortly entirely cease to be a place of much importance. The whole, if not gone, is going, and this consideration ought to make us less concerned about the particular situation (in regard to the public) in which we may be placed. The only glimmering of hope which I see is from the Court, when that shall fall into other hands, and the Court, without any invidious consideration of particular characters, is a miserable foundation to build a system of Reform and Liberty upon. However, if that opportunity does offer, we owe it to the country not to neglect it : and in such an event the want of you in the House of Commons will be a want indeed. Upon the whole, I consider the probability of your being obliged at some time to leave the House of Commons as of less importance than it would have been in former days. The unpleasantness of your father, to whom you are so much attached, receiving what he thinks a favour from these people is another question, and is, I admit, considerable; but the same affection for him, which in one view makes the thing more felt by you, must serve in another to reconcile you to whatever pleases him.

" My newspaper must, I am sure, have given very imperfect accounts of the debates on the Indemnity Bill, but I was not sorry to see in another article that the Attorney General has threatened to revive the Writ of Attaint against Juries. I suppose it was only a vapour, but even that vapour might do good if the indignation of the country were capable of being roused by anything.

"Yours affectionately,

"C. J. FOX."

TO THE EARL OF LAUDERDALE.

"*June* 17*th*, 1801.

"Dear Lauderdale,

"The pacific declarations of the 'Moniteur' cause a good deal of expectation in town, as I am informed, and certainly there is nothing easier than to make peace if the two sides wish it. Though the K. may be in a certain degree recovered, I do not think he will venture to interpose any difficulty in its way, which, if he were in the complete possession of his understanding, he most certainly would; but the Willises will certainly prescribe acquiescence, and he will not refuse their prescription.

"Your thirteen volumes folio frighten me, but I shall certainly like to see some of them by and by. If it would not be too much trouble, I should like to have a copy of that part of the Index which relates to the period between James's accession and his abdication.

"The Woburn party takes place on the fifth of next month. I suppose it is hopeless meeting you there, but change of air would be very good for you in recovering strength, and it would give many of us great delight. I have a great desire to compare our speculations upon public affairs, but after all it is only for amusement, for I do not think anything now likely to occur which would give even you, and much less myself, an opportunity of doing any good."

TO THE HON. CHARLES GREY.

" St. Anne's Hill, October 5th, 1801.

" Dear Grey,

" I did not receive your letter of the 24th of September till a few days ago, just as I was leaving Holkham, and could not find a moment to write till I came here. I do not think we yet know exactly the circumstances attending the breaking off of the nego- tiation, but, whatever they may be, and whether Ministers shall appear to be more or less blameable in their conduct of it, I feel no inclination to depart from the plan of absence, and am very glad that you are of my opinion. Whether the measure was ever quite right I have always had my doubts, but having taken it I think it far best to adhere to it, with the exception perhaps of going once in the Session to move either Reform or general Inquiry, but even in regard to this exception I am not very decided unless there should be great encouragement to it out of doors. I am very glad Wyvill is so sanguine about Yorkshire. I will try what I can do with the Duke of Norfolk, but he has of late been hanging back strangely. Nothing, however, is so likely to set him a going as a change of opinion, if it should be at all general, in the West Riding. I think the Reso- lutions, which I return you, very proper. You have heard probably of the violent measure they are taking

in Scotland of expelling from the Faculty of Advocates,
and consequently depriving of his practice, a man
because he is concerned in an opposition newspaper.
I think this enlightened age, as it is called, is as
much given to persecution as the most barbarous.
The transportation of the Deputies and Directors is
not perhaps quite so bad as that of Muir, Palmer, &c.,
because there is the pretence at least of danger from
their stay ; but such pretences are seldom wanting to
persecutors, and are always false.   Men persecute
because they love persecution, and so far am I from
believing fear to be the true cause of persecution, that
I begin to think that fear is the only motive that ever
can persuade men to suffer those who differ in opinion
from them to breathe the same atmosphere with them.
This is not pleasant philosophy, but I am afraid it
is true.

   " As you do not mention Mrs. Grey, I take for
granted that she is well.   I have had very good
sport in Norfolk, and have great delight in the
thoughts of passing the winter without going to
London except for a day or two.

" Yours ever affectionately,

" C. J. FOX.

TO THE HON. T. MAITLAND.*

" 1801.

   " DEAR MAITLAND,

      " I am much obliged to you for your two

------

* This letter seems to be addressed to the Hon. Thomas Maitland, afterwards General Sir Thomas Maitland, successively Governor of Ceylon, and
of Malta and the Ionian Islands.

letters, and entirely agree with you that the thing must have happened from some sudden turn here. However it may have happened, it is an excellent thing, and I do not like it any the worse for its being so very triumphant a peace for France, who, except Ancona, does not give up any part of her conquests. Indemnity for the past and security for the future are now evidently construed into Ceylon and Trinidad. I do not know why you should consider it, however, as a mere truce—I hope better. The sense of humiliation in the Government here will be certainly lost in the extreme popularity of the measure. I expect there never was joy more universal and unfeigned, and this rascally people are quite overjoyed at receiving from Ministers what, if they had dared to ask it, could not have been refused them at almost any period of the war. Will the Ministers have the impudence to say that there was any time (much less that when Bonaparte's offer was refused) when we might not have had terms as good? Bonaparte's triumph is now complete indeed; and, since there is to be no political liberty in the world, I really believe he is the fittest person to be the master."

TO THE HON. CHARLES GREY.

"St. Anne's Hill, *October 12th.*

"Dear Grey,

"You will probably have learnt from the newspapers that at the Shakespeare I expressed my perfect approbation of the peace.* I think I could do no

---

* The Preliminaries of Peace were signed on the 1st Oct. 1801.

otherwise, though upon this, as upon other occasions, I should have been glad if it had been possible to have known your opinion.

" I have, however, no doubt but that it is the language we ought all to hold, the question not being between peace now and peace years ago, nor even between these terms of peace and any others; but simply this peace, such as it is, and a continuation of the war. How Pitt will defend it, it is difficult to conceive; but it is universally believed he will; what indemnity or security he will find I know not, nor how he can deny that these, or better terms, were to be had long ago, and consequently that all the money and lives lost since that period at least have been squandered wantonly and wickedly. You will have observed of course that France does not give up one acre she possessed before the war or conquered during the course of it. Windham is said to be miserable; Lord Buckingham, &c., &c., are much against it; but whether Lord Grenville is included in this description I have not learned with certainty. I mean to give it my support some one day in the House of Commons, but whether that day shall be the day of the Address will depend in a great measure upon your plans. If you mean to be in the House the first day I will be there too, but if you defer your coming till the day the preliminaries are taken into consideration, I had rather be there the same day. I am sure you cannot differ materially with me about the line to be taken.

The worse the conduct of the late Ministry, the

more excusable an inglorious peace, and *vice versá,* the approbation of such a peace as this is the most decided condemnation of them. With regard to the present men, this should be put home, and that their only defence must consist in the desperate state of things produced by their predecessors. In regard to the public opinion upon the subject, my belief is that there never was more genuine and general joy upon any public event. I know that in London, and I heard too in Liverpool, there are some who abuse it; but in general it is far otherwise. Even those who are most dissatisfied only say that *every gentleman* is against it and every blackguard for it. I dare say Pitt has taken, upon the whole, the most judicious line, because both I and you, who do not wish him well, would rather have wished probably that he had taken a different one ; but, on the other hand, he must make a figure both ridiculous and odious. Pray write a line. I cannot attend more than one or two days at most ; but both in the choice of those days, and as far as I can consistently in the line I shall take when I do attend, I wish to be entirely guided by your wishes and opinion.

" Yours affectionately,

" C. J. FOX."

TO SAME.

" St. Anne's, *October 22nd.*

" Dear Grey,

" I do not know whether my speech was or was

not misrepresented, but I think it very likely that it
really was liable to the interpretation you deprecate,
and in that respect no doubt it was indiscreet ; but
you know that of late I have not considered much for
myself what in a political view may or may not be
judicious.   I feel however, as you do, that the power
of France is truly alarming, but the hope of diminishing or restraining that power has been, in my opinion,
long *gone by*.   Nor do I think that any arrangement
of those points which alone were (or indeed could be) in
discussion during the late negotiation, would much
have affected that question.   If, for instance, we had
retained Martinique, Sta. Lucia, the Cape of Good
Hope, Pondicherry, &c., I do not think we should
have been a whit less in danger from France in time
to come.   If I were inclined to cavil at all at the
terms, I rather think I should blame the having preferred Trinidad or even Ceylon to Minorca, or Malta,
for a port in the Mediterranean is something.   I have
heard nothing more of the probable conduct of individuals since I wrote last. Pitt will support the peace
certainly, but I do not agree with you that he is bound
to do so from his conduct respecting the Lisle negotiation.   He has since that time rejected two offers
from Bonaparte at periods when he could not doubt
but he might have as good terms as these, and has
disclosed that his proposal at Lisle, though sincere,
was rather in compliance with the public opinion than
from his own, and (he thinks) the rejection of it by
the French was an *escape* on our part.   Besides, the
French have carried their point, which he stated to be

so intolerable, of not negotiating concerning any territory annexed to the Republic. I wish, as you do, that the French had shown more spirit in preserving their own liberty ; but that is not, strictly speaking, our affair. The power of the Republic is certainly an evil, but it is an evil which has been the unavoidable result of the nature of the attack against it. If the war had continued, this evil would probably have become greater, or at least our means of resisting upon future occasions would most certainly have become less. I could have been very well content to stay till the day upon the preliminaries, but Fitzpatrick's opinion and yours seeming to be that the first day is the proper one, I shall attend on the Address, but not speak to *make* a debate, only in case one happens that gives me a proper opportunity. I fear, however, that whatever happens, I cannot with propriety be absent on the day when the peace makes the regular subject, and so I shall have two days instead of one, which is in itself bad enough, beside the increased chance of saying indiscreet things which I feel to be very great ; for the truth is, I am gone something further in hate to the English Government than perhaps you and the rest of my friends are, and certainly further than can with prudence be avowed. The triumph of the French Government over the English does in fact afford me a degree of pleasure which it is very difficult to disguise. I take for granted Sheridan will *not* be there, and that if he is he cannot abstain from abusing the peace. As to the ruin of England being sealed, I do not know how that may be, but what I am clear in is, that the only chance of her being saved arises from the peace having been made this year, every evil (and there may be many) which may be attendant on the peace, would have been ten times worse upon a peace which had happened later. As to your coming, if it is inconvenient to you, I am sure I have not the face to press it; but yet I own that upon the day of the preliminaries, I think you *ought* to be there, and may hereafter regret your absence.

" Yours affectionately,

" C. J. FOX."

TO THE EARL OF LAUDERDALE.

" January 7th, 1802.

" Dear Lauderdale,

" I do not like your account of yourself at all, but think you quite right to go Southward. Regrets are vain ; but I wish you had gone upon the first news of the Preliminaries, and escaped this vile winter. I certainly do believe this to be a healthy place, but we have not found it so lately, for Mrs. A. has been ill more than once since the beginning of the winter, and six weeks ago I had a fever, who never had one before. I shall be very happy to have two or three days talk with you here upon many subjects ; but I hope you will not delay your journey so long as to be in England during the March and April winds."

TO THE HON CHARLES GREY.

" St. Anne's Hill, *Wednesday.*

" Dear Grey,

" I had yesterday the enclosed letter from Wyvill, which rather embarrassed me. However, I have answered it as you see by the enclosed copy of my letter, which I send in the same paper with his. I did not quite like stating the fact, as I had it from you in confidence; but, on the other hand, if I had pretended ignorance of the existence of a transaction which has been so much talked of, it would have conveyed a notion that I was dissatisfied with what you had done. I have done for the best, and I hope you will approve. I have a letter from Lauderdale, who is just come to town, and I dislike his account of himself exceedingly. I heard from another quarter that he was nine days coming from Howick; I have seen nobody, nor heard anything of what is going forward; the adjournments are to me quite unintelligible—making Rose and Long Privy Councillors is to be sure ridiculous enough, but it is no matter.

" Yours ever affectionately,

" C. J. FOX."

MR. WYVILL TO MR. FOX.

" Burton Hall, *January 14th,* 1802.

" Dear Sir,

" Yesterday I received from a friend in the North the pleasing intelligence that Mr. Grey, finding a mild reform *would not,* or perhaps, to speak more properly, *could not* be conceded by the Minister, had refused the offer of a high office in Administration, and broken off the treaty for a coalition. It is impossible he could act more usefully for his country, more honourably for himself, or more worthily as your friend. Doubtless you, as the person principally concerned, would be the first whom he would inform of this honourable conduct, and I hasten to congratulate you upon it : and to express my earnest wish and hope that it will be steadfastly persevered in, and followed by every other friend of yours, and of reform, except the one who has already receded.

"With every good wish to you, I remain,
"Dear Sir,
"Most truly and faithfully yours,
"C. WYVILL."

MR. FOX TO MR. WYVILL.

"DEAR SIR,

"I did not till yesterday receive yours of the 14th. With respect to what you have heard, it is true that Mr. Grey, at the request of persons for whom he has the greatest deference, had some conversation with a member of the present Administration, but to say the treaty was broken off is not quite so correct a description of the transaction as to say that what passed in that conversation did not afford any ground for any treaty or negotiation. It would on many accounts be improper to enter into particulars any further than to express my perfect confidence that Grey never will, or ever can, either on the subject of Reform, or on any other, act otherwise than is consistent with his own honour and the good of his country. It is said the present Ministry promise very fairly upon many points, but I am not much inclined to give them credit.

" I am, &c."

TO THE EARL OF LAUDERDALE.

" January 20th, 1802.

" DEAR LAUDERDALE,

" I do not like your account of yourself; but think you quite right in your determination to go abroad if mere alteratives are proposed. I do not know Dr. Baily, nor indeed where to find a physician that has any sense. I think I have heard that Pitcairn has some, but I do not know him.

" I should like very much to have the conversation with you which you wish, but as it could not lead to anything to be done by either of us at present, it may be postponed till I go to town—when that will be is uncertain.   *   *   *

" I never remember anything more unintelligible than the adjournment. The truth is, I suppose, that Addington is a fool, and that there is no reasoning upon the actions of such, especially when they have got about them, as he seems to have done, a parcel of people as foolish as himself. Our old friend Pelham is, I think, the man of the most understanding in the set, and he I am told is a cypher."

Jan. 31, 1802.

" Dear Lauderdale,

" I am very sorry Grey is so much affected by
Sheridan's speech. I do assure you that though I
read it with attention, it did not strike me that there
was anything that could be supposed to allude to
Grey, nor does Lord Robert, nor any one else with
whom I have talked about it, conceive it otherwise.
I own, on the other hand, that Tierney and not
Canning seemed to me to be the person attacked, but
was there any harm in that? I shall go to town on
Friday—I leave this on Wednesday. I have a letter
from Grey which mentions Sheridan's speech much as
I suppose he did to you. He (Grey) does not mean
to come, and surely you must have mistaken me when
you told him I thought he ought to come."

Woolbeding, *January* 31*st*, 1802.

" Dear Grey,

" I received this morning yours of the 24th, and
am very glad you approve of my answer to Wyvill.
It is, I admit, very extraordinary, but it is true that I
have not heard one word from Erskine, nor of him,
but from common report. I suppose, by the manner
in which you mention it, that the newspaper report of
the Duke of Portland's going to Ireland is true, and,
if it is, it is certainly a great additional objection

indeed ; but the more I reflect upon what passed, the more I am convinced that there were many insuperable objections, and, consequently, that one more or less is not worth thinking of.* Perhaps even in our own views, supposing all we asked had been granted, we were too moderate ; and I am the more led into this opinion, from the stress which I perceive all the few friends whom I have heard hint at the subject, lay upon a *majority* in cabinet. However, it is now all over, and *alors comme alors* was exactly the right answer in the last conversation. Lauderdale must have mistaken me when he said, *I* think you ought to come. I never said anything like it—I only said that your not coming might occasion some things to be said ; but I added that I thought you ought to pay no attention to anything of the sort, and emphatically that *I* in your case should *not*. I am very sorry you feel as you say about Sheridan's speech. As I read it, there did not appear to be anything that could be construed as glancing at you—nor has anybody, I believe, so understood it. Lord Robert says he understood it exactly as I did. I thought it alluded to Tierney, and to him only, and I feel myself quite sure that it was so meant.

"If Burdett's motion is while I am in town I shall attend it, and shall write to him to day to desire he would fix it accordingly, but rather preferring the 16th or 17th of February to an earlier day, that you may have time to do as you please. I am very happy

---

* I have no information respecting this overture from Mr. Addington to Mr. Grey. It seems to have been at once declined.

indeed Mrs. Grey is got well again. I have heard from Lauderdale, who says he is better. When I have seen him I will write to you.

"Yours ever affectionately,

"C. J. FOX."

TO SAME.

"*February 9th*, 1802.

"Dear Grey,

"I write to you one line just to desire you to tell me whether or not you consider (as I have supposed you to do) all negotiation, and everything that can be called or miscalled negotiation, between you and the Minister to be quite *off* and done away. Your phrase of *alors comme alors* seems to be decisive upon that matter; but I should be very sorry to be mistaken.

"Yours affectionately."

TO SAME.

"St. Anne's Hill, *February 21st*, 1802.

"Dear Grey,

"I was in a great hurry when I wrote to you the short note in London, and concluded besides that Lauderdale had written to you all you would want to know about news, &c. With respect to Lauderdale himself, I ought certainly to have said something, and especially as what I should have said could not be otherwise than agreeable. After the two first days of my seeing him, he appeared to me to be so much recovered from the miserable state to which the violent operations of his medicines had reduced him, that he did not seem the same man, nor indeed to have any other complaint than that degree of weakness which, after what he had gone through, was unavoidable ; when I called upon him the day previous to my leaving town, viz., Wednesday, I was told he was gone out with Lady Jane Long, * which I was very glad to hear as it seemed a confirmation that he was going on mending as fast as possible.   In short, though I do not pretend to much skill as a physician, I feel quite confident that he is *now* in a very tolerable state of health, but if his complaint was, as is supposed, bilious, we all know how liable such disorders are to return.   His spirits were, every day I saw him (except the first), excellent.

" My reason for asking you the question I did, was not indeed anything like a *suspicion* (my dear Grey, how could such a word come from your pen?), but because I believed some persons understood the thing differently.   Even Lauderdale, though he agreed with me in thinking that *you* considered the thing as all over, had his doubts with respect to the construction put on what passed by others.   Now, what others thought was not of any consequence to me, but I wished to be quite sure, and authorised to *say* I was quite sure, with respect to your mode of considering the business.   I wished this for two reasons ; 1st, Because as I was resolved neither by anything I should

* Lady Jane Long, afterwards Lady Jane Houstoun, was sister of the Earl of Lauderdale.

say or do to thwart any plan you could form, it was
material to me to know most distinctly what was the
state of the negotiation, if it must be so called. 2nd,
Because I thought it possible that I might have
conversations with others (Lord Moira and perhaps
Erskine), in which I should like to have it to say
rather upon your authority than my own, that all
negotiation was over. As Moira did not say a word
to me upon politics, and as Erskine knew your
sentiments, this necessity did not occur. If I had
entertained any notion of your considering the thing
in any other way than that in which you do consider
it, I should have avoided threatening an opposition to
the payment of the Civil List Debt ; as it is, I think
you can have no objection to it, whether you attend
it or not. I mean to oppose the payment and aug-
mentation (if such be proposed) *in toto*, and so I think
you would if you attended, but if there is any wish to
direct the attack more exclusively to the late Ministers,
as contra-distinguished from the present, I think a
motion might be made to the following effect :—
' That it was the duty of the Lords of the Treasury,
when they first found the expenses of the Civil List
to exceed in any considerable degree the revenue
appropriated for that service, either to make such
reductions as would provide a fund for discharging
the arrear, or to state the circumstances to Parliament
for the purpose of taking the opinion of the Legislature,
in what manner such excess of expenditure should be
provided for.' Parliament might then have increased
the Civil List if they thought fit, or reduced the

expenditure, and surely, upon such an alternative, Parliament and not the Ministers were to decide. You know I quite despair of anything doing good; but if I were to judge from the experience of past times, profusion of this kind is more apt to strike people in general, than upon a larger scale. I cannot bear the thoughts of going to town again, but yet, I feel I must for *one day* upon this business. I need not say how glad I should be to see you there, but I adhere to the golden rule of doing as I would be done by, and therefore do not ask anything of this sort.

" Yours affectionately,

" C. J. FOX.

" P. S.—When I saw Erskine I had not received your letter ; and I think I understood you so perfectly that I did not judge it necessary to send to him for your letter to him, to which you allude."

TO THE EARL OF LAUDERDALE.

" *February* 23rd, 1802.

" DEAR LAUDERDALE,

" I hope you will stay more than one night on your way ; we want your advice very much on many farming points. My sheep are not like Grey's ox, for though they have had hay, &c., to an amount that frightens me, they are not at all fat. . . .

" From what Pitt said, it looks as if he meant to lay great stress upon what the King gave up for the annuity ; now I have no books here by which I can ascertain what is the King's *right* at his accession. Blackstone, who is commonly perspicuous, is very confused upon this subject; in one place he speaks of the hereditary revenue as if it was settled on the King by the particular Act regulating the Civil List; in another he speaks of the grant as an *addition* only to the hereditary revenue. If the King has at his accession a *right* to the hereditary revenue, it is material to know what that revenue is, as well as by what law or statute it became *his*. By the way in which Blackstone speaks of what he calls the *addition*, it is impossible he can mean only the £120,000 a year, for he calls it a truly royal addition, and says that without it the King would be too dependent on Parliament, nay afterwards hints that *with* it he is perhaps too powerful; now surely £120,000 would not make this difference. If it is an amusement to you (not otherwise) to look into this, and you will let me know what you think, I shall be obliged to you. I should suppose that an inspection of the Acts of Parliament settling the Civil List would make the matter clear at once—but I have them not."

TO SAME.

"*February* 28*th*, 1802.

"DEAR LAUDERDALE,

"Since I wrote to you I looked into the Annual Register 1777, where there is an account of our Debates. To judge from that account, the doctrine of the King's *right* to the hereditary revenue for the purpose of Civil List, was not ventured by the Ministers in the House of Commons; and when mentioned in the House of Lords (it is not said by whom) was scouted. It is very curious how Blackstone has evaded the question, for I am *now* convinced his indistinctness upon the subject is intentional. I have read D. Stewart's Life of Robertson, and like it very much; but it does not I think give the idea of such a man as you represent Dugald Stewart to be. I am very angry besides at what he says of Hume. Religion is one question; but it would require great abilities indeed to persuade me that Hume's system tends to destroy the foundations of morals. I suspect too that he has said this from mean motives. You know I am not very indulgent to such motives in politics, but I am ten times more hostile to them in literary men, and applied to philosophy.* I do not know to what he alludes in Horace Walpole's post-humous works, which I have never read, when he supposes his extravagant praises of Robertson to have been insincere. I know that in private conversation he used to speak of Robertson's works in the highest, and what I thought an extravagant, strain. He rated him as an historian far above Hume."

TO HON. R. FITZPATRICK.

"*March 9th,* 1802.

" My dear Dick,

"I had your letter yesterday, before Lauderdale

* There is no reason for Mr. Fox's suspicion of mean motives, Mr. Dugald Stewart might be timid, but was thoroughly honest and conscientious.

left me. He appears to me surprisingly well, and believes that the agitation he has undergone has rather done good than mischief to his health. As to the Writ, I am clear you would do it better than I, not that you feel less, but that you have more command of nerves and voice than I have in such situations ; I agree with you about the impropriety of Sheridan's being the person ; but it is quite clear that the moving of the Writ does give a good opportunity.* I have my doubts, but I will be governed entirely by the present Duke, yourself, Lauderdale, &c.† I am glad you like Lord Villiers ‡ so well ; he appeared to me, at St. Albans, to be really and deeply affected : and, from what I had seen of him before, I have a favourable opinion of him."

TO SAME.

"March 13th, 1802.

" My dear Dick,

" As, notwithstanding my objections, you have determined that I should move the Writ, I will endeavour to do it as well as I can. I should suppose that a material point on such an occasion is to be short, which is so different from my usual style that it adds much to the difficulty. I think Lord Robert (if he has no objection) the best person that could be thought on to come in now, as he has probably not the smallest wish to do so again. With regard to

---

* The writ for Tavistock on the death of the Duke of Bedford.

† Francis, fifth Duke of Bedford, died on March 2nd, 1802. The writ for Tavistock was subsequently moved by Mr. Fox, in a celebrated speech.

‡ Viscount Villiers, born 1773, succeeded his father, fourth Earl of Jersey, in 1805.

the Duke's intentions for Tavistock, at the general election, I know them, and thought he had mentioned them to Lord John.* His plan was that it should be kept for me in case of my not liking to stand for Westminster, and yet choosing to be in Parliament. This, I told him, I should never wish ; but he said, and I acquiesced, that there was no use in deciding prematurely, before the general election called for a decision. I do not believe he had settled in his own mind who should come in, in case of my refusal, and I believe he avoided doing this, according to his usual attention for the feelings of others, that I might not think I was standing in the way of his favour to any-one else, and be deterred by that consideration from accepting his offer. I should prefer Tuesday for moving the Writ. Write to-morrow to say when you will come. I hope to God the Civil List business does not come on very soon ; if any day next week, pray let me know, that something may be arranged accordingly, for I would not be two days absent from home for the world."

TO SAME.

"*March*, 1802.

"Dear Dick,

"I am rather disappointed at your not coming before Tuesday, because I should have liked to have had some advice with respect to what is to be said on Tuesday. I will be at Holland House soon after two, and if you will meet me there I shall be much obliged

* My father, John Duke of Bedford.

to you. If I do not find you there I shall proceed
directly to Arlington Street. I understand neither
what is expected to be said, nor how what I am to
say is to be introduced. If you can think of anything pray put down a note or two upon paper. The
worst of it is that any eulogium to be short must be
very general. I will do my best, however."

TO THE EARL OF LAUDERDALE.

" March 17th, 1802.

" DEAR LAUDERDALE,

" If you will send me by return of post the paper
in which my speech is taken most at length, and best,
I will look it over and send you a corrected, and may
be an improved, copy, which you shall have either by
the post or the coach on Saturday. Perhaps this may
answer the purpose of the character, as it would be
awkward for me to write so soon upon a subject, after
having spoken on it."

TO SAME.

" March 19th, 1802.

" DEAR LAUDERDALE,

" I shall have no scruple in introducing new
topics, if any occur, that I think I can manage
tolerably; but as there certainly will not be enough
new to give it the appearance of a new composition,
I think it is best it should be in the present form, and
that is the purpose for which I wanted the account of
my speech. I will send it by Sunday's post, which
by your account will be time enough. If there is any

particular topic or circumstance you wish to have
touched, or any which you wish to have treated
differently, if you write to-morrow I can try to
insert it, as I get my letters here, as you know,
early."

TO SAME.

"*March* 21*st,* 1802.

" DEAR LAUDERDALE,

" I thought the business would have been easier
than it is to me. I put off beginning too long, so
that I cannot send it you till to-morrow's post, or
Tuesday morning's coach; but at any rate you will
have it Tuesday morning." *

TO SAME.

March 22*nd,* 1802.

" I WILL send the thing by to-morrow morning's
coach. It will be ill written, and require a careful
correction of the Press."

TO SAME.

"*March* 25*th,* 1802.

" DEAR LAUDERDALE,

" We are very anxious to hear a better account of
you. I am glad you like what I have done; the truth

---

* The Speech on moving the Writ for Tavistock, and that on the Westminster Scrutiny, are the only two speeches Mr. Fox ever corrected. We
see by this letter how difficult the task was to him. Impetuous, rapid, and
hurried in speaking, he was careful, slow, and fastidious in writing.

is that I have taken very great pains with it, though
after all I am far from satisfied.   However, if you
like it, it has occurred to me that, besides being in the
Magazine, it ought to be published separately, and do
away Ridgway's account, which though perhaps full as
like the real speech that I made, is intolerably bad in
the reading, at least to my taste.   However do exactly
as you please, or if you are not well enough to *do*,
tell Adair and he will.   I wish you to *think* too about
the Whig Club.   They should do *something*—but
what ?   If anything were originated before they meet,
it would perhaps be easy to accede, but otherwise they
cannot do other (if they do anything) than originate
something. I am so sure that among the many who feel,
you are the person who feels most, that I would have
your wish implicitly complied with in everything that
is done."

TO SAME.

" *March 26th,* 1802.

" Dear Lauderdale,

" After all Grey must do something upon the
Civil List business; he had better have stayed in
Northumberland, than have been present and neuter.
If he has any intention to support it, he may do so
consistently enough, and lay the blame upon the late
Ministers for not bringing on the question sooner.   I
must oppose it *in toto*, but he need not consider me,
especially as I feel all but quite determined to cut
entirely at the general election."

TO SAME.

"*April 6th,* 1802.

" DEAR LAUDERDALE,

" I cannot help thinking something ought to have been done, and ought still to be done, about publishing my speech in a different way. I am sure, as it is, that vile publication of Ridgway's will be ten times more read than the Magazine. If another publication can take place, I send you two alterations, one is a false print in the Magazine. It is now too late to do what is right, but what ought to have been done is this : as soon as Ridgway's publication appeared, it ought to have been declared unauthentic, and the public desired to wait for an authorised copy of the substance, &c. Perhaps there is a little vanity in all this, but I excuse it to myself by the consideration that the credit of the subject is a little involved in that of the speech."

TO THE HON. CHARLES GREY.

"*May,* 1802.

" DEAR GREY,

" I am not sorry you did not come, as the weather was so very bad. The frost here has done, I am afraid, a great deal of mischief. It was very well I did not go to town for the debate, as I should exceedingly have disliked to have been kept the two days. I hear Sheridan did very well ; perhaps it was rather shabby in me to be absent, but I do not care, and the smallness of the minority makes it of less consequence.

All opposition seems to be out of the question, perhaps for ever; and we may boast, I expect, that we were the last of the Romans. I hope you will come. Can you tell me anything of Lauderdale? I do not know where he is.

"Yours affectionately,

"St. Anne's Hill, *Sunday, May*, 1802."   "C. J. FOX.

TO SAME.

"St. Anne's Hill, *Tuesday, May*, 1802.

" DEAR GREY,

"Though I hear your opinion is that Lord Belgrave will not bring on his foolish motion, yet I am sure you will agree with me in thinking that we ought to be prepared in what manner to act upon it. It appears to me that we may either decline attendance upon it, or make a serious opposition to it, as we think fit, without any great impropriety; but I own, I think we ought to do one of these two things. Between them I have little choice, but I am very desirous to do what *you* do, and wish you to be guided entirely by your own judgment.

"If it comes on at all, I suppose, from what Lord Belgrave said, that it will be in the course of next week.* I should like to know the day, if we are to attend, as soon as possible, on account of arranging my going to town. I suppose I must go to the Whig Club on Tuesday.

---

* Lord Belgrave proposed his motion of approbation of Mr. Pitt's administration as an amendment to a motion of Mr. Nicholl, on May 7, 1802. Both Mr. Fox and Mr. Grey spoke in the debate.—Parliamentary History. Lord Belgrave, afterwards Earl Grosvenor, was created Marquis of Westminster during Lord Grey's administration.

" Do you know whether it is understood that Ministers bring on anything on the Definitive treaty? If they do not, perhaps some of the Grenvilles will.

" Yours affectionately,

"C. J. FOX."

TO SAME.

" St. Anne's Hill, Friday, May, 1802."

" Dear Grey,

" I am very much obliged to you for your letter. Your decision is, I believe, quite right: though, I own, *I wished* the other, chiefly however from motives of laziness. I do not think if it were otherwise right for us to be absent, that the attendance of others would be any very material objection with me; but if *you* are present, I think it impossible, nay disgraceful, not to debate the question *à fond.* As to the manner of opposing, I incline in judgment very much to the plan of amendment; but then I hope you will draw, or superintend the drawing of, the amendment yourself. I will get Windham's and Grenville's speeches; and am much inclined to attend Windham's motion, but shall not think myself bound to do so, if the time of it should be very inconvenient to me.* It is not, I suppose, quite impossible that Belgrave may be still desired to waive his motion; or, after having made it, to withdraw it, by Pitt in public, and Addington in private. In such case, I should think we ought not to provoke debate; but to content ourselves with laughing

---

* Mr. Windham's motion for an Address on the Definitive Treaty, May 13th, 1802.

at the whole procedure, and perhaps commending
the prudence of it.   I shall be in town on Tuesday
for the Whig Club, and stay for Belgrave's motion, or
even for Windham's, if either of them come on
Friday ; but if your application to Belgrave succeeds,
and Windham's motion comes on later, I shall possibly
return on Wednesday or Thursday, and go back to
London for the business.   Pray above all things, my
dear Grey, do not fancy that it is possible for you to
be present on the occasion, and not to do your very
utmost.   I know it is very disagreeable to be told
such a thing, as it seems to be setting one such a
task ; but there are occasions where this must not be
minded.

" Yours affectionately,
"C. J. FOX.

"P.S.—Of course I shall be glad to know, as soon
as possible, the arrangement of the motions, but I
suppose you will hardly be in town to-morrow.
Though rather cold out of the sun, it is a delightful
day here : nightingales singing merrily, &c.   Pray
when all this nonsensical business is over, give me a
day or two here."

TO THE EARL OF LAUDERDALE.

"*June 27th*, 1802.

" DEAR LAUDERDALE,
" I have at least made up my mind to come in—
not convinced by reason, but finding the wish among

my friends so general. I am sure I am wrong, but I cannot go against the tide." *

TO SAME.

" *July* 28*th*, 1802.

" Dear Lauderdale,

" We positively set out to-morrow morning,† and I shall be very much obliged to you if you will write to me to let me know how you go on. I cannot help fancying you have a chance.‡ Any letter which you judge will leave London on or before the 10th of next month, should be directed to me at the Poste restante à Bruxelles, afterwards chez Perregeaux à Paris, where I hope to be by the 17th. Pray send me a list of any books that I may have a chance of getting for you, and a memorandum of anything else that I can do for you. Is there anybody you would particularly wish me to see ? I wish there was a chance of your coming yourself to Paris while I am there—suppose the moment your election is over. I advised Burdett to give up, which advice he has not taken, and has been gaining these two days, but I fear there is no chance. I have just learned that they have taken away the business of some of the offices from Coutts, and that it is expected some great individuals will do the same. This seems to be the foolishest thing I have yet heard.

---

* This letter evidently alludes to his coming again into Parliament. See *ante*, p. 363, respecting his coming in for Tavistock.   † For Paris.

‡ In the election of Scotch Representative Peers.

" As I think it possible that some awkwardness might arise to us abroad from Mrs. A.'s not being known to be my wife, I no longer wish it to be a secret that we have been married near seven years." *

TO SAME.

" *November* 18th, 1802.

" Dear Lauderdale,

" I arrived last night and found yours of the 10th. I hope it will not be long before I see you; in the mean time, as to war, I can only say that my opinion is clearly that it will not be. I can tell you my reasons for this opinion in two sentences. 1st. I am sure that Bonaparte will do everything that he can to avoid it. 2nd. That, low as my opinion is of our Ministry, I cannot believe them quite so foolish as to force him to it, without one motive either of ambition or interest to incite them. I have no time to write more.   *   *   *   *   *
I think I shall attend upon the Address, because though, if the Ministry is warlike, I have no hope of dissuading them; on the other hand, if they are pacific, I may serve in some degree to encourage them."

TO SAME.

" *November* 26th, 1802

" Dear Lauderdale,

" I write you one line just before I return to the country, only to tell you that if you are coming, the

---

* This note fixes the date of Mr. Fox's marriage in the summer or autumn of 1795.

sooner you come the better, for I see at least a possibility, if not a probability, of a state of politics arising within these three weeks even, that may make our party, weak and disbanded as it is, of some consequence, and enable us to (do) a real good service to the country. I shall write to Grey when I get home, not to press him to come up, for I suspect that would be in vain, nor am I quite sure that it is necessary at present, but to state to him my notions. Nobody knows anything yet about Pitt, and upon his determination a great deal will depend. The Grenvilles, &c., have studiously brought matters to decided hostility between them and Addington. It was evidently a measure to do so. Your brother spoke very well indeed, and if he had omitted the last two or three sentences, I should have thought his speech perfectly judicious."

TO THE HON. CHARLES GREY.

"St. Anne's Hill, *November 29th*, 1802.

" Dear Grey,

" As I hear Mrs. Grey is expected to lie-in soon, I conclude there is no chance of your coming to town, and you know I am the last man in the world to advise any friend in these times to sacrifice any private considerations to public concerns. It is true however, that there never has been lately a time when I so much wished to have some conversation with you on politics as the present. The state of things is not yet to me quite intelligible, but it must, I think, soon become so, and I see the possibility of circumstances arising in which you may be of more use to the country than I had lately thought it likely for you or any of us to be. The question of peace or war appears to me to be so clear, that I cannot bring myself to doubt of your opinion, though I heard it. Besides the mischiefs of war, in a constitutional view, of which we have had such ample experience, the certain misery it must occasion by the repetition of Income Taxes, &c., &c., and the imminent danger of bankruptcy, a most material consideration in this case is the moral certainty of failing in our object, and of aggrandising France still more than we have done. I therefore lay as a foundation, that the main object at present is to preserve peace, if it can be done with honour, and that it *can*, if our Government are so disposed, I have no doubt. The Grenvilles, &c., cry out for war—Addington *seems* at present inclined to peace, but both are waiting with anxiety, and I believe, *uncertainty*, for Pitt's decision. The Grenvilles seem determined to bring him to one as soon as possible, by declaring themselves (which they did not do accidentally, but as a measure) the determined enemies of the present Ministry, and by intimating that they would bring some question avowedly against them. How will Pitt decide? I think not for the Grenvilles—though, from their stating the necessity of his return to power, it looks as if they had hopes of him ; on the other hand, from what one hears, I scarcely think that he will decidedly support peace, nor perhaps will he be quite cordial to Addington.

In short, I cannot guess what he will do ; but, upon
the various different suppositions, it might be worth
while to consider what we ought to do.　If Pitt is
cordial for Addington and peace, they will not much
want me or even you, and then I suppose things will
go on just as they did last year, sometimes supporting
and sometimes opposing, bringing on or not constitutional questions as may be thought best at the time ;
but if Pitt either joins the Grenvilles or totally absents
himself, or wishes to hold a conduct between war and
peace, but which may be calculated to bring on war,
then Addington may really be in want of your support,
and the support given him may in every view be both
useful and honourable.　In such a case even I would
give something like a regular attendance (only something like however).　Then the arrangement that was
talked of this time twelvemonth might be exceedingly
desirable and practicable too—because, in that case,
Addington would not only wish it, but want it, and
of course would go a different way to work.　Remember that if things should take this turn, *I* must
be, as I was last year, out of the question ; but you
might successfully insist upon many right things
with regard to measures as well as men.　I mention
this because I think it is the best thing that is likely
to happen ; but even putting all ideas of arrangement
of any sort out of the question, if, by our acting with
some vigour in a body, we can prevent war, we shall
have done a most material service to the country, and
probably, too, add some little strength to the party,
if what remains can be so called.　It is the more

material to form some steady opinion upon affairs
now, because it looks as if this question of peace
or war was not, as such questions have usually been,
to be a temporary one, but a sort of controversy likely
to continue for years, unless war put an end to it.
With respect to men, you know my inclination would
rather be to the Grenvilles, as men of some spirit, but
the line they have taken with respect to war, and their
professed desire of reinstating Pitt make any junction
with them impracticable for the present.   If Pitt
should join Addington cordially, and, contrary to my
expectations, this war controversy should drop, then
the Grenvilles may, like all other oppositions, come
at length to popular measures, and then you might
act with them, but this is a distant view. The present
men are, to be sure, *dreadfully* foolish ; I say dreadfully, for they are so much so as quite to frighten one
with the thoughts of having anything to do with them ;
and yet perhaps some, or at least *one* of those we
should bring to them is quite their equal.   I have
seen him, and he seems not to understand or to be
capable of understanding anything that is going
forward, or even of deliberating what conduct he
ought to hold.   I understand (but not from the best
authority) that the Prince has still less opinion of him
than he had ; and I believe his influence in that
quarter has been always overrated.   In short, I begin
to be afraid that, unless you and Lauderdale come
forward, people will say that they must have Pitt or
Grenville, as the only candidates for power that have
common sense.   As for myself, you will have heard

or read in the newspaper what I have been doing.   I
was very anxious to take the first opportunity of
speaking strongly for peace ; among other reasons, for
the purpose of ascertaining what the prevalent disposition in the House of Commons was, and I found
it rather such as I wished than what I could hope.
I have not for many years, certainly not since the
Russian business,* found the House so much with me
as in my second and longest speech upon the Address;
and, as far as I can judge, notwithstanding the flash
in the newspapers, this part of the country is as much
inclined to peace as ever.   At Liverpool, I am told, it
is much otherwise, and, perhaps, in some other
places ; of the north I have not yet heard, but if
Wilberforce is any symptom of Yorkshire, he spoke
stoutly for peace.   I mean to attend whenever any
question on peace or war comes on.   On the army
day I shall state my opinions in favour of small
establishments, in which, however, I expect hardly
anybody to concur ; but I am sure I am right, even
with a view to external affairs, and, with a view to the
constitution, it is but too plain a case.   I was glad
to hear that Lord St. Vincent had said, that, let who
would go to war, *he* would not.   Maitland made a
very good speech, only a little imprudence at the end
of it.   Mrs. Fox desires to be remembered to you.
As to Paris and its wonders, museum, &c., when
we meet.

    " Believe me, dear Grey,
       " Ever most affectionately yours,
                " C. J. FOX."

        * In 1790.

TO THE EARL OF LAUDERDALE.

"*December 5th,* 1802.

" There can be no reason, I think, for your coming sooner than the time you mention. I know not a word more than when I wrote from London, only that by some letters I have to-day, it looks as if the Ministers last Thursday appeared more warlike than they had done ; but by some accident the newspaper, giving an account of that debate, has missed and I do not know what passed. I shall go to town for the Whig Club on Tuesday, and the Army on Wednesday, and, if I learn anything material, will let you know.

" Yours ever.

"C. J. FOX.

" I wrote a long letter to Grey, which, if you call there, and he has not destroyed it, I hope he will show you."

TO SAME.

"*December 8th,* 1802.

" DEAR LAUDERDALE,

" I have only time to write a line before I go down to the House, that you may get it before I set out. I shall be very glad of the potato oats you mention, and will certainly try them, though in some countries, as I am informed, they have failed.

" The name of the flower is Cypripedium, or Ladies' Slipper ; it is not to be had here, but, though rare, grows wild in Scotland."

TO THE HON. CHARLES GREY.

Tuesday, December, 1802.

" DEAR GREY,

" Since I received yours of the 17th, Lauderdale has been here, and I do not think your account of his healthy appearance has been at all exaggerated. He certainly, ever since I knew him, never looked near so well. With respect to your determination about yourself, I am very sorry, but that is all I can say. I did not mean to make you so foolish a compliment as to express a hope that you could do much in checking the career of despotism in these times, but simply that without you there would be no check at all, and so I fear it will be. The observations I have made since I wrote last, confirm me in the opinion that the time when you could be of real service is more remote than I imagined it to be when I wrote to you my first letter ; but yet it may, and I think must come in time. I agree entirely that an offer of the sort, to which you allude, must *come* and not be sought ; but I thought that so clear a point, that I did not think it worth mentioning. Nay more, it must not only originate from them, but from a full conviction in them of its necessity, or no good can come of it.

" With regard to the Consul, I am very obstinate in my opinion that he meant nothing insulting to England either in the German or Swiss business. The impertinent paragraph in the ' Moniteur ' was of a

subsequent date to those transactions, and was the
consequence of anger, either at our actual, or at our
intended interference ; an anger, by the way, not
unmixed with real surprise, which, however impertinent it may be, is rather in favour of my opinion,
that nothing was intended irritating to this country.
Perhaps I should go as far as you in thinking the
Swiss business a *just* cause for war ; but, on the
other hand, I am sure you will agree with me, that,
in this instance, it would have been nothing but a
base and hypocritical *pretence* which would not have
imposed upon one man of sense in Europe ; and that
the war, even if successful in general, would terminate
in our having Malta, or the Cape, or Cochin, or in
anything rather than Swiss liberty or independence.
When I said I thought Bonaparte right in the German
business, I meant as to manner, as well as matter, and
that so important a party to the treaty as France
was, had a right to insist upon its being executed in
some reasonable time. But, right or wrong, he could
not conceive England interested in the business ; as
you cannot but remember with what pertinacity both
Pitt and the Ministers maintained that they had
nothing to do with that treaty in any view, and that
it was best that they should not. My notion about
Bonaparte's politics is this—that when I first went to
Paris he was foolishly sore about our newspapers, but
not ill disposed to the Ministers, and still less to the
country. At this time he was out of humour with
Austria, and determined, as I suspect, not to give way
a tittle to her. Afterwards, when he suspected

(whether truly or falsely) that we should interfere,
he began to be terribly afraid of a war, which might
in France be imputed to his rashness. In consequence of this fear, he did make concessions by no
means inconsiderable to Austria, and immediately
felt bitter against us who were the cause of his
making them. But as that bitterness (according to
my hypothesis) arises principally from the fear he has
of our driving him into an unpopular war, I do not
think it will for the present prevent peace ; nor,
indeed, if pacific counsels and language are used here
that it is at all likely to be lasting. You may
depend upon it that commerce, and especially colonial
commerce, is now the principal object, and upon those
subjects they have a stupid admiration of our systems
of the worst kind, slave trade, prohibitions, protecting
duties, &c., &c., &c.* However, bad as their systems
may be, France must in some degree recover her
commerce, and the more she does, the more will she
be afraid of war with England. ' But what signifies
France ? Bonaparte can do what pleases *him*, without consulting the Nation.' This is not true in any
country beyond a certain extent, and I feel morally
certain that Bonaparte and all his friends are of
opinion that war with England is the only event that
can put his power in peril. An army is a most
powerful instrument of government ; but that it is
not in all cases one upon which dependence can be
had, is proved by the history of every country where

* Here is another proof that practically Mr. Fox was a sound political
economist, however much he disliked the name and the study.

very enormous armies are maintained ; and out of
the army he cannot expect the approbation of any
one individual if he engages in any war with us to
which he is not actually driven. Whatever ridicule
may be attempted to be thrown upon the title of
Pacificator, you may be sure that whatever hold he
has (perhaps no great matter neither) upon the
people of France, arises from the opinion that he
alone could make the peace, and that he will be the
best able to maintain it. Now, after I have said all
this, I admit the justness of your apprehensions that
the hostile language and *attitudes* (if one must use the
new-fangled word) of the two nations may produce
war even against the wishes of the two Governments ;
and to lessen that danger, as far as I shall at present meddle in politics, shall be my aim. The
question of Malta cannot certainly be brought on by
us, but will come on either by a specific address on
the subject from the new opposition, which however
is not likely, or the Government actually giving it up
and acquainting the House with their having done
so ; upon which occasion the Grenvilles must
certainly move some censure, or at least inquiry.
Your idea of dividing with Tom Grenville, who
certainly was in the right, was quite out of the
question ; for they made no motion, and would not
have voted for the chairman's leaving the chair if I
had moved it. Sheridan's speech has been, as you
will have observed, finely puffed.

> " Yours affectionately,
>
> "C. J. FOX.

" P.S.—I hear Pitt's language is decidedly pacific.
I hope, if you come, it will be pretty early.   It would
do my heart good to hear you make one good speech
in favour of peace.   I need scarce ask what your
Irish relations think about the question.   War for
them would, if possible, be still worse than for us,
though I really think there is no great difference."

TO R. ADAIR, ESQ.

" 1802.

" I HAVE your two letters ; and first as to the first,
as the lawyers say, I believe the Prince's intelligence
in substance true, or nearly so ; and some add that
Pitt's refusal is owing to *madness*, it seeming, I suppose, incredible that if he were in *his* right senses, he
should refuse to do what certainly would be the
greatest act of meanness hitherto exhibited, by coming
in without an arrangement of the Catholic business.
What would it be in effect but saying, ' I went out
because I did not think it right to stay in without
Catholic Emancipation, but I find I cannot bear it
any longer.'   My opinion of Pitt is not high, but I
own I do not think him capable of this.   That he
takes the proposal as any other than an insult is more
wonderful to me than anything else.   As to the
King's consent, is it quite sure that what was offered
with that consent was the Treasury ?   I doubt."

TO SAME.

" 1802.

" MANY thanks to you, my dear Adair, for your
letter, which is full of information, and especially

that part of it which relates to the apprehensions which are entertained of my manner of expressing myself. Between ourselves, the idea of expressing a warlike disposition, without going to war, appears to me to be rather the most absurd of all ; but anything to prevent war.   *   *   *   *

" I agree with the Duke about not submitting to humiliation, and think the line upon that subject easily drawn ; but what is there yet tending at all that way ? The conduct to the Swiss is odious, but how insulting to us ? or is it in truth anything else than a perseverance in that conduct which disgusted us before, but notwithstanding which we made peace ? Besides, is there any one who will, or can think of Switzerland as any other than a pretence ? "

TO THE HON. CHARLES GREY.

St. Anne's Hill, *Sunday, December 12th*, 1802.

" Dear Grey,

" Upon my return home on Friday I found yours of the 5th, which, notwithstanding some parts of it, gave me upon the whole the greatest pleasure. Your *openness* to me I never doubted ; but I do feel very much obliged to you for the detail you have gone into of your views of the present strange state of things. Those views appear to me wonderfully just, and, though formed at a distance, exactly such as if you had been nearer the scene, and heard all the debates, rumours, and intrigues, you would have entertained. I mean with regard to England—for as to France, I am obstinate in my opinion that

Bonaparte's wish is peace,—nay, that he is afraid of war to the last degree.

" Your notion of Addington is I believe quite right ; and his vapouring language is, besides the causes you assign, imputable to the uncertainty he is under with respect to the degree of support he is to expect from Pitt.   For that he expects some support from him is clear.   The danger is just what you say, that Pitt will temporise, that Addington will temporise also, and that by a middle conduct, on a subject which does not rationally admit of a middle conduct, the two countries may be in the situation you describe, which, if it be of long duration, must bring on War.   To encourage the Ministers therefore to avert such a situation, by holding language more decidedly pacific, and still more, by evacuating Malta at a proper time, and Alexandria immediately, is what I think of most importance.   Pitt cannot stay away much longer, for he is said to be quite well ; and the violence of the Grenvilles must oblige him, on the very first debate at which he is present, to declare himself for, or against, Addington. I have no doubt but it will be for Addington, but then I can hardly conceive that he will give him active support : and it is possible he may retire for the rest of the Session, or perhaps longer.   It is possible too that he may not come at all.   If there should be, as I think there must, a direct question on the evacuation of Malta, his staying away upon such a question must be considered as a declaration of entire secession ; and there are among his friends

(those) who say that it is his inclination. You will
easily perceive that most of the contingencies I state,
lead to the event at which I hinted in my last letter.
At present, Addington and Hawkesbury appear
rather shy of me, much more so than the first days
of the Session ; but the interpretation of this is, that
they avoid cautiously anything that might be stated
to Pitt in a way to warp him against them. Both
the Ministers and the Cannings are continually
sending embassies to sound him, and to prepossess
him against each other. (I cannot help interrupting
my statement to observe what a miserable and contemptible state of a Country and Ministry it is.)
What the result of these embassies will be, surely
cannot long remain doubtful. In the meantime the
King is supposed to be full as unwilling to restore
Pitt as ever ; and, indeed, from his nature, I am sure
it must be so. Now to the only part of your letter
which much concerns me ; and that is what relates
to your determination with regard to yourself. If
you persevere in it, only consider that all hope of
any good in the country—nay, of any alleviation
of evil, or any check to the career of despotism is
at an end. It is true the loss of our poor Duke
of Bedford is a great and just discouragement,
but then, on the other hand, it becomes the more
necessary that there should be some one man of
right principles ready to come forward ; and, besides,
though Lauderdale for many obvious reasons is
not in some respects so good a colleague for you
as the Duke of Bedford would have been, yet in

others he may be a still better ; and together
(with the assistance of some other *names* at least)
you might do a great deal.   However, all this is
more or less distant.   The present object is to
avoid the war ; and though you agree with me in
that, I do not know that you see the misery of
war now quite in so strong a light as I do.
Only reflect upon Ireland and Finance on one
side, and the impossibility of hurting France (or to
speak more properly, of diminishing her power) on
the other.

" Ireland *may* escape ; but the Finances, if they
escape without Bankruptcy, must be supported by a
system, which destroys all comfort and happiness in
the first instance, and in the result all independent
property.   Well, but if we are driven to war, why
then I say that, if we are driven to it by the enemy,
we must support, and support it in earnest ; but if,
which is far more likely, we are driven into it by the
folly of our own government, we must support it
also, but with a constant advice of negotiation and
peace.   As to your caution, you will see by the
newspapers and your letters, that I have acted in
that respect just as you would have wished me ;
indeed in some respects, in compliance with the
humours of others, I have been going a good deal
beyond my own opinion.   The truth is, I do not
feel half the indignation you all do.   Switzerland is
no doubt an abominable business ; but is it not one
of the same nature and character as a hundred
others, which have disgraced all sides and all

countries in the last ten years? Piedmont is literally nothing; and with respect to the German indemnities, I really and seriously think the French in the right; though I have not *said* so. The worst of all is the least mentioned; I mean, St. Domingo, and with respect to this, according to the vulgar phrase, he will not be damned for want of repentance. I suspect that your indignation is much more (as it ought to be) against Bonaparte for his conduct to the French than anything he has done externally; but according to our principles you must admit that it is not in any view a case of war. And, indeed, with respect to his foreign encroachments, whatever you may think of their wickedness, you must I think be very much prejudiced if you can see in them anything of intended insult to *this* country. I hope I shall soon hear that Mrs. Grey is quite well, and has brought you a son. As to leaving her at such a time, God forbid you should have thought of it. I conclude Lauderdale is with you, and this letter may do for him as well as you, though I will write a line to him if I have time to-morrow. Tell him I have seen his brother.

" Yours affectionately,

"C. J. FOX.

" Sheridan's speech, O Lord !!! gave more concern to his friends, and satisfaction to his enemies, than any he ever made."*

* Mr. Sheridan's speech on the Army Estimates, December, 1802.

TO THE HON. R. FITZPATRICK.

"St. Anne's Hill, *Monday, January* 10*th,* 1803.

"The violent reciprocal Billingsgate makes me a little alarmed for peace, but they say it is certain the Ministry mean peace. The Prince is to have his affairs settled by a message from the King to Parliament, in the manner most satisfactory to him, but in one that some people I fear will mock at. I never wrote that word before. The whole, however, is to be an inviolable secret, if the Prince can keep it so, till the message comes. Lauderdale is gone to Paris; he looks not only well, but a remarkably healthy man. Alexandria is, I hear; evacuated,* which is a very good thing; for, a little more delay, and Bonaparte might have demanded the evacuation in an unpleasant style. It is said he is to be called his Consular Majesty. I suppose under colour of representing the majesty of the French people. I shall go to town for the meeting of Parliament.† Lawrence has given notice of a foolish motion about Captain d'Auvergne; but, if one is made like that announced by Lord Minto, about the sending of Moore to Switzerland, I should think it a little difficult for Ministers to explain themselves. Pitt has been in town, but all is still in the dark.

"Yours ever,

"C. J. FOX."

---

* By the English troops.

† The session of Parliament began on the 16th of November, 1802, and after an adjournment at Christmas, met again on February 3rd, 1803.

TO SAME.

"*January 11th*, 1803.

"Dear Dick,

"Many thanks for your letter. Who your host of critics are besides Price * and Lady Caroline, I do not know ; but, *pace tantorum virorum,* if they merit that appellation, I think them completely in the wrong. First, as to brevity : if an inscription could be confined to a couplet, or two, it would certainly have a great advantage, because it might be carried in the memory of any one who had looked with any attention at the statue or edifice to which it belonged ; but, when that is out of the question, I see no reason why brevity is more desirable in a composition of this kind than in any other. † Next, surely we are not yet quite such philosophers as to consider a man's ancestry as forming no part of his glory, or at least of the splendour of his situation ; and in this case the ancestors are such, that one would refer to them if one did not in any other ; in short, I would as soon leave out all the rest as that part. You should answer as Stirling, the famous piquet player, did to one who, having made a singular discard, turned to him and asked whether he would have laid out that King of Spades. ' Sir,' said he, ' I should sooner have laid out the other eleven cards.' Pray be stout

---

* Mr. Uvedale Price, author of the "Essay on the Picturesque," of Foxley, Herefordshire, and his wife, Lady Caroline Price, daughter of the second Earl of Tyrone, afterwards Marquis of Waterford.

† This seems to refer to criticisms on General Fitzpatrick's lines upon my uncle, Francis, Duke of Bedford.

in this instance. I have laid by my copy so carefully that I cannot find it myself, and therefore cannot enter into so much detail as I could wish; but I remember I was very much against omitting the simile, as well as my wife. I had, I believe, some doubts whether one couplet towards the end might not be parted with. Will you send me a fresh copy? In a house where there are young ones you may make them copy. Apropos to young ones, I felt so much compunction at taking from Bob * the four verses I had given him that I have done the enclosed for him, which he will use or not, as he likes. In the mean time, if the critics you speak of are very savage, it may serve as a crust to them, for I am prepared, as Dr. Lawrence said, to defend every part; not the excellence, mind, but the Latinity and classical purity. I do not boast of my progress; the piecing in of several new bits, in consequence of my Parisian information, is a very troublesome job, and we have had a good deal of company during the holidays. By the way, I hope you are of opinion that, though to avoid notes entirely, as the ancients did, may be impossible, one ought to put as much into the text as one can,—even observations upon other historians, canvassing of authorities, &c. If this is not a material object I am sure I fling away much time and labour, but to my taste it is a very good matter. Your observations upon the House of Commons and upon politics are but too just. I am very much afraid, but yet I still hope that Bonaparte is afraid of a war, and

* Probably the present Sir Robert Price.

my intelligence continues to be that our Ministers are really earnest for peace. These are the grounds, and the only grounds whatever, I have of hope. I have not seen the Prince's Secret in the newspaper, but the very day after I had written to you I heard it was there.* If you have read Herodotus, and do not like him, I shall be quite disappointed. Rogers, the poet, has been here; I like him very well, but he is too complaisant (a fault of the right side) to have so much critical conversation with him as I like. I do not know how it is, but criticism is always my rage at this time of year. Did you ever observe that there is the same situation (and a very remarkable one too) in 'Britannicus,' in 'Aurungzebe,' and in Quinault's 'Thesée?' Query: Did the two last take it from Racine? or did they all three (which I think most probable) take it from some older play that I do not know? I do not know why I did not put these questions to Rogers."

TO THE HON. CHARLES GREY.

"St. Anne's Hill, *January* 17, 1803.

" My dear Grey,

"I have not been in a hurry to answer your

---

* "The Prince's Secret." These words apparently allude to the plan for an additional allowance to the Prince of Wales, which was proposed by Mr. Addington to the House of Commons on the 23rd of February, 1803. The "Annual Register" for this year, c. 6, contains a summary of all that passed during the session on this subject. Mr. Fox spoke on two occasions. See the letter of the 10th of January.

last letter, because in truth Bonaparte's expressions in the Speech you allude to, do appear to me more grating than anything else he has done : but you will remember that my proposition related to the time *before* we had interfered about the Swiss, and his anger afterwards is no proof that he meant hostility to us before.   On the other hand, you must agree that Moore's residence in Switzerland was a very foolish thing on our part.   I shall certainly be very slow in bringing you to town if you leave it to me.   But I am not at all of your opinion that pacific language on our part is like to do as much mischief as good, the contrary was evident before the holidays ; though as to the particular debate in the House of Lords to which you refer, I can say nothing, the account of it in my paper being so very short.   When Parliament meets we shall, I suppose, understand the state of things something better ; even if Pitt should not appear, and much more so if he does.   What a dreadful business St. Domingo has been, is, and is likely to be !   If Bonaparte is obstinate about it, (I think it probable enough that he may) his greatest enemies could not wish him worse.   I have not heard of Lauderdale since he went.   My brother, who has been all through Italy, confirms all the accounts of the abominable conduct at Naples, on the part of the King of Naples, as well as on ours.   I know you are a great admirer of Metastasio, and, I believe, I once before made you read Isacco ; but I have just been reading it for the fiftieth time, and want you to read

it again, and tell me whether is is not the best production of the last century.

" Yours most affectionately,

" C. J. FOX."

TO THE HON. R. FITZPATRICK.

"January 19th, 1803.

" I KNEW you would agree with me about notes,
nor is it on account of ancient example that I would
avoid them, unless the ancient histories were better
for the reader than the modern, which I think they
are. If the ancients did all these things better than
the moderns, I cannot help that ; and this example,
because it is better, not because it is older, ought to
be followed, as far as it can without flying in the face
of fashion too much. I am sorry you do not delight
in Herodotus ; but you will remember it was not
the four first, but the four or five last books, that I
expected you to be pleased with : therefore, pray do
not cut him ; and if the whole account of the Persian
war, the Athenian generals, &c., does not delight you,
I will never bore you again upon any subject of ancient
history. The end of ' Sydney Biddulph ' * is indeed
very good ; but a great part of the three first volumes
is very good also. ' Britannicus ' was acted at least
five years before ' Aurungzebe ; ' so that it is very
probable that Dryden may have taken it from Racine;
but yet I think it most likely that the situation is in

---

* The "Memoirs of Sidney Biddulph," a novel, London, 1761, 3 vols.
8vo., by Mrs. Frances Sheridan, wife of Thomas Sheridan. She was born
about 1724, and died in 1767.

some older play. Most assuredly Racine would not
have made the comparison you mention ; and why
should you suspect me of defending it, considering it
as belonging to a tragedy ? There is one line in
Quinault that delights me ;* but which it is just possible you may think over-done, in point of simplicity.
When Eglé, who is in the situation of Indamora and
Lindamora, appears cold to him, Thesée says :
' *Eglé ne m'aime plus et n'a rien à me dire !* ' "

TO THE HON. CHARLES GREY.

"CLARGES STREET, *February 28th,* 1803.

" DEAR GREY,

"I do not much understand how the affair of
the call, or rather calls, now stands. I charged Lord
Robert with the business, and also to enquire what is
to be done hereafter on the subject : and I will write
to-morrow. My cold makes me too stupid to answer
the other parts of your letter ; only be assured that
the state you ascribe to the Grenvilles is quite
universal, unless indeed death is a fitter description
than sleep for the general state of all political feeling
and sentiment. Of Despard nothing is said more
than of any housebreaker, who may have been
hanged the same day. Your observation that there
is every reason to suppose him mad, if his conduct in

---

* Philippe Quinault, born 1635, and died 1688, a dramatic poet, chiefly
celebrated for his French operas. Boileau's line—

"La raison dit Virgile, et la rime Quinault,"

is rather a jingle than a judicious satire.

other respects did not appear sane, is generally made, and then no more is said : no complaint on one side, no triumph on the other.   The Bark business, Do. The Prince, Do.   Peltier's, Do., to the end of the chapter.   The insipidity of the House of Commons is beyond conception, and I think it is catching, for the few times I have thought myself obliged to speak, I felt some way as if I was speaking like Addington, and I really believe I was.   I hope and believe this death-like state is likely to prevent the evil of war, and so far it is good ; as to everything else, I consider it as all over.   Unless the call forces me, you may trust me for not asking your attendance lightly ; but there may be a question, about Alexandria and Malta I mean, upon which I should state to you my very earnest wishes.   The most truly comical circumstance of all is that the Ministers (as I am told by some of their friends) attribute all the quiescent state I have described to their own superior management and abilities.

" Yours affectionately,

" C. J. FOX.

" P.S.—I have not heard from Lauderdale, but his brother has, and he is quite well.   You have heard of poor La Fayette's accident ; and Lord Maitland has *broke his hand* by a fall, but is doing well.   I never heard of such an accident before."

TO SAME.

"CLARGES STREET, *March 12th,* 1803.

" DEAR GREY,

"I have not written since Wednesday, because I have learned nothing more of this cursed business, than what is in every newspaper. I cannot help thinking that, however it may end, you ought to be present at the discussion that must follow. I think indeed you will scarcely feel pleasant at having been absent from it. In one event (I fear, alas, a very improbable one), I own I should be very anxious for your presence—I mean if matters should be accommodated : in that case an attack will certainly be made upon Addington, which, if not strong, will at least be loud, and I own to have you join with me in defending him upon this occasion, and to appear with whatever of force remains in the old party, would give me great satisfaction. You know I have no great expectations of the gratitude of the country, but yet the wish for peace among sober minded people is so general and so strong, that I cannot help thinking we should, in the *feel* of the country at least, be honourably distinguished from the other politicians and parties of the day, who so evidently make war and peace mere engines of attack upon a Ministry whom they dislike. What Pitt will do I neither know nor guess : whether Sheridan would be with us I do not *know,* and I suspect you do not *care,* or even that your wishes would be that he should not; Moira and Tierney would, I think, certainly join

upon this occasion the new opposition. Canning,
Morpeth, Lord G. Levison, &c., would no doubt do
the same, unless the first of these (for I do not think
the others could be restrained) were restrained by
Pitt. I ought not to omit that I have not had a
word of communication respecting the *assurances* I
mentioned, or of the present state of things, so that
my eagerness to support in the case I suppose, is
certainly not owing to any feel of personal kindness
or civility. Now let us look to the other, and as I
fear by far the more probable event. In that case
I wish your presence for a reason of a different nature
—not because I wish you to follow my line, or to
agree in my opinion, but because I wish you to take
one yourself, and to help me with your opinion ;
whatever that line and opinion may be, I will
implicitly follow it. The war of course must be in
some sort supported ; and whether you think it right
that we should mix that support with more or less
blame of the administration, with more or less concurrence of sentiment with the Grenvilles, &c., I leave
entirely to your judgment, promising only, that after
the first debate upon the breaking out of it, I should
be very loath indeed, nay, perhaps I could not even
by you be brought to give anything like regular
attendance. You have now all I know and all I
think. As to men, the folly and hollowness of
Addington is, you know, my aversion. With respect
to Moira, we do not, I imagine, much differ. I have
no liking for the Grenvilles or the Cannings : but
both of them have, I believe, notions of acting in a

party not dissimilar to my own. Windham has got
to such a pitch of absurdity that nothing can be done
with him. Fitzwilliam, to whom I need not tell you
how every motive of affection draws me nearer than
to all men else, may possibly, when he has got the
war he so longed for, get out of Burke's altitudes
into the regions of common sense.

"Though I have been led into all this, do not
imagine I see any prospect, by any junction whatever,
of forming such a government as *you*, much less *I*,
could be a member of. I see no such prospect, but
if there is war apprehensions from the imbecility of
the present men will be very great, and may lead to
new scenes ; and if our reliquiæ could be kept
together, if it were only Russells and Cavendishes
and a few more, with you at the head of them, not
only it would give me great satisfaction, but it might
be a foundation for better things at some future
period. Only consider what changes one event
might produce ; and in the jumbles that would ensue,
how very advantageous to the public it would be that
among the various knots and factions that would be
formed, there should be one at least attached to
principles of liberty. When I am in this train of
thinking, I sometimes feel that there are strong
political duties incumbent both upon you and myself.
As to call, &c., though we were within two of losing
a committee, Thursday, Addington has given no
notice of additional or more forcible compulsory
measures—so it is not worth thinking of for you, but
still I hope that you will come. As to my great

object of keeping something together, I am willing to hope that if we hit upon a proper language and system at the outset of the war, it may be compassed to sufficient degree without any constant attendance either on your part or on mine afterwards.

" Do you hear anything about Ireland ? I mean in case of a war. I do wish you and Lauderdale were here.

" Yours affectionately,

"C J. FOX.

" P. S. Some think that when Bonaparte hears of the message, he will fly out and immediately recall Andreossy. I rather think he will not, but he is so hot a man that it is by no means impossible."

TO SAME.

"CLARGES STREET, *Tuesday, March,* 1803.

" DEAR GREY,

" You decided right in not coming. The business was settled too late for the post yesterday, or I would have written. It is declared that if there are committees chosen, there is to be no severity, which amounts in my opinion to a declaration that the call *compulsitor*, &c., are all nugatory. The House, too, shows its spiritless character in this as in other things, for it is not very fair that the 300 members who happen to be in town should take the whole burthen upon themselves ; but submission in all things, both great and small, is our characteristic virtue. I persevere in earnest wishes that when the evacuation of Egypt and Malta comes to be considered, you should attend—but when that will be I do not know. I do not believe there is any concert between Pitt and Lord Grenville about finance business, and I do believe that the former was, for a time at least, very seriously ill again with the gout. The Prince goes on with his business, and Lord Porchester has given notice of another motion. I do not see what the great use of this is, yet I believe that the Prince will be strong, because in the rage of royalism now prevailing, a Prince of Wales being something like a King, will have a support which no other person or cause could have. In the meanwhile, the debates on this subject carrying, on account of the nearness of numbers, more interest with them than others, serve of course to display more strongly the *néant* of Ministers. I believe, indeed, there never was a sentiment of contempt so general—only the *spirit* (if it can be so called) of acquiescence is still more so. There are of course many who say this is owing to the old opposition and the new not being able to agree, but believe me, if they were to agree, which is next to impossible, they could do nothing except perhaps just in the Prince's business, which, even if carried, would lead to no consequences of moment. Nor do I believe that even *that* would be carried, though certainly near run. Mrs. Fox is still very weak after this influenza, but that is the case of most of those who have it. I am quite well : I trust that you and all yours are so ; and it is very good not to be here just now. The influenza spreads every day

more and more, and the weather is the most
intolerable that ever was felt. I hope you did not
begin to boast too soon of your climate, and that you
will escape these March frosts and snow, as you did
those we had in January and February. Though I
am still assured that Egypt and Malta are evacuated,
or evacuating, I observe that many persons assert the
direct contrary, and I am told the True Briton gives
countenance to those assertions. But still I am
assured in a manner I cannot doubt, notwithstanding
that sort of hollowness which is so remarkable a
feature in certain characters. The best part of the
present state of things is, that being wholly out of
every intrigue, and every connection, except with the
remnant of our old friends, it is of little importance
to me whether the things I hear on either side be
true or not. Cowper's letters, published by Hayley
in his life of Cowper, have not yet, I suppose, reached
Northumberland. When they do, I think you will
like them.

" Yours affectionately,

" C. J. FOX."

TO SAME.

"CLARGES STREET, *March,* 1803.

" DEAR GREY,

      " I am sorry to say that the result of further
reflection on what I heard yesterday, as well as what
I have learned this day is, that though there is
a chance of peace, there are many, very many more
for war. I have had some explanation about assu-

rances, which is not very satisfactory, but which, by laying the blame upon the inaccuracy of the person conveying them, who, it seems, gave me *his* opinion and not theirs, upon what was going on, exculpates the principals from any marked incivility. But all this is of no consequence. The material point to you is the time ; and I am told, and believe, that the business will in some shape come pretty soon before Parliament. Therefore, if you are not set out, pray lose no time. Peace or war—some system must be adopted by us for the sake of our characters—and I can adopt none, especially in case of war, without you. My belief, but it is only belief, is that war might have been, may still be avoided. If the representation on one side be true, it certainly may— and even from the very imperfect account I have heard on the other, I rather draw the same conclusion. In either event there will be a great cry (though perhaps an impotent one) against leaving the power in the present hands. How far we ought to join in that cry is a question quite open to us— and indeed I have been particularly cautious not to say a word that should preclude me from either joining in it or resisting it. Pray come, I know you are quite sure that I would not ask you wantonly, or make light of the inconvenience and unpleasantness of coming, in your circumstances.

" Yours most affectionately,

"C. J. FOX."

TO SAME.

"CLARGES STREET, *Tuesday, March*, 1803.

" DEAR GREY,

" I rather hope you are on your way up ; but, if not, you had better stay for the letter I shall write you to-morrow.   I have heard something to-day (not from the same quarter as the assurances) which makes me have better hopes, though not very sanguine ones, of peace.   This is no reason against your coming, rather the contrary ; but I shall hear something to-morrow (I am *told*) that may give me more insight into the time when *parliamentary* discussions are like to arise.   Perhaps I may hear nothing, but at any rate I shall write.   At present I am more convinced than ever that, if it is war, it is entirely the fault of the ministers, and not of Bonaparte.

" Yours affectionately,

" C. J. FOX."

TO SAME.

"CLARGES STREET, *Friday, March*, 1803.

" DEAR GREY,

" I have just received yours of the 15th, and think if you set out on Tuesday, as you propose, you will be time enough.   I am happy to think that (excepting in what relates personally to yourself) we are perfectly agreed in everything.   Where you suppose there is a shade of difference, there is in fact

none ; for what I meant was, not a support of
Addington's Ministry (which must depend on further
circumstances), but a support of Addington's *accommodation* with France—if he should make one ; and
the case, I suppose, in which such support would, in
my judgment, be so very becoming to us, and in
some degree useful to the public, is that of a smart
opposition being made, not to him in *general*, but to
the particular *convention* or *act* by which these
impending discussions shall be terminated, and in
consequence of which the armament shall cease.
You think this would not be the plan of the
Grenvilles, &c., and if it is not I agree with all you
say. Whether or not it will be their mode of attack
I know not. When I wrote last I thought it certainly
would, and that the prospect of being joined by
Sheridan, Moira, Canning, &c., would determine them
for that mode. From some little conversation I had
yesterday with T. Grenville, as well as from general
observation, I begin to doubt it. But probably their
determination will be influenced by events not yet
known, and at any rate it is not in our power to direct
it. All this is in case of peace—and I think you do
not differ even about the degree of propriety there
would be in supporting an accommodation. It is
material that the well-wishers to peace in the public
at large should have some authority beyond that of
the ministers to support and confirm them in their
opinions. In the event, too, of future opposition, it
is surely of importance that a great body of those
who form it should have the reputation of being

friends to peace. In the other, and, as I still think,
far more likely event, I see we equally agree, as far
as my judgment can be formed at present. If one is
to attend, it would certainly be a great relief to one's
mind to allow oneself to abuse Addington's pompous
nonsense as it deserves—it really is on all occasions,
both trifling and serious, disgusting in point of taste
to a degree almost intolerable. As to union of
parties in case of war, it is very difficult indeed ; but,
if decidedly called for, not perhaps altogether impossible. In that case, however, I should feel myself
obliged to intreat your reconsideration of what you
seem to have determined in regard to yourself. I
have not the smallest doubt (I almost wish I could
have any) of the sincerity of your determination ;
only consider that the circumstances of this world
are so variable that an irrevocable resolution is
almost a synonymous term for a foolish one. I have
a strong opinion that, if there is a war, you are the
only, literally the only, man capable of conducting it.
I lay aside all personal prejudices—but I think it
completely demonstrated that Pitt, with all his great
talents, is wholly unfit for it—indeed, he seems so
conscious of it himself, that he leaves the whole
management, in such cases, to others. Lord Melville,
who, by the way, is now talked of, besides being now
old, seems to be the worst hand that ever was employed. Lord Grenville is an able man, but not, I
think, for such a purpose : and Lauderdale, with all
his incredible activity, would be less fit for such a
task than any other. However, all this speculation

is in case of events, the chances against which are about ten thousand to one—not against war, but against our having any choice about the conductors of it. As to war or no war, the stocks rose yesterday and the day before—which, as far as it goes, is a good sign—but my hopes are very faint, I send you a paragraph from the 'Morning Chronicle,' which I think a more probable account of the matter, than any other I have heard. You will see we shall go to war, and be in the wrong in the opinion of all Europe.

" Yours ever,

"C. J. FOX.

" P.S.—By the way, I *know* that Whitbread means to be in town on Thursday for the Oakhampton ballot, and I do not *think* he will go back again for some days at least. I mention this as you speak of calling at Southhill. Do not imagine that I do not do ample credit to your virtue in leaving the country just now. I do not know that it is not the time of the year when I have the most enjoyment in it, when the weather is fine ; and when it is a vile east wind, I do not know any place where it is' more unpleasant than here. In short, the country is always best ; and, amidst the dreadful prospects we have, it is some consolation that I may possibly be allowed to live uninterrupted there. I am afraid I cannot say, *we*, because you may feel yourself obliged to do something in the military way. Adieu."

TO SAME.

"Clarges Street, *Wednesday, March*, 1803.

" Dear Grey,

" After my letter yesterday, concerning *assur-ances* and their value, you will be not a little amused at learning that about an hour after my writing, the message which you will see in the newspapers was delivered to both Houses.*   I suppose Malta is the discussion alluded to.   I did not know of the message till after it had been presented, though through the same channel by which I had my *assurance*, I might have been informed, one would think, that difficulties had arisen at least, even if it were not thought fit to explain to me the nature of them.   Mere folly is too charitable an account, surely, of such proceedings. But if the *manner* of all this is amusing, the business itself is by no means so ; and I am very much afraid it will end in war.   You know my opinion of the con-sequences of war—that opinion remains unshaken. I am sure the more you reflect the more you will agree with me.   Bonaparte has just now, as I am informed, *the whole continent*, Austria and all, with him ; but I do not know that that is not as well for us as to have Austria alone, for, besides the immense cost, I suspect that to support Austria in such circumstances would be absolutely impossible.   Many people think the effect of a war would be to restore Pitt—I doubt it much ; but I think the evil of war

---

* The King's message on the Armaments was delivered on the 8th of March.

so great, that to the lesser one of Pitt I am almost
indifferent.   I take it for granted Addington will be
all mystery to-day, and that we shall know no more
to-night than we do now.   If there is anything
material I will write again.

"Yours affectionately,

"C. J. FOX.

"P.S.—I hear our next division on the Prince's
business will not be so good as our last.   If this is so,
it is an additional reason why it should not have been
pressed again.   It is very foolish."

TO THE EARL OF LAUDERDALE.

"*April* 1*st*, 1803.

"DEAR LAUDERDALE,

"I did not, till the night before last, receive
yours of the 28th Ventose (that is the 19th March),
so that of course it does not give much new ground
for hope or fear.   Your account of everything exactly
tallies with my conjectures ; but, for some days after
the message, I own I was myself so far deceived as
to imagine something new and extraordinary had
occurred.   I did not, however, remain long in this
delusion : and, by what I hear, most people are now
recovered, or recovering from it.   How it will end
cannot yet be foreseen with any certainty ; but I
own my opinions are more with my fears than my
wishes.   The best thing I have heard is the immediate application from both sides to Russia.   As to

news from home, there is none. The contempt of
the Ministers rather increases, to which is added the
hatred and resentment of those who expected at least
pacific measures from them, and a good deal of ill will
from Carlton House. But whether or not all this will
produce anything is very doubtful—I think not.
There is some talk of Pitt, but I believe all idle. He
knows his insignificance, and does not like showing it.
Any junction would lower him (that is according to
the ridiculous ideas his friends hold out of him), and
without junction he is nobody. I could moralise a
little upon this, and I suppose Pitt does the same—
at least I hope so."

TO THE HON. CHARLES GREY.

"St. Anne's Hill, *Saturday, April 16th*, 1803.

" Dear Grey,

" I have good authority for saying that the negotiation with Pitt is at an end, and in a manner not
likely to bring on a renewal. This event will
certainly produce others, and probably some in which
we may have seriously to consider what part we
ought to act. I hope, therefore, you will be in town
on Tuesday, if not sooner—and Whitbread too. I do
not think you will suspect me of being partial to the
Doctor ; but, if we should have anything like the
power of turning the scale, it is surely worth thinking
of, whether we should, either by action or inaction, be
instrumental in restoring Pitt and the old Ministry.
As to the more important negotiation, from what I

hear, I believe in peace, though not from any particular information ; I believe what you heard upon
that subject at D. House * was exactly true,
and that the result has been rather favourable.   I
shall go to town on Monday.

" Yours affectionately,

"C. J. FOX."

TO SAME.

"St. Anne's Hill, *Friday*, *May* 21*st*. 1803.

" Dear Grey,

" I am much obliged to you for your letter, and
the confidential intelligence contained in it.   I had
heard so many different accounts, that I did not
know what to believe.   You say nothing of the
Grenvilles—probably you know nothing—but as in
the House of Lords, Lord Grenville must inevitably
be the person to take the lead, I should think
T. Grenville, Wyndham, and others, would have some
plan of acting in the House of Commons conformable
to his.   Pitt's mode of conduct will, I think, have
a different effect from what he proposes, and will
tend to add real strength to the Doctor, to whom
nothing can be more favourable than a demonstration
of the impossibility of any union of the parties out of
office.   But that is his affair ; and to me, except inasmuch as it shuts out all hope of peace, a matter of
perfect indifference.   What I think of the papers ?
Why I think as you do, and every man must, that
the case is weaker than it was possible for the most

---

* Devonshire House.

prejudiced man to suppose. If any sense or system
can be made out from them, it seems as if the whole
change of measures has turned upon Sebastiani's
report—a paper which certainly ought not to have
been published by Bonaparte, and which contains
some impertinences—but which, as a ground for war,
is weak beyond measure. It gives no *new* insight
into the Consul's wishes with regard to Egypt ; and,
if any surmises are to be drawn from it, they must
evidently relate to remote periods, and contingencies.
The most ridiculous part of the whole perhaps is
the way in which the poor King of Sardinia is
lugged in, especially as it is well known that we
refused joining the Russian application in his favour.
What precious nonsense, too, all about the Knights
and their languages ; and then no reason given for
rejecting the Emperor of Russia's offer to guarantee
upon the terms by him stated. How different, by
the way, Bonaparte's conversation with Whitworth
turns out from what we had heard. I do not know
what information you move for ; but I have no doubt
of its being right. With regard to the motion for
suspension of hostilities till the negotiation is fairly
finished, perhaps we may not be too late to make it
on Monday or Tuesday ; and I am very much obliged
to you for not fetching me up. Whitbread's house
will be best for our meeting, which, however, should
be a very small one. I think, besides us three, only
Erskine, W. Smith, and Sheridan. I name these
because I think Smith is a man who likes consultation,
and who is not unlikely to have made observations

on the papers which may have escaped me. Sheridan will probably not come; but I would not let him have it to say he was not asked. I shall be in Dover Street by two at latest.

> " Yours affectionately,
>
>> " C. J. FOX.

" P.S. Perhaps you know (which I do not) what was the state of affairs in Switzerland at the different epochs of

> THE TREATY OF LUNEVILLE.
> THE PRELIMINARIES.
> THE TREATY OF AMIENS.

I do not know that this is of great consequence, only I think the state of that business is not generally understood. Pray add Lauderdale to those who are to be at Whitbread's."

TO THE EARL OF LAUDERDALE.

" June 21st, 1803.

" DEAR LAUDERDALE,

" Thank you for the account of the election. The majority being so great almost gives one a notion that you would have succeeded, but of this you are of course the best judge. I heard when I was in town this day fortnight that W. Dundas had resigned, but I have not seen in the paper any successor appointed to him. Even I, who have had the highest opinion of the patience of the country, am a little surprised that such a budget should go down so quietly as it seems to do. The dissatisfaction at it

is, however, as far as I can learn, universal. There
is much of it I do not yet understand, and I conclude
it will produce far short of what Addington expects.
I hear reports that the ministers are serious in
endeavouring to make something of the Russian
Mediation, but these are mere reports, and I am
wholly ignorant of what they are at. The loss of
Hanover has, I am told, affected the King severely.
I hear it is the fashion to say it is not an *English*
concern, and yet I have not heard it asserted that in
case of a treaty, the restoration of it would not be
demanded and probably purchased with *English*
cessions or sacrifices. But there is a blindness and
apathy about everything that surpasses all belief.
Tierney seems to have been pretty well deceived
when he said there would not be an Income Tax * * *
I do not hear of any intention of making a serious
opposition to any of the taxes ; if such a thing were
to be, I would certainly go to vote against them.
I suppose the malt will be very unpopular in your
country. Were you surprised or not at Pitt's complete silence on the budget! Perhaps yesterday on
the arming scheme, he opened himself more. I
suppose that will operate as another heavy tax."

TO SAME.

"*July 7th*, 1803.

"DEAR LAUDERDALE,

"The defence plan is, I believe, generally dis-
approved, almost as much as it deserves, but that

nor anything else of the kind, is of any consequence.
The Prince of Wales appears (from what I hear) to
be the person in the whole country who at this
moment thinks most of public affairs, and as far as I
hear too, he thinks right.   He is in a rage about
Hanover and the Elbe, and has the greatest possible
dislike to the defence plan.   To augment the regulars
if we must have war is surely the only common sense.
Stocks fall as you see very much, but to what particular cause the fall is owing I do not think clear.
It seems, as far as it goes, to justify the plan of
making comparatively small loans, and raising these
War Taxes, but then again they are intolerable. * * *
These ministers, even if they had the impudence to
make what would in any hands be necessary sacrifices, could not, I think, make peace, and still less
keep it.   Pray tell me before the event, what you
think of the probability of invasion, its probable
success, &c.   It is very generally expected, and
though I still think it will not be attempted, yet the
language in France, which I must suppose to be
encouraged by Bonaparte, is such as to make the *not
attempting it* a sort of failure in the eyes of Europe.
If attempted, I have great confidence in the difficulty
of escaping our fleet with anything like a large
armament.   Then again, if once they land, with our
total want of preparation (a want by the way which
these nonsensical schemes of defence tend to make
more certain), with our generals and our military
counsellors, it is difficult to see how they can be
foiled.   I have had so many people here that I have

worked very slowly indeed, and I make no doubt but
you will publish first. I never thought of going in
my first volume further than the Revolution, and of
course shall not come to the times of the Bank, &c.
But if I did I think I could dispose of such subjects
by a general or what you would call a superficial
account of them, without going into your cursed
science. *A propos* to history, I wrote to Laing some
time ago, and have had no answer. I directed to
him as I did to you at Edinburgh, and perhaps
as erroneously, but let me know.

" My potato oats are coming up very thick in
most parts of my field; in some parts they have
totally failed, owing as they say to a damned worm
of some sort ; but where they are thick they are very
backward in comparison of others which were sowed
about the same time, and it looks as if they would
run very much into very coarse and thick straw.
My Swedish turnips come up well too, but though all
sorts of pains were taken to get the ground clear,
there are abundance of weeds, and particularly of
what we call Catlock, which unskilful hoers cannot
distinguish from the turnips themselves while they
are young, and it seems to be one of the qualities of
the Swedish turnip to grow slowly, and therefore to
retain their likeness to the Catlock longer than
others. However, we are doing our best. You
persuaded me last year to sow a greater proportion
of rye grass with the clover than is usual here. The
consequence has been that the rye has got quite the
better, and I shall have but little clover. Is it your

opinion that the Malt Tax will lower the price of barley as much as the farmers apprehend?"

TO THE HON. CHARLES GREY.

"St. Anne's, Hill, *Friday, July*, 1803."

" Dear Grey,

"I have thought of writing to you any time these six weeks, but have been deterred by the consideration that I had nothing to tell you that you would not learn as well from the common newspapers. From them you will have learned that I went to town last week to attend the defence plan as it is called—but *why* I went I do not know myself except that I was much pressed to do so by many friends, not one of whom gave any reason for their wish. There was so little in what I said, that of course you cannot much approve or disapprove of it. When in town I saw the Prince by his command, who talked a great deal to me upon the state of the country, upon which his ideas appear to be generally right—and he also talked (which indeed seemed to be his principal object) upon party politics with a good deal of earnestness. His object at present is to promote an union between Lord Spencer, Windham, and the Grenvilles on the one hand—with you and me on the other. He is as hostile to Pitt as ever. However, with all his eagerness he seemed satisfied, from what I said, and what I had before written in a letter which was shewn him, that it was impossible for much to be done this session—and that with respect to another, the only thing was to wait for events, and not to do or say anything to make junctions of any kind more impracticable than they are. With this view, and indeed from my own inclination, I spoke very civilly to Windham, whose notions as to defence here really appear to me to be the best of any I have heard. The army of reserve (here at least) is converted into a heavy tax upon gentlemen, as we are obliged to subscribe to enable the poorer sort to get substitutes. I for instance must subscribe five guineas, and my servants and labourers a guinea or more each, which will also fall upon me—and all this to get less useful soldiers than might be had by the common recruiting methods, with a larger bounty. This appears to me to be intolerable. As to the arming of the people they have hitherto done nothing here and will I dare say do nothing *right.* Now as to the miserable story of Ireland. Have you heard anything more than is in the papers ? What can it be ? It certainly has not the appearance of being a partial or accidental mob—but on the other hand if there was any concert one would think they would have waited till the French were either actually landed there, or here, or at least till they were supposed to be on the point of doing so. I can make nothing of it, except that it proves what I always suspected, that the accounts of the better state of Ireland were all delusory in the extreme. They say ministers are more despised every day, and some think Pitt rises—but I confess I saw no symptom of any particular respect for him in the House. It is true he made one of his very worst speeches. Sheridan goes on courting the ministers more and more every day —but the Prince seems, as you may guess from what I have already said, very averse to them. If he (the Prince) could be a little steady, there would be more chance of good than from anything else ; but the country is divided, and no good can ever come to it. The state of the stocks looks as if Lauderdale were right, and that the war could not be supported more than a year or two. Bonaparte must see this, and avoid a decisive measure. I still think therefore that Ireland, and not England will be his object. I hope your harvest looks as well as ours, though some croakers talk of a *silver blight,* which I never heard of before. I hear with great pleasure that Mrs. Grey and all yours are well. Mrs. Fox desires to be kindly remembered to you.

" Yours affectionately,

" C. J. FOX."

TO SAME.

" St. Anne's Hill, *August 8th,* 1803.

" Dear Grey,

" My going to town the first time was owing to the importunity of friends—but the last I went of my own accord, as, having once attended upon the defence, I thought I ought not to be absent on Craufurd's motion. It was not till I got to town that I heard of the Prince's wishes, that his offer and the rejection of it should be mentioned, which with me was an additional motive to attend. In this

E E 2

instance he certainly is on very good ground—his offer was to serve in any way as a Major-General, or, in short as they pleased. The ministers put the rejection entirely upon the King, *truly*, I believe,—but when such answers suffice what a mockery to talk of the Constitution! You know of course from the papers (though the doors were shut), that I moved a military council, and that Sheridan, (whether because I was present or for what other reason I knew not) voted against the ministry, and not only so, but spoke very well, and what is most wonderful of all, took no distinct line of his own. He did not like, I know, the Prince's offer, &c., being mentioned in the way it was, and as I heard the Prince was full of suspicions with regard to him—but I hear they have since dined together, and I should not be surprised if Sheridan had persuaded him that we all, who acted according to his declared and anxious wishes, had done him disservice, and that his policy was to support the Doctor. However, I *know* nothing of all this, nor have had a line of intelligence since I returned. I think they have been spoiling the defence bill, by turning it into a scheme for procuring volunteer corps, a sort of force of which I have no great opinion. The people hereabouts are very slack, but it seems to be chiefly owing to their fears of being made *real soldiers*. The army of reserve has besides caused much irritation, and they confound all the bills together. Nothing new seems to have transpired in regard to the Dublin business. One thing you will be pleased to hear is, that a Lieutenant of

Yeomanry, who flogged a man to make him discover arms, was dismissed in consequence, and the sufferer told he would be supported in a civil action, if he chose to bring one. I believe Lord Hardwicke, and I am sure my brother, will not consent to any cruelties—but this is little—there must be a fundamental change in the system of governing Ireland, to give even a chance of future quiet there. Oh! if you had heard the Doctor in answer to me on that subject! it was quite below himself. *What can I say more?* as the East Indians finish their letters. Sheridan is mad with vanity and folly—but what he is driving at I do not know, nor, I believe, does he. Some say he means to exhibit a sort of contrast to Tierney. I cannot help thinking how Tierney must laugh at him, if he hears this. Do you hear from the Ponsonbies about Ireland?

" Yours affectionately.

"C. J. FOX.

" P.S.—We have just begun harvest. The heavy crops of wheat are very much laid—and east of London, as I hear, far worse than here. Mine, not being heavy, have escaped. When you compare the account in my former letter of the Prince's conversation with me, and of my conduct at his desire with respect to Windham, with what you will have read of Sheridan's speeches since that time, it gives a good notion of Carlton House politics—does not it? "

TO SAME.

"St. Anne's Hill, *August 9th*, 1803.

" Dear Grey,

" You will have perceived that I had not received your letter when I wrote yesterday. It is impossible to agree more than we do about junctions. In a letter, which was shown to the Prince, I stated that whatever mutual concessions might be made on smaller matters, I never could be of a party with any men who did not hold that peace upon certain terms with the Government of France, whatever that Government might be, was desirable. Indeed, I think that Lord Grenville's speeches, as I have read them, are not against peace in general ; and the very words of their resolutions, that by *Remonstrances, &c., peace might have been* preserved, are inconsistent with the notion of the sort of war talked of by some, and hinted at, as I think, in Sheridan's speeches. I should be afraid that Windham might incline to the old *internecine*, but I should hope none of the others. With respect to an active session next year, I am at present very much against it ; but between this time and Christmas surely some events must take place which may influence materially our opinions on such a subject. It is unfortunate that the difference between our situations makes it almost impossible for us to act exactly on the same plan. My nearness to London exposes me to the constant attacks of my friends to attend on particular occasions, and these occasions over, I am naturally in a hurry to get away.

Now you are too distant to be called for, unless on very essential occasions indeed, and when you are come so far, and with your family, (for I hope you will not again come without) you of course stay some time, and have no objection to parliamentary attendance. Ireland is the subject upon which I feel the greatest danger of the necessity of attendance, and possibly that may be the attendance only of a day. However, everything is, I think, in a state of greater uncertainty than ever existed before. You will find they have spoiled their Defence Bill still worse than ever. Mrs. Fox desires to be kindly remembered. We are very happy to hear Mrs Grey and the children are so well. Remember me to her.

" Yours affectionately,

"C. J. FOX.

" P.S.—I think, if the French are wise, they are more likely to visit you than us. In London there was a strong opinion they were to begin their embarkation the 10th, *i.e.*, to-morrow ; but this is nonsense."

TO SAME.

"St. Anne's Hill, *August* 18th, 1803.

" Dear Grey,

" Your proceeding at Newcastle seems to have been perfectly right ; it will be reckoned of course rather cold, and the sting, as you call it, towards the end, would be considered by Sheridan as absolute disaffection. All your ideas about what is going on

agree exactly with mine ; and of all the follies, I
think the proposal of uniforms the worst.   Here we
have volunteers in plenty, learning on the green to
" *stand easy,*" &c., but not a single weapon, gun, or
pike, among them all—and this they call training.
I send you a letter from Lord Robert on account of
what is said in it of Lord Grey.   The gallery was
cleared, so he may have heard a false account of my
speech ; the fact is, I did not mention him at all, nor
even allude to him otherwise than by saying there
were several distinguished general officers, from whose
advice (considering the time of their life, and the
state of their health) more was to be expected than
from their actual service in the field.   This did not
point to him more than to Lord Howe and several
others.   It was Maitland who mentioned Lord Howe
and him, and said they differed in opinion on the
proper mode of defence—a circumstance of which I
was totally ignorant.   I am sure you are convinced
it is utterly *impossible* I should have taken an un-
warrantable liberty with *his* name—not likely, I hope,
with that of any other general.

" The Prince of Wales has been here, and we had
a good deal of conversation.   I have since written to
him, and wish I had kept a copy of my letter to
send to you ; but I was too lazy.   The sum of it was
this :—in regard to the bringing before parliament
his offer, and the rejection of it, I told him it was a
point on which he must determine himself, and upon
which I could not advise—but, if he did bring it
forward, I would support him—and he should do it

in earnest, so as to have all the support which could be obtained—and keeping no terms with the Ministry. Without considerable strength it would not be a measure suitable to the dignity of his situation. With regard to Irish affairs, if his Royal Highness would, upon consultation with the principal good-intentioned men of that country, form some system of Government in which Catholic Emancipation was to be included, and have that system brought forward in parliament, and well understood in the country, it might certainly, if steadily pursued, have a very good effect ; because, though it probably would be unsuccessful for the present, the Irish, having hopes from a new reign, would be less inclined to France, and less willing to join in any rash attempts at risings, &c. I think you will not disapprove of any part of this, and, if anything should be done in consequence, I should hope you would come. My opinion is, that nothing will be done, because I shall continue to state that, unless things are to be done in a style of which I think both the Prince and his confidential friends incapable, the whole had better be let alone. I am to see (so the Prince says) Moira in a few days. You know my opinion of him ; but, if he can be right about anything, it will be about Ireland ; and the Prince's ill humour with Sheridan seems, I think, to have increased his confidence in him (Moira). N.B.—I hope I shall not have such confused sentences in my history. I entered into a great deal of detail in my letter upon the communications to be made, and the manner of making them, to the different

knots in opposition ; but this not worth repeating,
One who had not seen so much of Pitt as you and I,
would imagine of course that he would support
Catholic Emancipation ; but my opinion is otherwise.
On the other hand, however, some of his old friends
may : Windham and Lord Spencer, I think, certainly.
I mean, in a few days, to write both to Grattan and
to George Ponsonby, to know their opinions upon
Irish affairs. This letter will look to you like
wonderful, and, for me, unnatural activity ; but, if
you think that to be my disposition, you will be
deceived. Only, if there is any chance, however
small, of good in Ireland, I do not know how, being
in parliament, I can refuse attending to it. Our
newspapers are full of the good dispositions of the
Emperor Alexander, but I know nothing authentic
on the subject, and doubt all that is said. I am
very glad your harvest has so good an appearance·
The turnips surprise me ; as in this country (excepting my Swedish) there is not a turnip-leaf so
big as a shilling to be seen. I have got in my
thin crop of wheat very well.

" Yours affectionately,

"C. J. FOX.

" I go to to Woolbeding on the 29th for ten days."

TO SAME.

"St. Anne's Hill, Sunday, September, 1803.

" Dear Grey,
    " I must write you one line to tell you that I

hear that on the very day I was writing my long letter to the Prince, he and Sheridan were getting drunk *tête-à-tête*, and that the latter boasts that he had convinced his Royal Highness that all he had done was right. It is not the *boast*, which may be all false, but the dining *téte-à-téte*, in the present circumstance, which makes an impression on me. I write this chiefly to save you the trouble of thinking at all seriously upon the contents of my last letter. If I should, which I think not at all unlikely (for my sins) hear any more, either through Moira or otherwise, I do not intend to give you so useless a trouble as to bore you with it. Ireland, however, is still a serious business, which you ought to think about.

" Yours affectionately,

" C. J. FOX."

TO SAME.

" ST. ANNE'S HILL, *October 19th,* 1803.

" DEAR GREY,

" It is a great while since I wrote, but, till I knew something to tell you, and especially till it was known when parliament was to meet, I made a pretty good excuse to myself for my intolerable idleness, which has certainly lately been something worse even than usual. I thought, too, it was the less pressing to write because I had seen nor heard nothing that altered the opinion given in my last short letter to you, on hearing of the *téte-à-téte* dinner given at the Cocoa-tree. I have since (seen) Moira, who came here about a fortnight since. I believe I owed his visit to his having heard I expected him ; but I never liked him so well ; for he was as frank and intelligible as he is usually the contrary. The result was that, all things considered, he thought the Prince would not take the *determined* part which he had once thought of—in short, I collected from this conversation, as well as from other accounts, that Sheridan had as much weight with him as ever, and had almost, if not quite, persuaded him that it was his intention not to break entirely with the Doctor. So you see Thurlow's opinion of the anchorage is very just. Now, with regard to ourselves—the Prince's doing nothing is, in some views, of great consequence ; for, whatever opinion may be generally entertained of his steadiness, still his name and interference would have great effect in smoothing difficulties, and facilitating junctions. An apparent reversionary prospect goes a good way with many, and, most of all, with that numerous class of persons who are never easy without something that is like royal favour. Whether, without such a *smoother*, the difficulties, which you are as well aware of as I, can be got over, is very doubtful : but parliament meets the 22nd of next month, and something must be determined. In your letter to Mr. B, which I have seen, you seem to state four plans to choose out of. 1st. Support of Ministers—which, however, you justly term impossible. For you and me I am sure it is— because, to hold out to the country that *they* have deserved well of it, or can administer it well, would be a base falsehood on our part. 2nd. To attack present and past conjointly. The *best* that can be said of this mode is, that it would be throwing away our time ineffectually, and sacrificing our ease for nothing; but, in reality, it would be worse, as such a conduct would in a good measure tend to strengthen the Court. 3rd. To act in a manner that may lead to the forming of a party against the *Court*, composed of the old and new opposition. 4th. To do nothing.

" The question therefore, as I see it, is only between the two last, and upon this question I do most sincerely wish that you would determine. Which is pleasantest there is no doubt ; but that is a reason the more why one should be upon one's guard against one's inclination. The strongest argument in favour of action seems to me to be the business of Ireland, with respect to which it does, I confess, seem to me that the appearance of anything like a strong party in favour of the Irish might be very useful in regaining the affections of some, and retaining those of others to this country. Besides, I have, I own, a little desire to rescue ourselves from the infamy of acquiescing in the baseness of conceding the most important of all national points to the private opinion of the King. But with regard to the main object, the *public* good to be derived from an apparent strength in this business, will not that depend upon what that strength will be ? and who knows what the new opposition would do in such a case ? I have a strong opinion that Pitt would do nothing right— perhaps the others might. This ought by some means to be ascertained. On the other hand it is a strong argument against this mode of acting, that our efforts may most probably not lead even to the forming of a party acting with fidelity against the *Ministers*, much less to one decidedly and honestly against the *Court*, which after all is the main object, whether we look to Ireland or at England, or to foreign politics. I have a strong suspicion that nothing will induce Pitt to make the *saut perilleux*, and jump into opposition. But others might (and I think very probably), *by degrees*, make up their minds to be in opposition without him. But all this is uncertain, and requires time ; and then whether it is worth while to put ourselves to inconvenience for such doubtful objects, is another consideration. Without your being on the spot as well as me, to take advantage of such occurrences as may arise, to watch openings, &c., I am sure nothing can be done. With respect to the fourth and pleasantest plan, the greatest objection to it is, that the bias of many of our friends being more against Pitt than the Doctor, it is to be feared that many will follow Sheridan whom* we should be sorry to lose ; but as we have no eager views to future politics, any more than to the present, this is of less consequence. Now let me repeat to you, my dear Grey, how very desirous I am that you should decide, and how certain I am that I shall think your decision, whatever it may be, right : whereas, if I am forced to decide myself, whatever I decide I am sure to think wrong. If you decide for

* *Quos* not *quem*—for that I consider as past praying for.—C. J. F.

inaction, the worst of it is that our respective situations make a necessary difference in our conduct; for instance, if anything is moved by Hutchinson, or others, about Ireland, being but twenty miles off, I must attend; and on the other hand, though you are 300 miles distant, constructions may be put upon your absence. If I go on the first day, which I suppose I shall, I will endeavour, of course, to give Windham a lift, and Sheridan a rub, and deal very much in generals. I mean this in case you are not there ; if you are, one might perhaps endeavour at some amendment in which old and new opposition might concur. I was, like you, a great while before I could be persuaded to read *the* pamphlet, which is as stupid as it is impudent and false. To *you* I think it is more particularly impertinent than to any one else, except perhaps Moira. Tierney and Sheridan, of course, deny its coming from the ministry ; but it could come from no other quarter, and I believe it certainly is Brother Hiley's. My newspaper has put off the invasion till next month : I cannot think it possible to come in any considerable force *in boats* in winter time, but what you say on the other hand of the persevering preparations has a good deal in it. People every day seem to be more apprehensive of Ireland being the principal object ; the only question seems to be, whether there are large ships in readiness for the purpose—for boats there are, I suppose, out of the question. Have you heard anything from the Ponsonbies about Ireland, particularly whether they think anything ought to be stirred in Parliament ? *

* Mrs. Grey was the daughter of the late Lord Ponsonby.

The Catholics here, as you saw by the newspaper, behaved rather better about their address than I expected from them. Mrs. Fox desires to be kindly remembered, and is, as I am, very happy to hear Mrs. Grey and the children are all well. We are surprised at your speaking of cold, of which we have had little or none. Do not imitate my sluggishness about writing, but let me hear from you soon, and the more decisively the better. *If* there were a fair prospect of a party *bonâ fide* against the Court— but that is a terrible *if.* If you mean to come to town at all, only recollect that, for political purposes, a month before Christmas is worth six after, as it will be the time for getting things into some shape, if that be possible, or if not, for satisfying ourselves that we have a right to be idle afterwards. It would, indeed, be a mode of putting off decision, which is always to my taste. To desire you to come 300 miles only to look about you, would be very unreasonable indeed, but if you do intend coming, to propose to you to come a few weeks the sooner for such a purpose is not quite so bad. At any rate, I hope you will not come again without your family. We go the 31st to Southhill, where we shall stay, as I guess, about a week. You can calculate posts, and direct to me accordingly either here or there.

" Your's affectionately,
"C. J. FOX.

" P.S. Terrible bad sport here."

TO SAME.

"St. Anne's Hill, *November 27th,* 1803.

" Dear Grey,

" The very day after I wrote to you last, I had a message from the Prince that he would come here, which was afterwards changed into a summons for me to go to town. I went, and met him and Sheridan at Moira's. As the last has been, I understand, at Howick, he probably related to you the nature of the conversation. The upshot was, that in order to get the Prince and his friends undeceived as soon as possible, I advised that the question of ' whether any junction upon honourable terms could be formed with the Doctor,' should be brought to a point immediately through Sheridan. Sheridan, to my surprise, undertook it ; and it has ended, as you may suppose, in *nothing.* The thing now stands as it should do. The Prince, if he can be undeceived, must be so now (I have not seen him since), and at least he can have no pretence to urge me to any tenderness towards the Doctor. In matters where his Royal Highness's name is concerned, I shall of course do, or forbear doing, as he wishes, and in other matters I shall follow my own course and the advice of my friends. I mean on the day of the Army, to support Windham, &c., cordially, and am very sorry you will not be there to do the same. I certainly do not think, at present, that I should be justified in pressing you to come, but if there were just cause, remember your syllogism is not made out—that you cannot come without your

family is granted ; and pray do me the justice to
recollect, that so far from pressing such a measure,
I always deprecated it—but that you *cannot* bring
your family (though the inconvenience of doing it
may be allowed) is not made out. Now comes a
point upon which I wish to have your opinion as soon
as possible. I mean· that which has been so often
agitated—whether we should bring on the business
of Ireland. Since the insurrection, the question
stands on very different grounds from the former,
since it is in a manner demonstrated that the country
is in the state in which we feared it to be, and not in
that which the Ministerial Irish members represented
it. Sheridan, as you may guess, is furious against
stirring a question which will embarrass himself, and
says that we shall not be fifty upon it—that we shall
exasperate the Orangists by the attempt, and drive
the Catholics to despair by the failure of it.
Fitzwilliam and I think on the contrary that we
shall not be so weak, and next, that by showing the
Catholics that there are men of name at least in this
country who espouse their cause, we shall teach them
to look to other quarters than Bonaparte for redress.
In a party view, Sheridan says we shall give Pitt,
who, he concludes, is against us, an opportunity of
ingratiating himself with the King, and so contribute
to his restoration. This argument we do not hold
to be worth answering, because it is obvious that if
listened to, it would bind our hands, not only upon
this, but upon all other occasions. And on the other
hand, we think the measure good in a party view, as

it would gain us the support of Windham, the
Grenvilles, and possibly of others of Pitt's friends.
Nay, further, if Pitt must be always considered in
our deliberations, against which I protest, I think
there is no measure more calculated to embarrass
him, and drive him to an option between acting fairly
and honorably, or losing a great number of his
friends, and disgusting the rest. I do not speak
without book of the Grenvilles and Windham.
I asked a fair question, and have had a fair answer.
If the question is to come on, I think Geo. Ponsonby
would be the properest person to undertake it, and
next to him you or myself. It should at all events
be one of our party, for more reasons than one, as I
know some doubtful votes among us that would be
decided, however foolishly, by such a circumstance.
I have written both to Geo. Ponsonby and Grattan
to ask their opinions. You will have perceived that
by what I said in the House of Commons I tried to
raise some expectations without pledging myself. The
affair of the 23rd of July may probably be discussed
on the Army day. The folly of the Castle appears,
from papers which I have seen, to have been beyond
belief; and the impudence of the government there,
if they really have (as my brother thinks) endeavoured
to lay part of the blame upon him must be beyond
the Devil's. My brother has a distinct approbation of
his conduct from the Duke of York, and is appointed
to command in this Home district, which is a pretty
strong mark of confidence. Lord Hardwicke is
continued, and has the Garter. I am told, too, that

Yorke says it was not Lord Hardwicke, but his Secretaries, *without his knowledge,* that expressed the wish for my brother's recall : a pretty respectable account of *his* brother, to be sure.   Surely all this is beyond the usual follies of foolish governments. *À propos* to the command in Ireland, I learn from undoubted authority that, upon my brother's return, it was destined for Lord Cornwallis, who accepted it, but that upon his coming to town, the Doctor excused himself, by laying the rejection of him upon the King.   And I have reason to believe that the Doctor had been informed that such an appointment would raise a rebellion among the Orangemen of course ; and yet he (Lord Cornwallis) passed the attainder against Lord Edward's children, &c. &c., and has been upon all occasions (God knows) complaisant enough to His Majesty.   But not to go all lengths is as bad as going none.   These examples are rather good than bad.

" As to Sheridan, I think him even more gone than I had supposed.   I dined with him one day at Brookes's, and one at Lord G. Cavendish's, and he certainly was rather run at, but he seemed to grow worse and worse.   The chief subject was, however the Irish question, and upon that alone I would not judge him ; but there are two symptoms which I consider as deadly.   1st. He would not own to me that nothing had come of what he had undertaken at Lord Moira's.   'If anything, what ? ' was a natural question on my part.   ' Can I see you to-morrow ? ' was his reply.   ' Why not go into the other room now ? ' said I. This was at Brookes's. He said he could not *just then*, and no more passed about it, though we met the next day : of course he had nothing to say, but his disowning this is a very bad sign. But the worst of all was his going out of the House on the day of the Report, because he had heard a report that Francis was to say something about the Prince's not being employed. If even where the Prince's name is in question, and on a subject upon which his (the Prince's) eagerness is well known, Sheridan does not differ from the Doctor—the inference is too plain. If I do not write often, you will at least allow I write long enough ; so God bless you : only let me have your opinion as soon as may be, that I may quote it, if necessary, in some *conciliabulum*, which I suspect must take place.

" Your's affectionately,

" C. J. FOX.

" P.S. Mrs. Fox desires to be kindly remembered. We had a very pleasant party at Southhill and at Woburn. The young Duchess is very gay and good-humoured."

TO THE HON. R. FITZPATRICK.

" St. Anne's Hill, *Tuesday, November 30th,* 1803.

" Dear Dick,

" We were in hopes to have seen or heard of you before this ; and may be that you and I should go to town together for the army. Pray let me know when it is to come on, and, even if you take no other part in it, think of saying something about the Prince. If the new Opposition attack the general system of defence, I am determined to support them vigorously ; but upon that subject I shall not begin. If you see Windham or Grenville, and the opportunity offers, you may tell them so. With regard to the great question of Ireland, I have written both to Ponsonby and Grattan, and should wish to have their answers before I decide, though rather for the sake of others than my own. If you can collect the opinion of any of our friends upon the point (I mean the propriety of bringing it on), pray let me know. At the dinner at B.'s and Lord George's, everybody was so glad to run at Sheridan, that no real opinion could appear. You had best come.

> " Yours affectionately,
>
> "C. J. F.

" P.S.—I saw Windham for a moment in the street, who seemed to have some notion of doing something previous to the Army : I did not rightly understand him what. If a general motion of disapprobation (which I should like exceedingly) were to be made, it should be after the Army and Navy, and growing out of the debates on those questions."

TO SAME.

" St. Anne's Hill, *Friday, December 2nd,* 1803.

" Dear Dick,

" I think differently from you, and that the Army

Estimates will probably have been presented to-day, and be considered this day week; and this is an additional reason, though none was wanting, why you should come sooner than you talk of—suppose the old day, Sunday. I have a letter from the Prince, which makes it all safe upon the subject of mentioning his business; and I am sure the more persons speak of it the more he will be pleased. I will speak to Francis * of this before the debate; but do not mention my having had a letter yet. What Sheridan said, though I knew it was a lie at the time, gave me an opportunity of asking orders, which I did, however, without naming Sheridan; but of this when we meet. I am not so attached to the Army day † that I should refuse attending upon any other occasion on which the defence system might be examined; but I own I prefer that day very much; first, because there is great convenience in a committee; and next, and chiefly, because it is much better that the first appearance of agreement with Windham, &c., should be on an accidental than on an apparently concerted occasion. Many of our friends would mock at supporting a motion of the N. O.‡ in the first instance, who might be easily brought to it if the motion arises out of debates in which we have our share, and in general the appearance would be better. We do not, in this case, concert a motion; but when

---

* Sir Philip Francis.

† The allusion seems to be to the intended debate on the Army Estimates, which took place on the 9th of December, 1803. Mr. Fox spoke on this occasion.   ‡ New Opposition.

public business is brought before us, we give similar opinions, which, if afterwards shaped into a question, must of course have the support of each party. You will agree with me, of course, that this reasoning might as well not be communicated. The Army's being the natural opportunity, and the advantage of a committee, are quite sufficient arguments in its favour. I have not seen even any extracts from the pamphlet you mention. Among the various accounts of the going out in 1801, the account I most credited was the same as you say this pamphlet gives; but why the meanness should be boasted of, one does not readily conceive, unless they think (and perhaps not very wrong) that things are fallen to that state that nothing is so disgraceful and unpopular as to stand in opposition to the King; and the only charge to defend oneself from is that of having forfeited his favour by disputing his will. He is a mean rascal after all,* and you, who have sometimes supposed him to be high-minded, were quite wrong. Mind and come soon. I hope you will have no relapse; but if you have one, have it here. Lady M. W. M.† has sunk in my opinion, from her letters and the new published poetry.

" Yours affectionately,

"C. J. F."

* Mr. Pitt seems to be here meant; and a pamphlet, published in his defence, mentioned in a former letter, is alluded to.

† Lady Mary Wortley Montague, of whose letters and writings a new edition had recently been published.

TO SAME.

"DEAR DICK,

"All you say concerning the Irish business is true; there is no chance of Grenville's bringing it on. Fitz. refrains from it; not, I believe, from his deference to Ponsonby or Grattan's opinion, but because he thinks (perhaps truly) that he has not the talents necessary for bringing on a question of such importance. I send you two letters, which of course are of the most confidential nature : they make me only regret the more that the business is not to come on. I think more than half of Pitt's friends must have been with us; and though he would have opposed it, his speech must have been substantially favourable to the question. I have told the duchess that, although I had intended, if the question had been to be moved, to give Pitt notice, it is impossible for me to make any communication to him about it, as things now stand. Send me back the letters. Monmouth would have been dead yesterday, if the fine weather had not saved him ; and, though I have had a terrible number of letters to write to day, so that I dare not quite say I will not dine before his head be off, I have hopes. N. B. I did not take the mode I mentioned to you; but, on the contrary, entered into the discussions, &c., which I had once thought of postponing till after his execution.*

"Yours affectionately,
"C. J. F."

* Mr. Fox alludes to the description of the execution of the Duke of Monmouth in his History. See the end of Chapter iii.

TO THE HON. CHARLES GREY.

"St. Anne's Hill, *December 17th*, 1803.

" Dear Grey,

"I have deferred writing till I had an answer from Ireland. I had one from Grattan some days ago, and I have one from G. Ponsonby to day. They are both against bringing on the question at present, and so of course I must give it up, but with more regret I must confess than I ever felt upon any political subject in my life. It is the only question that can be started to make what can be called a *cause* against the Court. We missed the opportunity very unwisely in 1801 ; the insurrection of last summer gives us another, and, when we shall have lost that, it is not easy to foresee when we shall have another. If the French land there, *tout est dit*, and if there is any long period of uninterrupted tranquillity, a fallacious security will take place, and all the arguments you mention of disturbing unanimity, &c., when things are quiet, will gain additional force. I am vexed, I own, very much vexed ; Ponsonby, whose hurry of business would not let him write at length, says, *not for these three months*—what he means by this period I cannot guess. In the mean time it may, though I rather think it will not be, taken up by the Grenvilles or others ; for I think I am bound to acquaint them that I have dropped the thoughts of it for the present. With respect to your apprehensions of the consequences of letting Sheridan be a *go-between*, I do not wonder at your

being alarmed, but I was convinced from circumstances that there was no danger, and perhaps I felt
the bolder from my own determination to have
nothing to do with the thing if it succeeded ; but, in
fact, I was morally certain that there could be no
success ; and my only object being to convince
others upon that point, it was necessary there should
be a go-between, and that the go-between should be
a person who wished a junction. So far from the
thing being in a state in which improper use may be
made of it, I strongly suspect Sheridan never did
anything in it. You will have heard of our debate
on the Army. I think Windham and I exposed the
volunteer system pretty well, and I think the House
were rather with us. Pitt's speech was very flat, and
his plan (of) making them *quasi* soldiers, and settling
fines, &c., without their consent, is very ill received
in general. Whether he will move it, or not, I doubt.
Erskine made a foolish figure, I hear, in the debate
on the report. What you say of the unpopularity of
the Grenvilles and Windham is, I believe, true, and
especially among our friends, but they are the only
part of the new opposition with whom we can
expect cordial and fair co-operation. You know I
always thought among all their faults, that they had
one good quality, viz., that of being capable of becoming good party men. Pitt, I hear, is more and more
bitter against the Ministers, and feels strongly what
he deems the embarrassment of his situation. I am
told he even expresses this sentiment (an openness
not very usual with him) to some of his friends.

The Grenvilles, &c., are, I suspect, very much out of humour with him; many of these circumstances would be good, if we were allowed, by bringing on the Irish business, to make use of them; but as it is—but I will not renew my lamentations. There is nothing in the present state of things that could make me press you, or even advise you, to come at the expense of any great inconvenience ; but if there were, I must still maintain that, Mrs. Grey being to be confined in March, was not a reason why the family could not come up in November or December— the difficulty will, as you say, increase. My situation is awkward enough to be sure without you; except Whitbread, and now perhaps Francis, not one friend whatever opens his lips in the House to support me ; and all my allies upon the bench next the bar attacked, when I am away, by my friends. I hope and believe I shall attend very little, but at any rate the state of things is very unpleasant. Every measure that has any thing like spirit in it thought imprudent, as if we had some fine situation which we were afraid of risking, The truth is, I fear that our friends are like Pitt, and, though they know that they have not, nor ever can have the King's favour, they do not like giving up all the hopes of it, any more than Sancho Panza those of his island.

" I think I shall not bear it much longer, but how I shall get out of it the Lord knows. I sometimes think I shall call a meeting, and tell them fairly that a great majority of the best opinions are against it, but that I must and will bring on the business of

Ireland as an individual, without any expectation of their support. In short, I do not know what to do. If some question is not brought on by some friend of ours, or some opposition to a Ministerial question headed by some of us, upon which a division can be had, you may depend upon it we shall crumble most incredibly, and what is still worse, all the shabby rascals will have it to say, whilst they are carrying on all sorts of coquetry with the Doctor, that they have committed no act of desertion : What can be done ?

" I hear from Lauderdale that he is in high spirits about his book. I hope it is not quite so paradoxical as you apprehend. I heartily wish it may succeed in public opinion, for his heart seems to be quite set on it. What a strange man Moira must be ! for when I saw him only two days before his departure, he thought as I did, that there was not the least *inclination* even in the Doctor, to solicit our support, so that your old friend Tierney could make a fool of him in one single conversation.

" Believe me, my dear Grey, with every good wish for you and yours,

" Yours affectionately,

" C. J. FOX.

" P. S.—Upon reading over my letter, I am afraid you will think that all my friends are against the bringing on of the Irish question, which would be a great error. Fitzpatrick and Whitbread are for it, the former very eagerly indeed. Fitzwilliam of course and all the younger ones, Lord King, Lord Archibald Hamilton, &c. Our numbers would, if our friends stick by us, be good. Wilberforce and others would support us; and though Pitt I think would not, I doubt whether he would prevent some of his friends, Canning, &c."

THE PRINCE OF WALES TO MR. FOX.

" DEAR CHARLES,

"Yesterday's post brought me your kind and friendly letter, for which I beg you will accept of my best acknowledgments. So far from not meeting the question with respect to the indecent treatment I have experienced on the subject of the military situation in which I am placed, and so far from my not wishing it fairly to be understood by the country, nothing can be more conformable to my inclinations than that the topic should be revived, as I consider it a point of absolute duty on my part to the country, that my character should stand quite clear in its eyes, especially as the correspondence has been subject to much gross misrepresentation. As, for instance, instead of the King's having told me, as you know in his letter that he did, that my place was at the head of my regiment, the courtiers, not the Ministry, have artfully and intentionally circulated, that my being here at my post was entirely contrary to his Majesty's will and pleasure, and arose solely from a wilful *opposition* on my part, the King having desired *me to be on his right hand* whenever he took the field.

I feel quite secure in your hands, and therefore wish you to follow exactly what your own excellent judgment will suggest ; and, from what has dropped from the King, in his last speech, of his determination to set *a personal example*, I think it affords you the fairest and most inviting opportunity whenever the army estimates are brought forward. It is not my intention, unless something very particular should arise, to be in town for some time. Pray remember me most kindly to Mrs. Fox, and tell her I have not forgot her wine, but that as soon as I entertain my family in London, and my butler consequently returns, I will instantly despatch it to St. Anne's Hill.

" I am ever, with great truth, my dear Charles,
" Very affectionately yours,
" G. P.
"Brighton, *November 29th*, 1803."

" P.S.—I am afraid you will hardly be able to read this horrid scrawl, but I have not time to copy it over."

TO THE HON. CHARLES GREY.

"St. Anne's Hill, *January 6th*, 1804.

" Dear Grey,
" I have deferred writing since I received yours in hopes of being able to tell you something authentic respecting Pitt's politics, but I have not got the intelligence I expected. I cannot say how much obliged I am by your letter. You perceived, no doubt, that mine was written in a moment of ill humour and vexation, and there is nothing omitted in yours

that could tend to make me better pleased. I send you Grattan's letter, which you will return me. Ponsonby's was quite short, and referring me to a future one, which, however, I have not had. At present I shall do nothing, but I consider the question as open, and a little more encouragement will make me decide for the attack. It would be no small additional motive that you would have no objection to be the mover. As to giving you, in the Eton phrase, sense, I should think it quite unnecessary, but would do anything in that way that you desire. That there should be a part of the United Kingdom to which our laws nominally at least extend, and which is nevertheless in such a state as to call for martial law, &c., so repeatedly, is of itself ground for reconsidering, at least, the system by which it is governed. I hear there is a wish in the Catholics here to have the question stirred, but whether this be true to any extent I do not yet know, but probably shall have further information upon that point in a few days, which I will communicate to you. In a letter I have from the Duke of Bedford, urging me to bring on the question, he alludes to a pamphlet of Mr. Tighe's addressed to me. I have not seen it ; but, from the way in which the Duke mentions it, I suppose that it is unfavourable to my opinions. Have you heard anything of it ? He is, I believe, a cousin of Mrs. Grey, and was quite connected in politics with his uncles.

" I wonder Lauderdale's book is not yet out ; I hope it is less paradoxical than you expect it to be.

The invasion is to be (at least so say the Ministers) this week or the next. If it is true that the troops in Holland are actually embarked, that is something ; but I am still confident that their landing in force is next to impossible. As I know now what I may, or may not, ask of you in regard to attendance, you may depend upon me, that I will not exceed your permission. Indeed I think it very possible, if the great business does not come on, that I may not attend myself above two or three days in the session. I have been making a very bad job of fatting two oxen. If you, upon your large scale, were to do as ill, it would be sad work.

" Yours ever affectionately,

" C. J. FOX."

TO SAME.

"St. Anne's Hill, January 29th, 1804.

" Dear Grey,

" I never wished more earnestly that the distance between us was less than at this moment, for I have a matter to communicate which would be much easier and better done in conversation than by letter, for every reason. However, as I cannot afford to go six hundred miles, I must, in spite of all objections, attempt it in the only other way. I have had a direct communication (wholly unsought by me) from that part of the opposition which sits at the bar end of the House, to the following effect. That it is their wish to join with us in a systematic opposition, for the purpose of removing the Ministry, and substituting one on the broadest possible basis. Stowe

and all his appendages,* Lord Spencer, and Windham
are the *proposers* : of Carlisle and others they have
no doubt ; and Fitzwilliam, as you know, is eager for
such a plan. There was an openness and appearance
of cordiality in the manner of making the proposal
that much pleases me. Upon the subject of Pitt
there was no reserve ; it was stated that he, for himself, peremptorily refused entering into anything that
could be called opposition, and that a full explanation had taken place between Lord Grenville and him
upon that point. The result of this explanation was
that all political connexion between them was off, and
that, if the proposed plan took place, no consideration
was to be had of Pitt or his opinions at all, except as
far as, in a prudential view, one might sometimes
shape a question, for the purpose of availing ourselves of his support, as one would of any other
individual. It was admitted, too, that Pitt's plan
might be to let the Doctor fall, and then to avail himself
of the merit of not having been in opposition, in order
to make himself the most acceptable person to succeed him. It was admitted further that this was
an objection to the plan ; but it is one, I believe,
which neither you nor I much regard. With respect
to the Irish question, it would be left to my judgment ; but a most important question will, it is said,
come on immediately, in which, at any rate, we shall
join. I mean the revision of the volunteer system,
and, in general, of our military force. The Ministers,
it is said, intend to bring in a *declaratory* Bill to

* The Duke of Buckingham, Lord Grenville, Mr. Thomas Grenville.

confirm the Attorney-General's opinion, and condemn Erskine's. This *I* do not believe, but they
will certainly bring in some bill to assimilate volunteers more to regular forces, and thereby to increase
the incredible burthen of them to the country. The new
opposition will, if we concur, (and perhaps whether
we do or not,) bring forward a plan which appears
to me to be a good one, but which I cannot detail on
paper. The general drift is to follow in general
Windham's ideas and mine in regard to arming *en
masse*, to diminish the militia, to enlist regular soldiers
for terms of years, to put an end to bidding for
substitutes, &c., &c. My answer was that I must
consult friends before I come to any determination,
and particularly *you*. I own I lean very much to
such a junction—but then, what they say is true,
that it is idle to look for the full effect of it unless
both you and I attend ; the inconvenience of this
to both of us is certainly very great ; but is it not
perhaps *right* to sacrifice our convenience ?

Pray think this well over, and answer me upon
this as well as the other points of this letter. My
only doubt is between the two following answers.
1st. A direct yes. 2nd. That though I approve the
plan, I do not see sufficient prospect of real good to
make me give that sort of attention to public affairs
which is inconsistent with my private comfort—but
they will occasionally have my support and especially
in this volunteer business. By the way, in this affair
I should think Erskine and even Sheridan must be
with us as far as opposing the Ministers' Bill. Pitt

will, I believe, take the opportunity of trimming the Doctor for the *confusions, misunderstandings,* &c., &c., and even oppose his Bill if it is declaratory. Perhaps he will have a measure of his own—but I hear from all hands that his (Pitt's) ideas on this subject are so singular, that they are approved in no quarter. Pray lose no time in writing. What would I not give that you could without intolerable inconvenience come with your family to town for two or three months. Adieu. If Lauderdale is with you let him know my difficulties, for I have not time to write to him this post.

I have not yet heard again from G. Ponsonby, which, considering what I heard from you relative to my supposed misunderstanding of his opinion, surprises me ; indeed in his letter he said he would write more fully. The person from whom I had the communication knew nothing of what would be the conduct of Canning and that knot.

" Yours most truly,
"C. J. FOX.

" P.S.—I believe it is certain that Pitt offered to stay in without pushing the measure of Catholic Emancipation, and equally so that he concealed his having made the offer from all his colleagues except Dundas. What a man ! "

TO SAME.

" DEAR GREY,

" I received your second letter just as I was
leaving St. Anne's yesterday. I am sorry Lauderdale's opinion is so strong as you describe it, though
all I have done is telling them that I have every
inclination to act with them, but I think it would be
better to agree first in public, and so let the thing
come on naturally, rather than by any compact. But
it is useless to trouble you with more upon this
matter at present, as a new scene arises. The King
is as ill as in the worst moments of 1788. I think I
know this, and the bulletin indeed does not deny it,
' *much indisposed*' yesterday, and ' *much the same*'
to-day. Some are of opinion that his dissolution is
certain and near, but though this is the general belief,
I do not know that it is so well grounded as that of
his derangement. If this had not been the case, I
would have pressed you very much to come for
Monday or Tuesday se'nnight, when a motion was to
have been for a committee to consider of volunteers,
army, militia, &c. The nothingness of the present
bill would have made this a very advantageous
question ; but *now* I suppose all attention to all
questions will be suspended. You know that an
inquiry into the 23rd of July is to be moved on
Monday by Sir J. Wrottesley, a Pittite ; yet I hear
from good authority, Pitt will not be there, though
he is in town. Probably, however, this motion, with

all others, will be postponed. It is curious to see
how long these men, at such a time, a time as they
say of impending invasion, will venture to go on
without legal authority. The Doctor acquainted the
Prince of the King's illness the day before yesterday,
but did not state it, I believe, to be so bad as it
then was, much less as it *now* is. In some shape we
must have to act ; and therefore if you *can* come, for
God's sake do ; only wait for to-morrow's post, when I
may be able to tell you more, though I am not
certain. I wish for Lauderdale almost as much as
for you, but will he leave his book ? Whitbread, I
hear, made an excellent speech on Wednesday. I
was kept at home by Mrs. Fox's being very ill indeed
—not dangerously indeed after the first day, but in
dreadful pain from a bilious attack, and I had neither
heart nor composure to write to you or Lauderdale,
or indeed to do anything, till Sunday, and then I
thought I might as well put it off till I got here. Tell
Lauderdale this, if you see him, for his letter certainly
required an answer. Make up your mind to be what
you must be, if things take a turn that I think not
improbable. I will give every assistance, but you
must be at the head.

" Yours affectionately,

" C. J. FOX."

TO SAME.

" *Thursday Evening* (*near nine*), *March*, 1804.

" DEAR GREY,

"In case I should not see you, or see you only
in a crowd, before we go down to the House to-

morrow, I wish you would set down on paper some of
the names of those who you think ought to be
convened on Saturday, to decide finally (or at least
for the present) upon what I call the great question.
I should like such a sanction, not only in the case of
our doing something, but in the more probable one
of our being forced to submit silently. I will endeavour to see Sheridan or at least Moira, and bring the
question of the Prince's support to a point. As to
Pitt, I think, you must form the same conclusion from
the Duchess's paper that I do—He is a mean, low-
minded dog.

" Yours ever,

" C. J. FOX."

TO SAME.

"St. ANNE'S HILL, <i>Wednesday, March</i> 28<i>th</i>, 1804.

Vile weather.

" DEAR GREY,

" I am much honored by Mrs. Grey's request,
and accept with great pleasure. You will have
heard, of course, of the cessation of the bulletins
without the announcing of recovery : things go on
step by step, in such a manner, that how to remedy
the effects of our submission is a very difficult
question. Your plan of discussion in the papers is a
very good one, and I will endeavour to get it
executed. The person whom you name is the
properest for it. The division on Pitt's motion did,
I own, surprise me—not so much on account of our
numbers, as of theirs ; and it is a strong proof how
far less than any former House the present is

influenced by debate, for it was decidedly in favour,
if not of the question, at least of the Admiralty.
Pitt's opening was vile, and even in his reply, though
some of the declamatory parts of it were good, he
did very little. The Doctor gave out, and so did
some of his friends for him, that he saw the combina-
tion against him was too strong, and that he should
give up. I never believed him, and if what is
reported is true, that he is offering Erskine to be
Attorney-General, and forming other arrangements
of the like nature, it seems out of the question. To
propose to a man to come into an Administration
who are just about to resign, would rather exceed
even the Doctor's extraordinary mode of proceeding.
The decision of conduct which you wish, will not,
I think, take place with regard to Sheridan; with
regard to Erskine and the Duke of Norfolk it will.
Sheridan was a good deal badgered at Parsloe, and
looked in his most sheepish and down manner. What
was his motive for attending there I know not,
unless he had hopes of some support, which failed
him. Our meeting was small, but very good in point
of zeal. Coke made a warm speech, which gave
great satisfaction, and even those who did not quite
stomach our junction, if such it can be called, with
the Grenvilles, were as eager against the Ministers as
could be wished. With respect to future business,
my intention is to bring forward several questions
after Easter, in some of which Pitt will (speaking of
him, one must always say, ' *I believe*,') support me—
in others, *not*. I had meant, if I had not had your

letter to-day, to put off writing to you for a few days till I had something more arranged in regard to these measures than I yet have, and till I had received some communications from London ; but as I have begun I must go on. Russian Mediation, Ireland, and Military Defence, are the three general points I thought of. On the last of these three *only*, I expect Pitt's *active* support ; but on the others he may not possibly interfere. You know his sort of hydrophobia upon the Catholic question, but my motion might, I think, be simply directed to the necessity of inquiry in consequence of martial law, &c., as well as of the new fact, brought out on Wrottesley's motion, of Lord Hardwicke having applied in vain for extra- ordinary powers. To the Russian business, I hear, there is some particular objection, on account of some supposed transaction now pending, of which I know nothing, but am enquiring, It is very much the wish of Canning, &c., that we should begin, at least, with the motion which Pitt will support—*they* thinking it a great object, with a view to public effect, that he should appear with all his strength in support of a motion made by *me*. I say let him show how much he strengthens us, and welcome ; but let us show that without him we are not inconsiderable ; and this, I think, if proper pains are taken, we might show. You will perceive by all this how very desirable every possible attendance is, *and* that for weeks at the very least. I do not push the conse- quence at present, but I fear I must shortly. If you are here, you will, of course, make such of the motions as you like yourself. I cannot yet fix, but I fear we cannot open the campaign later than the 16th of April, as Parliament meet again on the 5th. Pitt is, I believe, as far as temper goes, completely exasperated against the present men, and consequently desirous of making conjointly with us as strong an opposition as possible ; but then again his views are so narrow, and his fear of committing himself against the Court and its corrupt interests, meets him so at every turn, that he cannot act like a man. Lord Camden's, Lord Castlereagh's, and Lord Carrington's influence with him is, I take it, all nonsense ; but the Court! the Court! he cannot bear to give up his hopes there, and upon this principle, wishes to narrow every question of opposition, so as to be pledged to nothing but the insulated questions, or questions of detail. This is a sad state of things ; but forcing even him in, is an inroad on royal power, and as such, good, come what may afterwards. I am told Lord Saint Vincent is very angry with us who voted for the motion. He ought to be angry with those who advised him to resist the production of the papers : for if he had taken the other course, Pitt must have moved his Address, and the division would have been triumphant for Lord St. Vincent.

" Yours ever most affectionately,

"C. J. FOX.

TO SAME.

"St. Anne's Hill, *August 2nd*, 1804.

" Dear Grey,

"I have only time to write you a few lines to-day. I know little more concerning my three motions than when I wrote last, except that I have reason to believe that upon the defence, or army in mass, or whatever shape I may give to *that* question, Pitt will support me and take real and unusual pains to appear with great numbers. I have not therefore decided the *order* of my motions, nor shall till I go to town on the 10th. I think probably the first of them will be on the 17th or 18th, but if you can come, you will easily believe I can manage to put it off for a few days. In the mean time, reports are that the King is much worse, and I find by your letter to Whitbread that you feel as I do about the difficulty, if not impossibility, of submitting without an effort. Adieu.

" Yours, ever,
" C. J. FOX.

"I hate to press you, but I really think the next six weeks must bring matters to a crisis, both with respect to the King, and to the getting rid of these rascals. I go to town the 10th.

" No. 9, Arlington Street."

TO SAME.

"St. Anne's Hill, *Friday, April 6th,* 1804.

" Dear Grey,

"Things are just in the same state as when I wrote last, at least as far as I know, and our operations will begin as I told you, I think the 18th the latest possible day for the first motion. I do not know whether I mentioned in my last the question of the exorbitant prerogative claimed by some of the bills, by which the King is supposed by common law to have a right in case of invasion of sending any individual into the ranks of any regiment he thinks fit. I think there must be a separate question on this point, but as I shall see Lord Grenville in a few days, who takes it up in the House of Lords, I shall determine nothing till I have talked with him. The King is supposed to have been very ill again on Tuesday. In these circumstances, my dear Grey, whatever my wishes may be, I cannot answer to myself not telling you how very material I think it is that you should come as soon as you can. We shall be, I hope, strong ; I am told on some occasions very strong ; but it is only the more desirable that both in numbers and debate we should appear to have our full share in the business. You must brave the expense and inconvenience, and bring Mrs. Grey for a month or two. Make Lauderdale come too if you can. Sheridan has been here, and as I judge is very desirous of getting right again, but you will easily believe my dependence on him is not very firm. He

is certainly out of humour with the Doctor. I think
you said Brandling would vote against Ministers—
can you do any thing towards getting him up ? or
can you point out any other channel ? Lauderdale
seems justly uneasy about our Government's apparent
share in the Paris plot. If anything comes out we
must, I think, take some opportunity (perhaps by a
direct motion) of expressing our detestation of the
transaction, even though we should have no other
support than our *old* friends. Indeed, I think I
should feel quite miserable not to have done it. It
is not necessary for me to repeat with what extreme
reluctance I press you to do what in your case I
should hate doing as much as you can. They say
even the Duke of Norfolk is to come back, but I
doubt it.

" Yours affectionately,
"C. J. FOX.

" It is a sad business the Duke d'Enghien being
taken—if Bonaparte would pardon him handsomely !
but I fear. . . . . I go to town, as I said, on Tuesday.

" No. 9, ARLINGTON STREET."

TO SAME.

"ARLINGTON STREET, *April* 13*th*, 1804.

" DEAR GREY,

" I received yesterday yours of the 8th, which,
if you had directed to this place, I should have
had it a day sooner. I cannot bear, my dear Grey,
to press you ; but to say otherwise than that I think

your attendance of the greatest consequence is impossible for me, consistently with what I think and feel. As to anything like a certainty of the effort against the Doctor being successful, I am sure I am far enough from entertaining any such notion ; but, that there is really a chance, and a very good chance too, is my decided opinion ; that chance would, no doubt, be far better if Pitt were different from what he is. With respect to the particular questions, there is much in what you say ; but the fact, I understand to be, that Pitt will, *totis viribus*, support the motion I have mentioned. I think now, too, of connecting with it, as preparatory to any practicable general arming of the people, the question Lord Grenville has started concerning the assumption of the prerogative in the Defence Bill, and consequent enactment. The argument will be in this order. I wish a general arming, not as a threat for the purpose of raising volunteers, but for real defence. I must begin, therefore, with getting rid of a statement of prerogative which I think false, and still more of an enactment that cannot be endured, viz., giving the King the power to send you or me into the ranks of any regiment he pleases, subjecting us to the Mutiny Bill, &c. When I shall have got rid of these impediments, I would have an act empowering the King immediately to arm us, and, in case of invasion, to direct in what manner he shall call on us for service. Then will follow the propriety of some new modes of increasing the regular army, which, notwithstanding all their statements, is very deficient. I think the infantry, for *field* service, does not amount altogether to 25,000 men. I have detailed all this because I think it will in some measure answer your objection. If, indeed, we were to carry the Committee, I do not differ with you in being afraid of some of Pitt's vagaries ; but, such is our condition, we must agree where we can, and take the chance of how soon we shall be obliged to separate. This unfavourable state of our condition applies, I fear, to more than the management of parliamentary questions : but let us first get rid of the Doctor is my first principle of action, in which I reckon you as concurring with me as much as any one. Whitbread did send me Belsham's Letters—my answer was, that I cannot stomach his ideas about the treasury, and still less that of making overtures. As far as there is anything of the sort yet, the overture certainly came from Pitt, but confined, of course, to parliamentary proceedings at this particular time. As to the King's state, I have heard very little these last two days ; but he is not well, that is certain, and that he will not become so is my clear opinion. What this ambiguous state will produce is very difficult to divine ; but that if Ministers do propose anything, they should, at their time of proposing it, be in as weak and decried a state as possible, seems to me to be clearly desirable for the Prince's interests in particular—and in this instance our interests, and those of all who wish well to the country, are the same with his. Lauderdale's notion of questions, preparatory to a motion for dismissal, I entirely approve ; but are not some of the

questions I have stated of this nature ? He has, of
course, mentioned to you his opinion, that, after a
good division, in which Pitt and we concur, petitions, &c., might be easily obtained in Scotland. I
suspect this is equally true with respect to England ;
but then the question ought to be something of more
importance and *body*, if I may so say, than Pitt is yet
up to. Oh ! he is a sad stick. Our divisions these
three days have been shabby, which I am sorry for,
as they may hurt future ones ; or, if they do not,
the contrast of our numbers, when Pitt is in town, to
what they are when he is not, will be more striking
than one would wish. Comparatively, indeed, to
those of the majority, our numbers yesterday were
good. Lord H. Petty made one of the neatest and
best short speeches I ever heard ; and its being in
answer, and indeed a complete answer to Grant, who
is held so high, made it the better—to be sure Grant
was flimsy beyond expression.

" I was just going to conclude this letter when I
received yours of the 10th. What can I say ? I hate
the thoughts of your coming alone, almost as much as
you can do. But, in short I know not what to say.
Our first division of great consequence will probably
be on Friday next, the 20th, but that probably will
be followed (unless we should make a very bad figure
indeed) by others of equal importance. How long
such a battle may last it is impossible to say, and
with regard to the King's health, and any measures
to be taken on that subject, it is still more difficult
to conjecture. If you *do* come, I think you will

agree that the sooner the better ; and no pains shall be wanting to accelerate everything as much as possible, with a view to your release. Indeed, everything that does not depend on the King's illness may easily be brought on as rapidly as you please. Now referring you to the former part of this letter, and to others, I will say no more on this distressing subject. Come or not come, only remember that on you, and Lauderdale, and Whitbread, must now and always be my only real dependence in politics. This would lead me to say something to that part of your letter which relates to Sheridan, but I have not time, and must now conclude this long prose.

" Yours affectionately,

"C. J. FOX.

"I will if possible write a line from the House of Commons about the particular days of business ; one of which may be fixed to-day."

END OF VOL. III.